Sixth Edition

SURVIVAL
A Sequential Program for College Writing

Robert M. Frew
Nancy A. Sessano
American River College
Sacramento, California

T. H. Peek Publisher
P. O. Box 50123, Palo Alto, California 94303

Copyright © 1974, 1975, 1985, 1989, 1995, 2003
Robert M. Frew, Richard C. Guches, Robert E. Mehaffy, Nancy A. Sessano

ISBN 0-917962-46-X

07 06 05 04
35 34 33 32

Manufactured in the United States of America

Contents

Preface to the Sixth Edition

Welcome to the sixth edition of *Survival*. Within these chapters are the tools for successful writing, enhanced by sample essays written by students and professional writers. As always, it is our hope that *Survival*'s carefully constructed exercises will serve as your stepping-stones to thoughtful, creative essays.

We have retained the strengths that have made *Survival* an effective composition textbook. The step-by-step, sequential approach is still here: each chapter focuses on a particular writing assignment, and each exercise takes you a step toward mastery of that assignment.

In this edition the step-by-step approach is integrated into a three-phase writing process: planning, writing, and editing. We believe these techniques will help you to approach your writing projects with skill and confidence. In *Survival* the writing process encourages collaborative feedback and revision; the process always leads to a polished product, possible because you have mastered the details of the final document format.

As requested by instructors, we have changed some of the chapters in this edition. "Sentence Structure and Mechanics" has been moved into the appendix. Chapter One, while still reviewing basic essay structure and the writing process, also includes a variety of organizational strategies. Chapter Two, which concentrates on argumentative structure, incorporates more successful techniques for using the Internet and library for research. Chapter Three stresses further techniques for analyzing and evaluating different types of research materials and producing a longer essay. Chapter Four walks you through the steps of successfully reviewing a film, restaurant, etc. Chapter Five leads you through the process of researching and writing a literary analysis of a poem, short story, or novel. Chapter Six then teaches you how to investigate a problem and present viable solutions. Chapter Seven completes the text by reviewing and presenting tips for successful test-taking, either in-class or out-of-class.

All of the chapters more carefully concentrate on critical thinking, active reading, and computer literacy skills. This new edition also frequently discusses what plagiarism is and how to avoid it, a growing problem within the writing world.

Furthermore, we have added a new technique to keep you, the students, well organized—the Project Folder. In this folder you will place all your preliminary work, your research materials, preliminary drafts of the essay, along with the final draft of your essay. Our philosophy in requiring this folder is that it will keep you better organized, and it will help your instructor better understand the process you went through to produce the final document.

This textbook is still about survival, your survival in your writing classes and in the "real" world of writing. We are confident that this text will help you do just that. As always, the goal of every edition of *Survival* is to illuminate the writing process in all of its phases and to help students realize their writing potential.

Acknowledgments

We would like to thank the staff at T. H. Peek Publisher for their support and expertise. We would also like to give special thanks to the English Area staff here at American River College—Sandra Cleary, Mary Higgins, and Jocelynn Bahr—for their patience and encouragement. Furthermore, we certainly could not have completed this revision without the help of our students and our colleagues, especially Lyn Case, Harold Schneider, Rod Siegfried, Paula Kitching, Betty Monsen, and Marni Nakamoto. Bob Mehaffy and Dick Guches have earned our gratitude and appreciation, because without their partnership *Survival* would not be the success it is today; we wish them friendship as they sail the world's seas.

As always special thanks must go to our spouses, Pat and John, for their love and understanding throughout this process.

Bob Frew and Nancy Sessano

1

Essay Structure

Objectives

When you have completed this chapter, you will have:

1. practiced the three-phase writing process.
2. demonstrated an understanding of basic essay structures.
3. created thesis sentences.
4. selected an organizational strategy.
5. written topic sentences.
6. written primary and secondary support sentences.
7. composed introductory, body, and concluding paragraphs.
8. written and revised a 500–750 word paper about a social problem.
9. created a Project Folder.

Essay Structure 1

In the contemporary world, the ability to write well is still of paramount importance in our lives in spite of the predominance of visual imagery and sound in the media, in advertising, and on the Internet. Moreover, the need for absolute clarity in written communication, especially in areas such as school, science, government, business, and diplomacy, has obligated us to agree to apply certain conventions in constructing and punctuating sentences, developing paragraphs, and creating whole compositions. And even though we may operate in a variety of language communities at home, school, and work, these conventions dictate that we use **Standard American English** when writing. These conventions ensure a clarity of communication that would not otherwise be achieved.

Survival is a textbook that will help you learn the form of writing most widely assigned in the academic world: the essay, or paper, as it is commonly called. The fact is that your instructors in a variety of subject areas will assign essays and expect you to deliver high-quality written work. As you work your way through *Survival*, you will master a writing process that will enable you to manage almost any writing project with skill and confidence.

Writing skill is absolutely necessary for your success. This skill goes hand in hand with reading, oral communication, mathematics, and critical thinking, making up the five basic skills crucial to your survival in this complex, competitive world of continuous change. Furthermore, you must learn to adapt your writing for different audiences and situations encountered in school and at work. For example, in school you are often assigned to write term papers, book reports, lab reports, and written exams. Your reader is usually your instructor, but often other students in your class will read your essays as well, offering their responses and editing suggestions.

At work you may need to write letters, memos, different types of reports, feasibility studies, grant proposals, competitive proposals, instruction manuals, promotional literature, and other types of writing, each with a different purpose and audience. Frequently you will be asked to work collaboratively on writing projects, for example, peer editing or co-writing with other employees. In these situations the success of your group with its project depends on your ability to handle your part of the writing assignment competently.

LESSON ONE—*The Writing Process: Planning, Writing, Editing*

Whether writing for school or work, you need to know a process you can rely on for each writing project. *Survival* recommends a writing process that moves back and forth among three phases:

PLANNING
WRITING
EDITING

Your ability to produce successful writing projects will increase dramatically if you adopt this process.

The writing process you will practice in *Survival* is a step-by-step process—step one, step two, step three, and so on, but it is also a recursive process. The rhetorical path is clear: choose a subject to write about, propose an idea about the subject, then explain and defend that idea. However, along the way the process becomes nonlinear. You will find yourself planning and replanning, writing and rewriting, thinking your essay is finished, and then discovering it isn't. Each of the three phases includes different stages. You will find yourself interrupting one of the phases to loop back or ahead to a different phase or stage. The overlapping characteristics of the process can be represented by the illustration below:

Three-Phase Writing Process

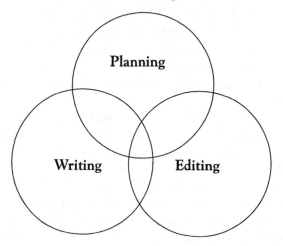

The Planning Phase

The planning phase of the writing process is often called the prewriting phase because it includes all of the activities completed before you actually begin composing the essay. Essentially, you are organizing in order to begin writing. You are clarifying the assignment, finding something to write about, gathering information, and formulating your main idea for the essay along with an outline to follow in developing that idea. Within the planning phase you complete several steps:

DISCOVERING A SUBJECT
NARROWING THE SUBJECT TO A TOPIC
RESEARCHING THE TOPIC
WRITING A THESIS
DEVELOPING AN OUTLINE

The Writing Phase

The first or preliminary version of a piece of writing that will be revised, corrected, and retyped in a desired format is called a **draft**, often the rough draft. Any succeeding version of the original draft is also called a draft—second draft, revised draft, and on to the final draft. During the **writing phase** of the process, you write a series of drafts, proceeding step-by-step:

DRAFTING
REVISING
RECEIVING FEEDBACK
REWRITING

Of course, the computer has somewhat blurred the distinction among first, second, and successive drafts. If you use a computer, you know how easy it is to rewrite. The glowing screen beckons you again and again to tinker with the text just one more time before you print a final copy. For the sake of definition, therefore, you can say that a draft is produced each time you actually print a new version of your paper or retype it or write it over with pen or pencil.

The procedure for writing the **first draft** is simple: Find a quiet place or sit at your computer and write steadily and rapidly, without stopping, if possible, until the first draft is complete. As you write, do not worry about punctuation, spelling, or proper grammar; you will go back over your paper to remove the errors later. Whenever you stop to look up a word in the dictionary or check a punctuation rule, you run the risk of losing your momentum and forgetting what you were trying to say. Concentrate on what you want to say in your essay.

The Editing Phase

During the **editing phase** of the writing process, you prepare your final draft. Your main concern will be the final appearance of your document. You will present the finished document to be read by others, perhaps seeking the response of your classmates and, most important, evaluation by your instructor. Therefore, your goal should be to turn in an essay that is carefully edited, free of errors, and attractively presented in an appropriate format. Three steps must be completed in the editing phase:

EDITING
PROOFREADING
DOCUMENT PREPARATION

EXERCISE 1.1

1. Describe the process that you typically use when you are given a writing assignment (the one you used before reading *Survival*).

_____

_____

_____

_____

2. What are the three phases of the writing process advocated in *Survival*?

(1)_____

(2)_____

(3)_____

3. Explain why the writing process is not entirely a step-by-step linear process.

_____

_____

_____

_____

_____

Have your answers checked.

Now that you have read about the writing process and done some thinking about your own writing, read the following essay by Peter Elbow, a respected teacher of writing and a published author. In this essay he tells how he gets started on a writing assignment, more specifically, how he overcomes his initial panic: "I know I am not alone in my recurring twinges of panic that I won't be able to write when I need to, I won't be able to produce coherent speech or thought."

The method he explains is his personal brand of free writing, covered later in this chapter. After reading Elbow's essay, you will try his method to better understand how the writing process is made up of techniques that you can learn and practice.

As you read Elbow's essay, underline or highlight the main ideas, circle words you don't understand and look them up in a dictionary, and write your reactions to what Elbow is saying in the margins. You may need to read the essay more than once to fully grasp its content. Approaching a reading assignment this way is called **active reading**, an approach you should use in all of your academic reading, as it will help you comprehend and remember what you read.

Desperation Writing

by Peter Elbow

I know I am not alone in my recurring twinges of panic that I won't be able to write something when I need to, I won't be able to produce coherent speech or thought. And that lingering doubt is a great hindrance to writing. It's a constant fog or static that clouds the mind. I never got out of its clutches till I discovered that it is possible to write something—not something great or pleasing but at least something usable, workable—when my mind is out of commission. The trick is that you have to do all your cooking on the table: your mind is incapable of doing any inside. It means using symbols and pieces of paper not as a crutch but as a wheel chair.

The first thing is to admit your condition: Because of some mood or event or whatever, your mind is incapable of anything that could be called thought. It can put out a babbling kind of speech utterance, it can put a simple feeling, perception, or sort-of-thought into understandable (though terrible) words. But it is incapable of considering anything in relation to anything else. The moment you try to hold that thought or feeling up against some other to see the relationship, you simply lose the picture—you get nothing but buzzing lines or waving colors.

So admit this. Avoid anything more than one feeling, perception, or thought. Simply write as much as possible. Try simply to steer your mind in the direction or general vicinity of the thing you are trying to write about and start writing and keep writing.

Just write and keep writing. (Probably best to write on only one side of the paper in case you should want to cut parts out with scissors, but you probably won't.) Just write and keep writing. It will probably come in waves. After a flurry, stop and take a brief rest. But don't stop too long. Don't think about what you are writing or what you have written or else you will overload the circuit again. Keep writing as though you are drugged or drunk. Keep doing this till you feel you have a lot of material that might be useful; or, if necessary, till you can't stand it any more—even if you doubt that there's anything useful there.

Then take a pad of little pieces of paper—or perhaps 3 X 5 cards—and simply start at the beginning of what you were writing, and as you read over what you wrote, every time you come to any thought, feeling, perception, or image that could be gathered up into one sentence or one assertion, do so and write it by itself on a little sheet of paper. In short, you are trying to turn, say, ten or twenty pages of wandering mush into twenty or thirty little crab apples. Sometimes there won't be many on a page. But if it seems to you that there are none on a page, you are making a serious error—the same serious error that put you in this comatose state to start with. You are mistaking lousy, stupid, second-rate, wrong, childish, foolish, worthless ideas for no ideas at all. Your job is not to pick out *good* ideas but to pick out ideas. As long as you were conscious, your words will be full of things that could be called feelings, utterances, ideas—things that can be squeezed into one simple sentence. This is your job. Don't ask for too much.

After you have done this, take those little slips or cards, read through them a number of times—not struggling with them, simply wandering and mulling through them; perhaps shifting them around and looking through them in various sequences. In a sense these are cards that you are playing solitaire with, and the rules of this particular game permit shuffling the unused pile.

The goal of this procedure with the cards is to get them to distribute themselves in two or three or ten or fifteen different piles on your desk. You can get them to do this almost by themselves if you simply keep reading through them in different orders; certain cards will begin to feel like they go with other cards. I emphasize this passive, thoughtless mode because I want to talk about desperation writing in its pure state. In practice, almost invariably at some point in the procedure, your sanity begins to return. It is often at this point. You actually are moved to have thoughts or—and the difference between active and passive is crucial here—to *exert* thought; to hold two cards together and *build* or *assert* a relationship. It is a matter of bringing energy to bear.

So you may start to be able to do something active with these cards, and begin actually to think. But if not, just allow the cards to find their own piles with each other by feel, by drift, by intuition, by mindlessness.

You have now engaged in the two main activities that will permit you to get something cooked out on the table rather than in your brain: writing out messy words, summing up into single assertions, and even sensing relationships between assertions. You can simply continue to deploy these two activities.

If, for example, after the first round of writing, assertion-making, and pile-making, your piles feel as though they are useful and satisfactory for what you are writing—paragraphs or sections or trains of thought—then you can carry on from there. See if you can gather each pile up into a single assertion. When you can, then put the subsidiary assertions of that pile into their best order to fit with that single unifying one. If you *can't* get the pile into one assertion, then take the pile as the basis for doing some more writing out into words. In the course of this writing, you may produce for yourself the single unifying assertion you were looking for;

or you may have to go through the cycle of turning the writing into assertions and piles and so forth. Perhaps more than once. The pile may turn out to want to be two or more piles itself; or it may want to become part of a pile you already have. This is natural. This kind of meshing into one configuration, then coming apart, then coming together and meshing into a different configuration—this is growing and cooking. It makes a terrible mess, but if you can't do it in your head, you have to put up with a cluttered desk and a lot of confusion.

If, on the other hand, all that writing *didn't* have useful material in it, it means that your writing wasn't loose, drifting, quirky, jerky, associative enough. This time try especially to let things simply remind you of things that are seemingly crazy or unrelated. Follow these odd associations. Make as many metaphors as you can—be as nutty as possible—and explore the metaphors themselves—open them out. You may have all your energy tied up in some area of your experience that you are leaving out. Don't refrain from writing about whatever else is on your mind: how you feel at the moment, what you are losing your mind over, randomness that intrudes itself on your consciousness, the patterns on the wallpaper, what those people you see out the window have on their minds—though keep coming back to the whateveritis you are supposed to be writing about. Treat it, in short, like ten-minute writing exercises. Your best perceptions and thoughts are always going to be tied up in whatever is really occupying you, and that is also where your energy is. You may end up writing a love poem—or a hate poem—in one of those little piles while the other piles will finally turn into a lab report on data processing or whatever you have to write about. But you couldn't, in your present state of having your head shot off, have written that report without also writing the poem. And the report will have some of the juice of the poem in it and vice versa.

EXERCISE 1.2

Answer the following questions, using complete sentences. Write or type your answers.

1. How does Elbow get started with a writing project? Write a short summary of his essay (no more than five sentences).

2. Who is Elbow's audience in this essay?

3. Elbow has written his opening sentences in first person. Explain why this point of view is or is not effective in this essay. Before the end of the first paragraph, he switches to second person. Most writing instructors advise students not to use second person in academic writing. Why, nevertheless, might Elbow's use of second person be effective in this essay?

4. List the steps in the process of getting started that Elbow advocates.

5. Elbow uses an analogy (a comparison) throughout his essay. What are the two things he compares? Is the analogy effective? Explain why or why not.

6. In punctuating some of his sentences, Elbow frequently uses the dash (—). Why do you think he uses dashes rather than commas in those sentences?

7. Using some concrete examples from your own experience, describe a time when you had to write something and had writer's block (the inability to start writing). How did you overcome the block and complete the assignment? Was the technique you used one you would want to use again, or are you looking for a more effective technique? Would Elbow's method have been helpful? Why or why not?

LESSON TWO—*Managing Your Writing Projects*

Assignment Analysis

As soon as possible after you are given a writing assignment, analyze the assignment by asking a set of questions and then writing down the answers:

1. What is the assignment? Required length?
2. What type of essay is it, and what is its purpose?
3. When is the essay due? Are there other deadlines? What are the consequences of missing any of these deadlines?
4. Is there a recommended organization and format?
5. Are library research and documentation required? Interviews? Focus Groups? Surveys?
6. Who will be reading your essay, and how do you want to affect them?
7. Are any oral reports required in connection with the project?
8. Will collaborative work such as peer editing be required? If you will be working with co-authors or on a writing team, what are your responsibilities?
9. Do you have the skills you need, or will you need help?
10. How will your performance be evaluated? Will revisions be allowed?

Work Schedule

In order to finish your essay on time, you will need to organize a work schedule that includes completion dates for each task in the project. If you are working by yourself, the schedule is essential to help you determine whether you are working fast enough to complete the essay on time. This schedule becomes even more important if you are working with a co-author or on a writing team because each person needs to know when his or her part of the assignment is due so that everyone's work can be integrated and reviewed. Sometimes your instructor will break down the assignment for you, assigning a due date for each part. Often, however, the scheduling will be your responsibility. Because no schedule ever works perfectly, you must learn how to adjust your schedule to cope with unanticipated difficulties and temporary setbacks. Every day you should study your work schedule for the writing project, noting in writing the parts of the project you have completed and any changes you find it necessary to make.

Audience Analysis

Who are you writing for; who is your audience? What is the technical expertise of your readers? Are they likely to be biased by a particular point of view? How do you want to affect them? Should you adopt a particular writing strategy to affect your readers in the way you want? These are questions you must consider whenever you embark upon a writing project, usually as part of the planning phase.

How you want to affect your readers will mainly depend on your purpose. Is your purpose to explain, compare, analyze, evaluate, propose, or argue? If your purpose is to explain, your basic assumption is that your readers do not completely understand something. If, on the other hand, your purpose is to argue in favor of your opinion on a controversial subject, your assumption is that you can persuade your readers that your view is worth considering. Your purpose may be to go even further, persuading your readers that they should take a particular course of action. Whenever you write, you should create the impression that you are knowledgeable, objective, organized and articulate, sometimes humorous, but always honest and sincere.

Writing with Computers

Computers can make your writing projects more manageable. To be a successful writer in school or on the job, you need to master word processing on a computer. If you are not now using a computer for one reason or another, you will be before long. It's inevitable! You can compose, revise, and format written documents on a computer with relative ease. You can also use computer technology to search electronically for information in the library and on the Internet. You can communicate with others through computer networks, electronic mail, and fax. Some instructors require their students to turn in their essays on disks or electronically instead of printed out on paper.

Collaborative Writing

Working with others to do a project is called **collaboration**. One of the advantages of collaborative writing is that it encourages planning and review among the writers and can lead to improved writing performance. You probably already have some experience with peer editing sessions where you provide feedback to others and, in turn, receive feedback about your own writing. Your instructor may schedule collaborative learning exercises into your class, especially during the feedback step of the writing phase.

You may also be required to work on a **team writing project** at least once during the course. Participation on project teams in classes is required more now because some academic disciplines and businesses frequently use this approach for many types of projects. On a writing team you usually help write certain sections of the final product, but you also contribute to the team your particular expertise, such as a talent for editing or the ability to produce computer graphics. Almost all college graduates write with co-authors on some projects.

LESSON THREE—Planning Your Essay

Discovering a Subject

When students are asked why they are having trouble starting a writing project, one of the most frequent responses is, "I don't know what to write about." Actually, fear of failure may be preventing them from being logical, creative, and enthusiastic about what should be an engaging task. There really are so many subjects about which to write! Your problem should not be that you can't find a subject but rather how to choose a subject from several that interest you.

Usually when writers talk about the **subject** they have chosen for an essay, they mean the general category, such as crime or computers. When they talk about the **topic** for an essay, they mean the narrowed aspect of the subject about which they have chosen to write, for example, the magnitude of the money laundering problem in Florida for crime or the impact of computers on the teaching of writing for computers. Some writers use the terms *subject* and *topic* interchangeably. In *Survival*, however, the term *subject* will refer to the larger category before it is narrowed to a more specific concern, the *topic*. Think of them as two stages in the planning phase: discovering a subject (broad) and narrowing it to a specific, manageable topic (specific).

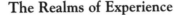

Select a subject ⟶ Narrow it to a topic

Consider three realms of experience while you are discovering a subject: personal experience, reading, and discussion. The three realms of experience overlap. In fact, the ideal subject probably involves all three. A personal experience of yours might lead you to seek out some reading material on the subject, and in turn your reaction to the reading material could lead you to a discussion with family, friends, or classmates. Or, to look at the process another way, any time you read something, your reaction to that material is always influenced by your previous experiences as well as by any prior reading and related discussions you may have had.

The Realms of Experience

Searching for a subject is often a skimming-and-scanning exercise—looking through local newspapers, paying attention to the news on television, scrolling through the subjects on the electronic periodical index in the library, or searching through your own memories or your journal if you keep one. What have you read lately that might be the source of a subject? Look through news magazines like *Time* or *Newsweek*. Go to the library and consult the electronic indexes, contemplating the different subject categories. Recall recent conversations you have had with family, friends, teachers, classmates, or fellow workers. Tune into a talk show or news program. Look over your lecture notes from an interesting class. Think creatively. For example, if you could launch a campaign to include an initiative on the ballot during the next election, what would it be? Is there something you have experienced that you could write about, something you have done that your classmates might want to know more about?

Try to select your subject quickly, the one that interests you the most. The best advice anyone can give you at this point is to pick a subject and start working with it immediately. Look over your list of candidates, select the winner, and save the rest for another time. (See Appendix D: Suggested Subjects, for a list of 400 subjects.)

EXERCISE 1.3

Select a social problem as the subject for the essay you will complete by the end of this chapter. Before making your choice, list from three to five potential subjects; then choose the one that interests you most.

Possible Subjects

1._____

2._____

3._____

4._____

5._____

Subject Chosen_____

Discuss your subject choice with your instructor.

Narrowing the Subject to a Topic

After you have discovered a subject for your essay, the main problem is narrowing it sufficiently. Most of the essays you will write will be reasonably short essays from two to seven pages in length (250 words per page, double-spaced). The social problem essay you are writing for this chapter will be from two to three pages long. Therefore, the topic for any short essay must be carefully limited.

By using various creative and analytical processes, you can narrow your subject to a manageable topic. Although you may already have a method for narrowing the subject, you should experiment with a number of widely used techniques until you find the one that works best for you.

Brainstorming

Begin by writing the subject you have chosen at the top of your screen or sheet of paper; then list anything that the original word or phrase brings to mind. Words or phrases that follow may relate to the original or to subsequent items. There is no time limit; however, at first see how productive you can be in a short time—fifteen minutes is a good start. Since this activity attempts to release the flow of creative ideas, anything that comes to mind on the subject should be recorded. No response is wrong in this exercise. When you are finished, examine your list, looking for a word or phrase that seems interesting and narrow enough in scope to be a good topic for a short essay.

Example

Crime

capital punishment	insanity plea	plea bargains
increased juvenile crime	jury system	violence in schools
road rage	alcohol-related	white collar
identity theft	domestic abuse	shoplifting
home safety precautions	child abuse	forensic science
underage drinking	hate crimes	juveniles tried as adults
murder rates	criminal profiling	home invasions
carjacking	DNA testing	costs of incarceration
drug use—prison or rehab?	three-strikes law	self-defense classes
parole	gangs	terrorism
	date rape	

Keep in mind that brainstorming is not just a prewriting technique. Brainstorming can and should occur anytime a writer is stalled and needs more ideas.

Freewriting

Start by writing the subject at the top of your screen or sheet of paper. Then write what you know about the subject as fast as you can without worrying about correctness of grammar, spelling, and the like. As with brainstorming, there is no set time limit, but try limiting yourself to twenty or thirty minutes. Freewriting is a great limbering-up exercise and can start you thinking in writing by producing phrases and sentences on the subject. This method works especially well for students who need to actually begin writing an essay before they can do much planning. As soon as you stop freewriting, look over what you have written and decide what your narrowed topic will be. Usually you will have written enough on the subject to discover the actual topic that you will use in your essay.

Example

Anorexia

Anorexia is a psychological disorder, found mostly in young women. They think they are overweight, but often that is just their perception, often they are far too thin and look unhealthy. There are physical signs: loss of hair, shallow skin tone, loss of energy, heart problems, kidney problems, bleeding gums. Really is a control issue. Many times family and friend are unaware of the eating disorder because anorexics get very, very good at hiding their problems and pretending to eat, push food around on their plate, claim to have already eaten, claim to be ill, etc. Causes could include lack of self-esteem, ads in the magazines—Cosmo, Teen, etc.—TV—models are a size 2, are 5'10" & weigh 100 lbs! Karen Carpenter died as a result of anorexia—Traci Gold admits to having this problem as do many other Hollywood stars. Calista Flockhart from Ally McBeal looks too thin, but she says she doesn't have an eating disorder. The media keeps printing stories about it though. Many female students from my high school also seemed to have anorexia—not eating was often all they talked about, especially before a dance or prom—don't eat so I can fit into a smaller size dress—Sometimes even with treatment these women still die. Treatments include counseling, forced eating, drug therapy, hospitalization, etc.

Clustering

Begin by writing and circling your subject in the middle of a page. (You won't be able to cluster on your computer unless you are quite adept at graphics.) Then draw a line with an arrow extending out from it, and write a word or phrase suggested by the first. Continue to build your graphic system of circles with arrows as one thing suggests another. Along the way a word or phrase may give rise to a whole new set of words and phrases. With this graphic system you can quickly and easily see how each word or idea relates to the others that you have developed. Try to limit yourself to fifteen minutes for this exercise. At the end of fifteen minutes, study your clusters to find your narrowed topic.

Illustration of Clustering

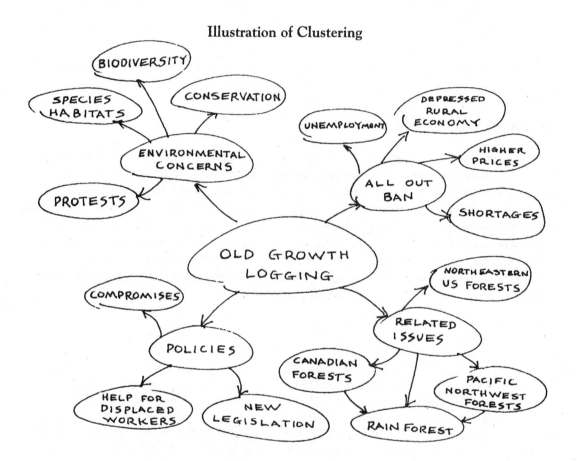

Analytical Questioning

Although many writers rely on the informal discovery techniques of brainstorming, freewriting, and clustering to narrow their subjects, others prefer a more analytical approach. One of the most effective ways to a find manageable topic is to ask yourself a set of questions about your subject.

Examples

    1. Is there a controversial aspect that will allow you to write either for or against something? If so, can you limit your subject by writing about just one side of the controversy, for example, by attacking or defending?

Example

Crime ⟶ Lenient sentences for white-collar criminals

2. Is there a good way to narrow a subject by restricting it to a particular time or place?

Example

Water shortages ⟶ Growing threat of salinity in Western soils

3. Is there some way to limit the subject through natural divisions?

Example

Pollution ⟶ Underground water pollution

Focused Questioning

If you already have a general topic, you can turn the topic into a question and then brainstorm answers to the question to arrive at an even narrower topic or possible ideas for paragraphs in your essay. Limit your time to ten to fifteen minutes.

Examples

Question: Should college students move out of their parents' home?

too expensive	need a job	bill paying
more freedom	roommates	less emotional support
scary	food	less time for studying
laundry	fewer rules	too much responsibility
homesick	mature faster	more time with friends
self-identity	safety concerns	parking

EXERCISE 1.4

Narrow the subject you selected in Exercise 1.3 to a topic suitable for a 500–750 word social problem essay. Use one or more of the prewriting strategies: brainstorming, freewriting, clustering, analytical or focused questioning.

Narrowed Topic:_____

_____

Have your topic approved.

Researching Your Topic

Before beginning to write, you will probably need to learn more about your topic. By gathering information and analyzing and evaluating it, you become knowledgeable enough to write convincingly. Your need to research your topic will vary with the assignment. For this first essay, for example, you will not need to conduct systematic library research. Perhaps all you will need to do is discuss your topic with friends or family members or read a few magazine or newspaper articles to increase your background knowledge. Your textbooks and class notes are other potential sources of background information for this first essay. For other assignments you may need to spend many hours in the library conducting an organized search for the information you need.

A simple starting point you shouldn't overlook is an inventory of your memory on the topic. Brainstorming, freewriting, clustering, and analytical and focused questioning are useful in this process, just as they were in narrowing a subject to a topic. After reviewing what you know about the topic, library research is usually the next logical step.

Within the library, or wherever available, computers have greatly increased your ability to conduct research. Encyclopedias, dictionaries, and other research sources are now routinely installed in computers. Computers can be used to search for bibliographic information in books, magazines, professional journals, government documents, and newspapers. Abstracts and full texts of articles and other printed materials can be obtained by electronic retrieval from computer databases. Gathering information from the Internet is introduced in Chapter Two and discussed further in Chapter Three. Research in the library, including the use of electronic information services, is covered in Chapter Three. Interviews and focus groups, research techniques you can use, are explained in Chapter Six.

Ask yourself again, what is your purpose in writing the essay, and what will your readers need to know for you to accomplish your purpose? Your purpose may be to inform your readers about something you want them to understand or to persuade them to adopt a particular point of view or to take action. Posing questions to yourself as you prepare to do your research will help you get organized. Either Analytical Questioning or Focused Questioning techniques described earlier can be helpful here.

Examples

1. What background information will I need to include?

2. What don't I understand, and what is it that the readers probably don't understand?

3. Can I explain the problem that needs to be solved? Are there solutions that might work? Is one of them better than the others?

4. What are the alternate points of view on a controversial subject? Which position do I favor? Are most of my readers likely to be in agreement with me, or will they oppose my point of view?

5. What are the arguments I can make? What are the arguments that my readers might raise to counter mine?

6. What evidence can I include to support my arguments and defeat the opposing arguments?

7. How will I give credit to my sources of information? Is any of the information worth quoting?

Plagiarism

Plagiarism is using someone else's material without giving proper credit. You must not use material from other sources in your essay without giving credit to the author and source of that material. This is true even if you don't quote other sources verbatim. You absolutely must give credit to your source whenever you include any ideas or information taken from the Internet, books, newspapers, encyclopedias, magazines, journals, pamphlets, essays, CDs, DVDs, films, speeches, lectures, or e-mails. Anything summarized, paraphrased, or quoted must be properly acknowledged with a lead-in, quotation marks around a direct quote, ellipsis marks for omissions, and accurate documentation in the MLA (Modern Language Association) format. Plagiarism is never acceptable, and the consequences of being caught are very severe.

For help in properly giving credit to your sources of information, consult the following pages:

Internet	Chapter Two	Pages 51–53
Printed Materials	Chapter Three	Pages 117–132
Surveys and Interviews	Chapter Six	Pages 240–244
Summarizing, Paraphrasing, Quoting	Chapter Three	Pages 128–130
Lead-ins, Quote marks, Ellipsis marks	Chapter Three	Pages 146–152, 154
Documentation	Chapter Three	Pages 119–121
	Appendix C	Pages 331–348

Research Procedures—Be Organized and Be Prepared

If you intend to conduct research to locate ideas and information for your essay, plan ahead to make the job of giving credit in your essay easier:

- Obtain a folder in which to organize your materials. This will be your **Project Folder.**

- Print out or photocopy all pages containing any ideas or information included in your essay. Also keep newspaper clippings (write dates and page numbers on them), pamphlets, brochures, and any other materials used.

- Use a highlighter to mark any passages used, or make marginal notes and underline passages with a pen or pencil.

- When helpful, use index cards, notebook paper, or a computer to take notes.

- Remember that whenever you use the exact wording of one of your sources of information, you are quoting, and you must place the copied words in quotation marks (" "). You must also give credit to ideas or information put into your own words by summarizing or paraphrasing.

- Place all printouts, photocopies, newspaper clippings, notes, and other materials you have gathered in the Project Folder.

- Compile a list of lead-ins you can use to introduce researched information, such as, According to Gwendolyn Brown, . . . Researchers discovered that . . . Nakamoto disagrees, saying, . . .

- Keep your Project Folder until your essay has been graded and returned, and be prepared to review any of your research material with your instructor.

- See Chapter Two for more detailed information.

EXERCISE 1.5

Using the questions on page 16 as a guide, conduct any research you think you will need to write the first draft of your essay. Keep in mind time constraints so that you won't plan more research than is necessary or expected for this first essay. If possible, limit yourself to some brief background reading, the Internet, some magazine or newspaper articles, or some class notes. (Have your research checked, and place it in your Project Folder.)

Basic Essay Structure

Every essay you write must have a beginning, a middle, and an end. The beginning section of any essay is referred to as the **introduction.** Its purpose is to prepare your readers for what is to be explained or argued in the body of the essay. The introduction, which may include one or more paragraphs, does this by narrowing from a broad opening sentence to a specific **thesis sentence** usually located at the end of the introduction. The **body paragraphs** follow this introduction. These paragraphs explain and support what is said in the thesis sentence. Finally, a **conclusion** of one or more paragraphs sums up the essay. The conclusion restates the thesis idea or summarizes the entire discussion without sounding redundant and then ends with a generalization that brings the essay to a close.

The number of paragraphs in an essay is not set by a formula. The number in any given essay will vary according to how much you have to say and where you decide to break the paragraphs, making them long or short. The diagram below shows how the structure would look in a short essay that might include five paragraphs.

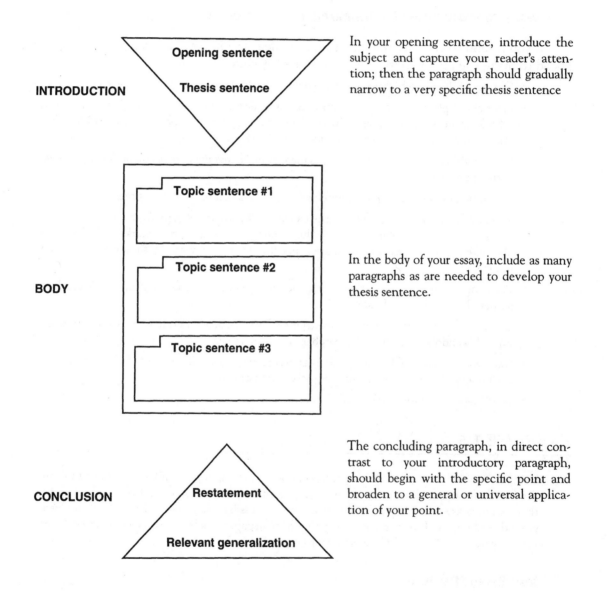

INTRODUCTION

Opening sentence

Thesis sentence

In your opening sentence, introduce the subject and capture your reader's attention; then the paragraph should gradually narrow to a very specific thesis sentence

BODY

Topic sentence #1

Topic sentence #2

Topic sentence #3

In the body of your essay, include as many paragraphs as are needed to develop your thesis sentence.

CONCLUSION

Restatement

Relevant generalization

The concluding paragraph, in direct contrast to your introductory paragraph, should begin with the specific point and broaden to a general or universal application of your point.

Writing a Thesis Sentence

After you have narrowed your subject to a topic, you are ready to write the **thesis sentence**. It is the most important sentence in any essay you write because it communicates the main idea of your essay. For this reason, your thesis sentence should be the first sentence you write. You may write what writers call a **working thesis**, which is a temporary version that you will perfect later.

Although the thesis sentence should be the first sentence you write, it will not be the opening sentence of the essay. Normally the thesis sentence is placed at the end of the introduction of your essay. In a short essay, such as the 500–750 word essay you are writing, the introduction will consist of a single paragraph. In such a case, the thesis will usually be the last sentence in that paragraph.

What is the main idea you want to communicate to your readers in your paper? That is your thesis idea. It underlies all of the discussion that follows it, and everything that is said relates back to it. Moving from your narrowed topic to your thesis is not difficult if you can answer that question in a single sentence. Without telling your readers, "I'm going to tell you about . . ." or "The purpose of this paper is . . . ," make the statement and you have your thesis.

Examples

Question: Do computer games interfere or threaten literacy?

Thesis: Unlike television, computer games do not pose a threat to literacy.

The Divided Thesis

Often the surest way to move smoothly from a narrowed topic to a thesis sentence is to read your narrowed topic and ask, How or why is this so? What are the reasons?

Examples

Narrowed topic:	How farmers and ranchers are threatening the wolf
Question:	How are they threatening the wolf?
Answer:	They are threatening the wolf in many ways.
Select three ways:	They are threatening the wolf (1) by using pesticides. (2) by converting wild lands into farms and ranges. (3) by waging war on the wolf.
Thesis sentence:	Farmers and ranchers have driven the wolf to near extinction by using pesticides, by converting wild lands into farmlands, and by waging open war on this most misunderstood of all wild animals.

The thesis above has refined the answer to the question. The thesis tells exactly how farmers and ranchers have caused the near extinction of the wolf: by using pesticides, by converting wild lands into farmlands, and by waging open war. This thesis is called a **divided thesis sentence**. By narrowing the thesis to these three points, all other ways farmers and ranchers have driven the wolf to near extinction are eliminated. For example, the writer developing this thesis could not discuss how fences and roads also helped push the wolf into its present precarious state.

The divided thesis technique is perfect for short essays of 500–750 words in length. It allows the writer to inform the reader openly what to expect in each body paragraph.

Here, body paragraph one would be about pesticides; body paragraph two would be about converting wild lands, and body paragraph three would be about waging open war on wolves. Such a technique makes the writing of short essays faster and easier than using any other type of thesis. More examples of divided thesis sentences follow:

Examples

1. Organized groups of city residents are fighting to save their neighborhoods by patrolling with video cameras, documenting the activities of drug dealers and buyers, and reporting to police representatives regularly. (list at end)
2. By patrolling with video cameras, documenting the activities of drug dealers and buyers, and reporting to police representatives regularly, organized groups of city residents are fighting to save their neighborhoods. (list at beginning)

Should You Always Write a Three-Part Divided Thesis?

No, not necessarily.

The three-part thesis works well in many essays, especially essays no longer than 750 words, but it is not mandatory or even desirable in all essays.

1. You may need a four- or five-part thesis.

   Example

   Each of the economic systems in Russia, China, Vietnam, and Cuba is different.

2. A divided thesis may be too long and therefore difficult to read. You can write a short version implying that the body of the essay will be divided into sections.

   Example

   Many questions about the Robert Kennedy assassination remain unanswered. (Each paragraph would address a different unanswered question.)

3. A thesis can assert the main idea of an essay without pointing to divisions.

   Examples

   Although nuclear energy seems to be the most promising source of energy for the next three decades, only a few experimental nuclear power plants should be allowed during the next ten years.

   OR

   The drought-stricken African countries bordering the Sahara Desert have failed to develop nearby water resources.

EXERCISE 1.6

Develop the thesis you will use for your social problem essay. Try writing different versions of your thesis before you decide which to use.

1. What is your narrowed topic?_____

   _____

2. Convert your narrowed topic to a question._____

3. Write a one-sentence answer to the question (an undivided thesis statement).

_____

_____

4. How or why is that so? List three to five reasons for the idea you stated above.

(a)_____

(b)_____

(c)_____

(d)_____

(e)_____

5. The next step is to experiment with versions of your thesis that incorporate some or all of the reasons you have listed. After writing several versions, write the one you have chosen for your essay in the space provided.

_____

_____

_____

_____

6. Consider the order in which you have stated the main idea and the reasons in your divided thesis. Do you want to state your main idea before or after listing your reasons? Put your reasons in a logical order; you will usually save the strongest idea for last, but you may arrange your reasons in a time or geographical order. Also make sure your final version is not too wordy.

_____

_____

_____

_____

Have your work checked.

Organizational Strategies

Besides having an introduction, body, and conclusion, you must give serious thought to the internal organization of your essay. Before you outline your essay, you will need to think about which organizational strategy you will use. This need holds true for the essay overall and for its individual paragraphs. The obvious strategy to choose for the whole essay may be suggested by your working thesis.

Examples

Thesis: Community colleges are better suited for local workforce training than state universities. [Strategy: Comparison/Contrast]

Thesis: Campus parking problems can only be alleviated by the construction of a multilevel parking garage next to the stadium [Strategy: Problem-solution]

Narrative Strategy

When you write a **narrative**, you are telling a story, recounting in detail what happened to you or others during an incident. Of all of the modes of writing, narrative writing is the most natural and informative. It is a primary way we relate to others what we have experienced and the meaning of that experience. We can narrate something very personal such as an encounter with racial prejudice or something that happened to someone else. In academic writing, narrative is usually used in introductions or in supporting examples. When used as the primary organizational pattern, it is usually accompanied by an analysis of the meaning of the experience described in the narrative; you would not just be relating a story. Two things are needed for effective narrative: accurate chronological order and descriptive details.

Illustration Strategy

One strategy that is easy to employ is **illustration**. It allows you to develop your paragraphs using **examples**. If you were attempting to persuade your readers that more fuel tax money should be used to fund rapid transit systems, you could illustrate your point with examples of serious traffic congestion, inadequate public transit systems, how fuel tax expenditures are actually increasing traffic problems, successful rapid transit systems, and of affordable funding plans. You can use short examples, explained in a few sentences, or extended examples, developed in one or more paragraphs.

On occasion, use of an anecdote may be effective. An anecdote is a short narrative about an incident or story—a summary of a personal experience, used as an example. For example, a writer might summarize his or her experience on the Bullet Trains in Japan or being caught in a local traffic jam.

Comparison or Contrast Strategy

Another easy organizational strategy to employ is **comparison or contrast**. When you compare two or more things, you explain how they are alike. When you contrast two or more things, you explain how they are different. When comparing or contrasting, you must first decide on your points of comparison or contrast. If, for example, you were advocating the advantages of community college over four-year universities for the first two years of college, you might contrast costs of tuition and living costs, entrance requirements, quality of instruction, facilities, campus life, and parking.

You can arrange your comparisons or contrasts two different ways. You may cover one side of the comparison or contrast in its entirety and then go on to cover the other side. Thus, you would cover your points for four-year universities and after that cover your points about community colleges. On the other hand, you may alternate your comparisons or contrasts, one point at a time. You would discuss the costs of community colleges and four-year universities, then discuss the differences in entrance requirements for both, and so on.

Definition Strategy

Your purpose may be to **define** something, explaining what something is or what something is like. On a larger scale, you might devote an entire essay to defining a concept or a problem. On a smaller scale, you might need to define a term central to your essay. For instance, if you were writing about white collar crime, you would need to define the term, or if you were writing about date rape, you would have to define the term carefully. Most writers who are defining concepts combine explanation and specific illustrations. They also contrast examples of what something is like with examples of what something is not like.

Analysis Strategy

Much of your writing for school will be analytic and requires a higher level of critical thinking. **Analysis** involves separating something whole into its parts, examining them, and interpreting their meaning or significance. For example, you could write a very detailed narration of a powerful memory from your childhood and then explain the significance of that event as an influence on your later development. In your English class you might analyze the setting, plot, characters, and symbolism of a short story and their importance to the story's theme.

More specifically, in analysis you can **divide** your topic into its components and discuss each one. On a political science test you might be asked to explain the functions of the three branches of the federal government: the administrative, congressional, and judicial branches. In analysis you can also **classify** the parts of the whole by grouping them in categories. Music, for example, is usually associated with categories such as classical, rock, folk, rap, jazz, country, religious, instrumentals, vocals, and so on.

Frequently in analysis you will be discussing **cause-and-effect** relationships. Whenever you explain why something happens, you are explaining the causes of that event. If, for example, you explain why fuel prices rise when a war breaks out, you are dealing with causes. In contrast, if you explain what happens as the result of something else happening—the consequences of another event—you are dealing with effects. You could, for instance, explain the detrimental effects of excessive television viewing by young children. In analytical writing, absolute separation of causes and effects is not necessary. Often your discussion of what happened, why it happened, and even how it happened will be intertwined.

Problem-Solution Strategy

In a world full of problems, it seems quite natural to analyze a problem and then discuss possible solutions. Although you could simply analyze a problem to increase your reader's understanding of its makeup and ramifications, it is usually advisable to propose and evaluate one or more solutions, either endorsing or recommending against each one. For example, you could analyze the parking problems on your campus and then evaluate several solutions to the problems.

Combining Strategies

You may decide to combine two or more organizational strategies. In a problem-solution essay, for instance, you might use a narrative based on your personal experience or observation in the introduction, then begin the body of the essay with a cause-and-effect analysis of the problem, and then follow that with a comparison of possible solutions. Furthermore, you will often use various organizational patterns within the paragraphs, especially illustration, because you will need to support your points with examples. Nevertheless, as you plan your essay, you should have an overall organizational plan in mind.

EXERCISE 1.7

1. Circle the main organizational strategy you will employ in your essay. If you plan to combine organizational patterns, explain how.

   Narration   Illustration   Comparison or Contrast   Definition   Division

   Classification   Cause-and-Effect   Analysis   Problem-Solution

Combined: _____

_____

_____

2. Do you need to revise your working thesis to reflect the organizational strategy you plan to adopt?
         Yes   No

Revised thesis: _____

_____

_____

Have your work checked.

Developing an Outline

In the last step of the planning phase, you will develop a particular kind of outline known as the **thesis-topic sentence outline**. After you have developed a thesis sentence that expresses the idea you intend to support in your essay, you are ready to begin writing your topic sentences. But before attempting to write a topic sentence, recall what you already know about paragraphs.

The construction of body paragraphs differs greatly from that of introductory paragraphs. The most important sentence in the introductory paragraph—the thesis—concludes the paragraph. However, the most important sentence in the body paragraph—the **topic sentence**—usually begins the paragraph. Yet this is only a superficial difference. In the introductory paragraph. All sentences except the thesis serve only to give background material for the thesis; consequently, these sentences are more general than those found in the body paragraphs. By contrast, each body paragraph must thoroughly develop the subject introduced by its topic sentence, with detailed explanations and numerous examples.

The topic sentence is to the body paragraph what the thesis is to the essay: the controlling force. The topic sentence controls in three important ways. It focuses on a particular aspect of the subject about which you are writing. In addition, the topic sentence limits what you may include in the paragraph. Finally, the topic sentence makes it easier for the reader to see how your paragraph supports the essay's thesis.

When you begin writing your topic sentences, you will realize how important your thesis sentence is. For instance, if your thesis sentence is divided, you will be able to see what each body paragraph should include. The sample thesis sentence about the wolf—a divided thesis—shows clearly how a writer's point can be made. The divisions make it easy to see what to expect in each body paragraph. Consider that thesis and its topic sentences:

Example

Thesis:	Farmers and ranchers have driven the wolf to near extinction by using pesticides, by converting wild lands into farmlands, and by waging open war on this most misunderstood of all wild animals.
TS #1:	The pesticides farmers have used to control insects and rodents have entered the wolf's food chain since the wolf dines primarily on rodents, and the wolf's offspring and general health have suffered because of it.
TS #2:	Every time more wild land has been deforested and converted to farmland, the wolves that once hunted there have been reduced to homeless wanderers, often unable to find enough food to survive harsh winters.
TS #3:	Unquestionably, the most serious threats to the survival of the wolf have been the rifle, poison, and the bounty system used by farmers and ranchers who mistakenly blame the wolf for all their dead livestock.

The ideal time to write topic sentences is immediately after completing the thesis statement; however, some people prefer to write topic sentences after writing the entire introductory paragraph. The topic sentences help you the most when you can see them in a list before you add supporting sentences for each paragraph. If topic sentences are written before support is added, an outline or framework develops that helps you envision your complete composition. If you can construct a thesis-topic sentence outline of the entire essay, you can often see irrelevant or misplaced material before it becomes a serious problem.

As you write topic sentences, you must incorporate some kind of focus in them. If your topic sentences are too broad, your paragraphs may constantly wander off the subject and cause you and your reader unnecessary frustration. A good way to control your paragraphs is to be sure every topic sentence has a **controlling idea** you can point to. As the phrase suggests, the controlling idea is the word or phrase that limits the content of the paragraph. The following topic sentence would be difficult to develop because it lacks a sufficiently focused controlling idea.

Example

Moving from the parents' home into an apartment or dormitory is an experience few young people forget quickly.

To control the paragraph in this case, you would only need to insert a single word in the topic sentence to focus on the kind of experience it is.

Examples

> Moving from the parents' home into an apartment or dormitory is a *liberating* experience few young people forget easily.

> Moving from the parents' home into an apartment or dormitory is a *frightening* experience few young people forget easily.

> Moving from the parents' home into an apartment or dormitory is a *social* experience few young people forget.

Any one of these controlling ideas would make the paragraph far easier to write. For instance, if you were to write about how moving out on your own is a frightening experience, you could explain how being alone at night for the first time is frightening. In the same paragraph, you could explain how fear takes over when the rent is due and you have spent the money for other things. But with that paragraph so defined, any reference to anything except frightening experiences would clearly be irrelevant.

EXERCISE 1.8

Develop a thesis-topic sentence outline for the final version of your thesis. When you are satisfied that you have a workable outline, copy it here or print a copy for your instructor.

Thesis:_____

_____

_____

TS #1:_____

_____

_____

TS #2:_____

_____

_____

TS #3:_____

_____

_____

Have your work checked. Include a final copy in your Project Folder.

LESSON FOUR—*Writing Your Essay*

Creating an Opening Sentence

Since you have already written a thesis-topic sentence outline for your essay, you have the thesis, the last sentence of the introductory paragraph. Now you need to write the remainder of that first paragraph—a paragraph that should be a minimum of five sentences.

The first sentence of the introductory paragraph is called the **opening sentence**. Not just any sentence will do for an opening sentence; this sentence must have impact on your reader. Because it is the first example of your writing the reader will see, the reader's opinion of your writing will begin to form at this point. For this reason you must use extreme care as you write it. The opening sentence must accomplish two purposes: It must attract your reader's attention, and it must lead into the subject of the essay. The following opening sentence was taken from an article by a very successful writer:

Example

Motherhood is in trouble, and it ought to be.

Notice how you immediately wonder where the essay is heading. How could motherhood be in trouble? If it is in trouble, the human race is in trouble. And who would speak against mothers? Creating this type of provocative feeling is important because it pulls your reader into your essay.

The opening sentence above is also good because it is general enough so as not to give away the thesis of the essay, yet it introduces what the writer wants to talk about in the essay: the weakening of society's demand that every young couple have children whether or not they want them. This type of opening sentence is called the **provocative opening**.

Another type of opening sentence is the **rhetorical question**, the question for which no answer is expected. For instance, the following opening sentence is from an essay on politics:

Example

When are Americans going to learn not to believe the promises of politicians?

In this case the writer assumes the reader shares certain experiences and feelings of frustration regarding politics. There can be no concrete answer to the question because some Americans will always believe the promises of some politicians.

Using a **quotation** from a famous person or authority on your subject is also a good way to begin. If the quotation you offer is powerful, it can be effective. But you must be certain it is so relevant to your thesis that your reader can instantly grasp the significance. For instance, if you were writing an essay on euthanasia, a quote from Shakespeare might work as follows:

Example

"To be, or not to be—that is the question."

This essay would then go on to relate the thought behind Hamlet's famous soliloquy on suicide to the subject of the essay, euthanasia.

The following are other examples of effective opening sentences:

Examples

Play is the work of children. (provocative)

How many mothers think they are helping their babies when they are actually doing them more harm than good? (rhetorical)

Edward James Olmos, Hollywood actor, says, "Education is the vaccine for violence." (quotation)

You can use other types of opening sentences, but master these three most common ones first. Remember that the purpose of the opening sentence is to get your reader to want to read what you have written. It must be interesting, or your reader may assume the rest of the essay will be boring and stop reading.

EXERCISE 1.9

For your first draft, experiment by writing one of each type of opening sentence. Then mark the one you want to use for your essay with a check mark.

Provocative: _____

_____

_____

Rhetorical
Question: _____

_____

_____

Quotation: _____

_____

_____

Have your work checked.

Developing the Introductory Paragraph

For a 500–750 word essay like the one you will write in this chapter, a one-paragraph introduction will be sufficient. Longer essays such as those in later chapters may need introductions that are two, three, or even four paragraphs long. But however long the introductory portion of your essay, remember that the last sentence of the introduction is always the thesis, unless you have a good reason for placing it elsewhere.

Between the opening sentence and the thesis, writers customarily give some background to prepare the reader for the thesis message. In a short essay the total length of the introductory paragraph is usually no more than five or six sentences, so you must be brief. You should, however, form a smooth connection between the opening sentence and the thesis. This transition can be accomplished by a number of different methods. Perhaps the most popular introduction gives a historical review of the events leading to the current state of affairs on the issue being discussed. The following paragraph was taken from a 750-word essay on the need for a solution to the problem of radioactive waste disposal.

Example

Some scientists and environmentalists fear that in the very near future the state of Washington may become the most unhealthy place on the planet Earth. As a possible storage site for radioactive waste, central Washington may soon be receiving huge amounts of this notoriously unstable substance that has been accumulating since 1944. When considering

Washington as a storage site for waste, one must be aware of the December 1957 disaster that took place within the Ural Mountains of the Soviet Union at what was once the city of Kyshtyn in the District of Zapadno. Radioactive waste, stored in mine shafts, percolated into the surrounding soil causing a nuclear chain reaction. The resulting explosion spewed contaminated soil for more than 1,000 square miles, and prevailing winds carried the contaminants even farther. American scientific leaders are confident, however, that this catastrophe will never be repeated and are preparing for testing at Gable Mountain, near the city of Hanford, to determine whether or not the bulk of this country's radioactive waste can be stored safely within the ancient basaltic lava flows of the Columbia Plateau. Unlike the highly fractured Ural Mountains, the great basaltic plateau of the Columbia Basin is a solid formation with an average depth of 3,000 meters; this seemingly ideal formation of dense igneous rock, therefore, will provide the United States with the best possible location for storage of radioactive waste. Viable but costly solutions to the momentous problems of radioactive waste include recycling by means of proton bombardment, storage in space orbit, and deep sea burial; however, at the present there is no workable alternative to a project such as the proposed storage facility at Hanford.

Here the writer goes from a provocative opening sentence to a historical example; the writer tells what scientists hope will not happen in Hanford by telling first what happened in Russia in 1957. After giving this historical example, the writer explains how it compares to the Hanford situation and then leads the reader smoothly into the thesis.

Sometimes writers find it more suitable to give their readers a more complete historical sketch. Consider the following introduction. It contains three paragraphs, so it is an example of the kind of introduction you could use for a longer essay, for example, a library research essay.

Example

"Gold and land abundant," was the persuading call which reached the ears of America's eastern populace from the new land called California. Storekeepers sold their shops and bought wagons and horses. Farmers packed up their families and farming tools. All made ready for the trip to California. The year was 1849, and the progression of California's population had begun.

In the century that followed, there was much turmoil over the ownership of California's rich soil, impeding many an individual's dream of owning land. The problem lay in the confusion over land holdings by the Southern Pacific Railroad and its stockholders, and those of the land speculators who unscrupulously acquired large parcels of land through the purchase of Spanish land grants. The legal battles were long and complicated, and the courts were sympathetic to the speculators and robber barons. As a consequence, the average squatter was shut out, and the control of California's real property was guaranteed to the beneficiaries of these magnates. The injustice seen in California in those early days appears to have been catapulted through time and into an urban setting as descendants of those squatters can be seen living in the rundown apartment complexes owned by many of these same old families.

Oblivious to the economic distress the renter feels, these owners periodically increase the rent demanded, an action justified by the fact that they themselves continue to pay rising property taxes, increased utility costs and steeper interest rates on borrowed money. Due to an over-inflated economy, the legacy of these land holders and speculators, a housing shortage has been developed, and the building industry has been thrown into a recession. There are ways, however, to help renters and to curtail this downward economic spiral. A well-defined system of rent controls, complemented by tax credits and low-cost loans to property owners and tailored to each of California's economic populations, would not only provide the reasonably priced housing but would also stimulate the sagging building industry economy.

Although this is the introduction for a longer essay than you will be required to write in this chapter, you can easily see how the writer's use of historical material leads from a quote in the opening sentence to the thesis. A shorter essay would require a shorter introduction, of course, so much less material between the opening sentence and the thesis would be included.

EXERCISE 1.10

Draft an introductory paragraph for the thesis you wrote in Exercise 1.7. Use the opening sentence you selected in Exercise 1.9. Then copy your introductory paragraph in the space provided or print a copy, either in its rough form or in a more polished form, whichever you prefer.

_____

_____

_____

_____

_____

_____

_____

_____

_____

_____

_____

_____

_____

_____

Have your work checked.

Writing the Body Paragraphs

Once you have written your topic sentences, writing the **body paragraphs** is just a matter of following a standard procedure. Read your topic sentence and ask "how?" and "why?" Every answer is a **primary support sentence**, so called because it directly elaborates upon the basic idea put forth in the topic sentence. For instance, if you were writing about anorexia nervosa, you would begin by developing a thesis statement and its accompanying topic sentences. Study the following thesis-topic sentence outline. Notice that this thesis is not divided. Although it is an effective thesis, it must be accompanied by strong topic sentences. As a rule, the more general your thesis is, the more specific your topic sentences have to be.

Example

Thesis: Anorexia nervosa is an eating disorder that severely affects many adolescents.

TS #1: First, there are many reasons why anorexia nervosa numbers have increased.

TS #2: Next to adolescence, society's obsession with being thin plays an enormous part in the continuing increase of anorexia cases.

TS #3: In addition, socioeconomic and race factors play an important role in the incidence of anorexia.

TS #4: Knowing the symptoms can help an individual and or family members recognize this disorder.

TS #5: Fortunately, over the years, some treatments have been discovered to help the victims overcome anorexia nervosa.

After working up this thesis-topic sentence outline, the next step would be to develop the topic sentences into paragraphs, one paragraph at a time. Suppose you were writing body paragraph #5.

Your first task would be to write your **primary support sentences (PS)**, for example, as follows:

TS #5: Fortunately, over the years some treatments have been discovered to help the victims overcome anorexia nervosa.

PS #1: One method of treatment requires hospitalization because the patient is fed intravenously.

PS #2: Another method of treatment is eating groups that are designed for victims who suffer from anorexia but are not in eminent danger of dying.

PS #3: In addition to these two treatments, other effective methods of treatment are trying to prevent eating disorders from occurring in the first place.

(Note how easy this outline is to follow because of the **transitions**.)

Obviously, if you joined the above topic sentence and primary support sentences, you would find you had created a paragraph. At first, the paragraph might look good to you, but rest assured that your instructor would not be impressed. Details are missing everywhere. Details that explain or clarify the primary support sentences are stated in **secondary support sentences**. Secondary support sentences are absolutely necessary whenever a primary support sentence does not explain your point with clarity. The details or examples in the secondary support sentence can make the difference between your readers' understanding or not understanding what you are saying. Notice how different the paragraph looks at the beginning when the first primary support sentence is reinforced by secondary support sentences. (**TS**=topic sentence, **PS**=primary support sentence, **SS**=secondary support sentence)

Example

     TS Fortunately, over the years some treatments have been discovered to help the victims overcome anorexia nervosa. **PS** One method of treatment requires hospitalization because the patient is fed intravenously. **SS** In the majority of cases, families bring adolescent girls to the hospital. **SS** In the hospital doctors will treat the victim by encouraging her to eat. **SS** If the victim does not eat willingly, sometimes it is necessary to force feed the patient. **SS** Unfortunately, this form of treatment is not usually effective because by the time the patient is brought to the hospital, the victim is beyond the help of doctors. **PS** Another method of treatment is joining eating groups that are designed for victims who have suffered from anorexia nervosa but not to the point of impending death. **SS** These groups are designed to be interactive and allow the victim to share her experiences with others who have encountered similar situations. **PS** In addition to these two treatments, other effective methods of treatment are trying to prevent eating disorders from occurring in the first place. **SS** Both middle schools and high schools are educating children about the effects of eating disorders and the seriousness of these diseases. **CS** Although there are some treatments, anorexia nervosa is very difficult to treat, and too often patients seek treatment too late.

Your instant clue that a paragraph lacks secondary support—one that every instructor recognizes instantly—is a short paragraph. If you write a paragraph that has fewer than five sentences, usually that paragraph lacks secondary support.

THE FIVE-SENTENCE RULE

Count the sentences in each paragraph you write. A paragraph containing fewer than five sentences is too short and should be expanded.

The following paragraph is taken from a college essay. The sentences have all been labeled to help you recognize them.

Example

     TS Space storage of radioactive waste, however, could result in the removal of all living matter from this planet. **PS** The most minute human or mechanical error could result in a shroud of radioactive material that would encircle the earth for as long as 4,000,000 years. **SS** Major accidents within the space program have been few; however, ten percent of all space flights have malfunctioned in some way. **SS** A malfunction aboard a space vessel containing radioactive waste would be the most devastating event the world has ever seen. **SS** Elements such as plutonium-239 and cesium-246, with a half-life of 250,000 and 2,000,000 years, respectively, would be released into the troposphere, causing all life to cease. **PS** Astroscientists contend that radioactive waste within ceramic containers can be transported into space via space shuttle; they are reluctant to admit, though, that a proven container does not exist. **SS** The Oak Ridge Laboratory in Tennessee, after years of testing and millions of tax dollars, has yet to produce a ceramic container that will withstand the intense heat produced by radioactive waste. **SS** Production of a container that will withstand the heat of a premature burnout is not even within the scope of the project. **CS** Storage of radioactive waste in space orbit is a distinct possibility; however, it is useless to even consider such a concept within the next few decades.

Notice that the paragraph above ends with a **concluding sentence** (CS) that sums up the position taken in the paragraph. Not every paragraph you write will need a concluding sentence, but you can often give a paragraph a more complete appearance by including a sentence like the one above.

You should also be aware that not every primary support sentence needs a secondary support sentence. If a primary support sentence is clear and a secondary support sentence would be so obvious it would bore the reader, you can go on to the next primary sentence. But, as a general rule, try one or more secondary support sentences before making that decision.

Example

TS Because of the increased use of technology and the World Wide Web, instructors have seen an increase in plagiarism in student work and have to use a variety of methods to combat it. **PS** One way instructors try to eliminate plagiarism is by creating unique assignments. **SS** No longer can they rely on asking traditional types of questions for essay assignments because samples of these essays are as available as the click of a few computer key strokes. **SS** Therefore, they often create assignments that link two or more readings and create original essay question topics. **PS** Another safety measure that instructors use is to check all preliminary work, from the initial brainstorming, to the outline, to a series of rough drafts. **PS** Once an essay is turned in and the instructor suspects plagiarism, another avenue available to instructors is the use the Internet to check for stolen sentences. **SS** By using search engines such as *Google* to hunt for words and phrases, the plagiarized source is often rapidly found. **SS** More instructors are using commercial anti-plagiarism services such as turnitindot.com. **SS** An instructor can merely submit a student's essay to the service electronically, and within twenty-four hours receive a report showing which passages have been plagiarized. **PS** Furthermore, publishers are helping instructors prevent cheating. **SS** These publishers and other computer-based companies are creating software to help block access to some applications on the computer, such as e-mail and web browsers, when the students are taking computerized tests. **CS** Instructors are dismayed at the time, effort, and technical expertise needed to track down plagiarism, but most are resolved to persevere in the task.

EXERCISE 1.11

Label the sentences in the following paragraph (**TS, PS, SS, CS**). (Answers on page 46)

_____Aquatic life, especially the anadromous fish, has been adversely affected by the pumping stations at the southwest corner of the Great Delta._____Pumping causes fast current flows._____Thus, invertebrates on which the fish feed cannot grow properly because of the increase in water flow._____In addition, small fish usually drift to their food supply, reaching it at the time their bodies need it._____The increased flow often interferes with this cycle, and many of the small fish die. Pumping also changes the direction of the water flow in some Delta channels, causing confusion for migrating fish, especially salmon returning to their spawning grounds._____To make matters worse, because the Southern Delta section is a nursery area for striped bass, fish are present there most of the year._____The pumping action draws fish to the export pumps, and fish too small to be adequately screened, striped bass in particular, along with the organisms on which they feed, and fish eggs are drawn through the pumps where they are either destroyed or transported south with water._____Salmon and other large fish do not go through the pumps, but because they become trapped in the screens, they have to be literally picked out by hand and transported to the Western Delta._____This handling is hard on the fish, causing many losses, and it is expensive.

EXERCISE 1.12

Write the body paragraphs for your essay, following the thesis-topic sentence outline you developed in Exercise 1.8. Then, either in rough or polished form, copy one of the paragraphs in the space provided, or print a copy of that paragraph.

To increase your understanding of the structure of this paragraph, label each sentence as **TS** (topic sentence), **PS** (primary support sentence), **SS** (secondary support sentence), or **CS** (concluding sentence).

Have your work checked.

Drafting the Concluding Paragraph

After you have written the introductory and body paragraphs, the **concluding paragraph** should be easy. The first sentence of the conclusion sums up everything you have said in the essay, and then the remainder of the paragraph makes a general statement about the significance of the subject. This is also your last opportunity to convince the reader that your position is the correct one. When you have summed up the content of the essay as briefly as possible in the first sentence or two, you should end your paragraph with a few sentences commenting on why anyone should care about the topic.

Example

In an age of increasingly scarce resources, careful studies should be made on how best to solve the water problems without destroying fish and wildlife or the environment. There is enough water in the state to provide for everyone's needs. However, water hoarding by a handful of landowners for self-serving reasons does not benefit the population as a whole. Eventually, a limit as to how much water can be removed from the Delta must be set so that rivers can continue to flow. Moreover, preserving the natural beauty of the state is a responsibility that must be accepted for the benefit of future generations.

Example

Anorexia nervosa is a very serious eating disorder that for the most part could be prevented. Anorexia nervosa could be prevented if the media would not constantly portray thinness as beautiful, and any size over a three as ugly. Also, parents and family members could help alleviate the problem if they would allow their children to be children instead of making fun of weight, putting children on restrictive diets, or putting extra pressure on them. If these two suggestions were taken seriously, the number of cases of anorexia nervosa would be drastically reduced. Even though anorexia nervosa is becoming one of the most common disorders in adolescence today, there are treatments available. Society needs to start protecting our adolescents from this disorder instead of encouraging them to think that thin is beautiful.

EXERCISE 1.13

Write a concluding paragraph for the introductory and body paragraphs you wrote in Exercise 1.10 and Exercise 1.12. Copy your concluding paragraph in the space provided, or print a hard copy. If you are writing on a computer, print out a copy of your entire essay.

_____

_____

_____

_____

_____

_____

_____

_____

_____

_____

_____

_____

_____

_____

_____

_____

_____

_____

_____

Have your work checked.

EXERCISE 1.14

Read the following essay carefully, looking up the meanings of any words you do not know. Read actively, highlighting main ideas and reacting as you read by making marginal notes. Read the essay more than once to fully grasp its content and style.

Introduction to Sample Student Essay

The author, Laura Burt, views young people's susceptibility to influence from others as a social problem. The material for her essay comes from two realms of Burt's experience: her reading and discussion experiences.

Burt's essay is well-written. Her introductory paragraph begins with a provocative opening sentence and leads to a clear thesis sentence. All of Burt's paragraphs are well developed and present convincing examples and details. Her conclusion sums up her main ideas and concludes with an idea for the reader to ponder.

Laura Burt

Professor Nakamoto

English 1A

16 Apr 2003

Don't Follow the Leader!

(1) College-age young adults are some of the most likely of all people to be swayed by an influential person or group. (2) People of college age feel more independent than ever before in their lives because they are leaving their families and hometowns for the first time and taking responsibility for themselves. (3) They are making new friends, joining fraternities and sororities, and learning many exciting things about the world. (4) However, these very reasons for feeling independent and strong are the main factors in young adults' susceptibility to being led astray and influenced by people with poor motives. (5) While most young people believe their values are too strong to allow them to be persuaded to follow another's instructions against their own best wishes, research has proven otherwise.

(6) The idea that college-age people are susceptible to influence from others is controversial because it implies that they do not have control over their own actions. (7) More than anything else, young adults want to assert their independence and authority over their lives. (8) Yet, people of college age are the group most easily indoctrinated into cults and are also most likely to slip into roles of authority or subservience, depending on the situation. (9) In a famous study conducted on the Stanford University campus in 1971, Philip Zimbardo asked a group of students to participate in an experiment for two weeks in which they either played the role of a "prisoner" or a "prison guard." (10) By the flip of a coin, the students were split into these two groups, given the uniform of each respective role, and put either in charge of "prisoners" or into a makeshift cell in the University Psychology Department. (11) The first and second days went by with most participants play-acting their roles

good-naturedly, but by the third day, the role-playing had started to overtake the students' personalities. **(12)** Some of the "guards" began humiliating some "prisoners," becoming cruel punishers even though they were fully aware that the "prisoners" had done nothing wrong. **(13)** Some students in the role of "prisoner" became zombie-like and apathetic, or rebelled and demanded their freedom. **(14)** After only six days, Zimbardo and others called off the experiment because of the aggressive nature of the now fully formed "guards" and "prisoners" toward each other (Myers 138). **(15)** The disturbing results of this study reinforce the idea that it is easy for young adults to lose their inner sense of direction and moral compass under certain circumstances.

(16) Even though young people may think their values will not allow them to do harm to another, it is rather easy to persuade one to perform certain tasks if the correct influences are in place. **(17)** People are more easily influenced by someone who they think of as an expert on a subject than by someone who seems to know as little about that subject as they do themselves. **(18)** If the leader of an organization is charming, persuasive, and knowledgeable about the group, that leader will be very influential. **(19)** According to Myers, "we tend to like people who are like us" (250). **(20)** Someone who portrays himself or herself as an expert is also easy to believe. **(21)** However, "expertness" does not necessarily mean having intelligence or authority over a particular subject. **(22)** To convey a sense of being an expert in one's field, one only needs to speak at a high rate of speed or be physically attractive. **(23)** Surprisingly, these simple ploys work very well. **(24)** First, speaking fast does not allow audience members enough time to gather their thoughts into a cohesive counter argument, making it seem to them that one does not exist. **(25)** Effective speakers throughout the years have used this method, including John F. Kennedy, who sometimes spoke at a pace reaching three hundred words per minute. **(26)** Second, physical attractiveness is appealing to the eye, and people look longer at someone who is appealing to behold, therefore giving him or her more of their attention.

(27) When presented with circumstances where personal responsibility for the outcome of a decision has been removed, young adults are more likely to submit to the requests and orders of influential leaders. **(28)** A lack of personal responsibility in certain situations can make people more likely to follow requests or orders from group leaders. **(29)** Cult leaders make it easier for their members to harm themselves or others by telling the members that they are not personally responsible for their actions because they are acting for the good of the group. **(30)** In an organizational setting, group members do not feel as accountable for actions as they would if each member were solely responsible for his or her own decisions. **(31)** Therefore, young adults make excellent candidates for indoctrination into social clubs, militaries, cults, and other organizations that heavily influence personal beliefs.

(32) Personal responsibility for one's own actions may be limited in other ways. **(33)** For example, when in a large group of strangers, such as while attending a sporting event, the crowd mentality can replace one's individual sense of responsibility. **(34)** Being in a group arouses people while at the same time diffusing responsibility. **(35)** According to the text *Social Psychology*, "Groups can generate a sense of excitement, of being caught up in something bigger than one's self" (Myers 295). **(36)** The physical arousal caused by being surrounded by so many other human bodies is enough to cause any calm person to be carried away. **(37)** The excitement from the crowd can even cause one to act in ways one would normally avoid, such as jeering the referee of a game or calling out insults to opposing team members. **(38)** "Because 'everyone is doing it,' all can attribute their behavior to the situation rather than to their own choices" (Myers 296).

(39) Granted, there are some circumstances under which the argument for the susceptibility of young people to outside influence may not apply. **(40)** In a psychology class lecture, Professor Stewart indicated that certain people may ask important questions of the leaders or organizations with whom they are unfamiliar, making these young adults less susceptible to manipulation. **(41)** Examples of these questions are: Does this group take away choices and alternatives for living or provide them? **(42)** Does the group deny access to information, family members, and friends, or facilitate that access? **(43)** Is ultimate responsibility for members of the group given to the individuals or to the group leader? **(44)** These questions make some young adults safer than others because one who asks them is likely to be skeptical or cautious in regard to an organization or leader who professes to have all the answers to life's traumas.

(45) When leaders do not allow people to think about the absolute magnitude of their actions, but only of the individual steps involved, it is called the foot-in-the-door approach. **(46)** This method begins by requesting a small favor. **(47)** In the case of the People's Temple cult led by Jim Jones in the 1970s, members were originally asked if they could simply take a few minutes to fold envelopes while they were at work. **(48)** In the beginning, all money donated to the church was given voluntarily, but soon members were asked to tithe ten percent of their income. **(49)** That figure soon jumped to twenty-five percent; then they were asked to donate everything they owned and work sixteen-hour days for the church. **(50)** Eventually, Jones had his members calling him "Dad" and pitting themselves against one another for his attention. **(51)** In the end, all the members who followed him to Guyana (ironically, in order to escape the evils of the world) committed suicide in a mass tragedy (Myers 270). **(52)** Some of them were beaten into drinking the poison cherry Kool-Aid laced with cyanide (Levi 172).

(53) There are also examples of the foot-in-the-door approach in a more typical society. **(54)** For instance, one may be asked to wear a lapel pin sponsoring a local candidate for office. **(55)** The wearer feels good about doing this small action because he or she controls it. **(56)** The next step in the process escalates a little; perhaps the volunteer will now be asked to put a sign with the candidate's name in his or her front yard. **(57)** Because the volunteer already supports the candidate publicly on his or her clothing, it will not seem like a very large jump to begin showing neighbors which contender he or she supports. **(58)** This step is only a beginning to something much larger, however. **(59)** The next step might involve the person answering phones on the weekend for the campaign, then donating small sums of cash to fund the campaign. **(60)** As the favors build in intensity, the volunteer will feel that he or she has done quite a bit of work and is well-liked in the organization, so a leap to something as radical as donating a third of his or her monthly income to the campaign will seem perfectly normal. **(61)** This new level of normalcy will prevail until an outside influence brings reason back into the life of the volunteer. **(62)** "When people commit themselves to public behaviors and perceive these acts to be their own doing, they come to believe more strongly in what they have done" (Myers 141). **(63)** They then feel obligated to do successively more extreme activities in order to keep up with their original sense of accomplishment.

(64) College-age adults are especially susceptible to influence by powerful leaders. **(65)** People of college age are just beginning to form their own personal values, and the newness of these values makes them easily molded and shaped by the hand of a powerful influencer. **(66)** The teens and early twenties are important formative years, partly because experiences during these times "make deep and lasting impressions" (264). **(67)** "Young people might therefore be advised to choose their social influences—the groups they join, the media they imbibe, the roles they adopt—carefully" (263-264). **(68)** The people in this age group should be wary of anyone offering them a life without sadness or pain because these emotions are a part of everyone's life. **(69)** Accepting the pain or loneliness in one's life is certainly easier when an influential leader is saying he or she will take all of the burdens off of one's shoulders; however, working through this very pain and loneliness is what causes one to become an independent adult with strong values.

EXERCISE 1.15

Reread Laura Burt's essay, "Don't Follow the Leader," studying its organization and development. From the list on the right, select the letter of the term which describes each sentence designated by the numbers in the parentheses on the left. (Answers on page 46)

 1. Sentence   (1) _____   a . Topic sentence

 2. Sentence   (5) _____   b . Thesis sentence

 3. Sentence   (6) _____   c . Opening sentence

 4. Sentence   (8) _____   d . Primary support sentence

 5. Sentence   (9) _____   e . Secondary support sentence

 6. Sentence   (15) _____   f . Concluding sentence

 7. Sentence   (16) _____

 8. Sentence   (27) _____

 9. Sentence   (28) _____

10. Sentence   (32) _____

11. Sentence   (33) _____

12. Sentence   (39) _____

13. Sentence   (45) _____

14. Sentence   (53) _____

15. Sentence   (64) _____

EXERCISE 1.16

Before you prepare the final draft of your essay, you should review it, or better yet have it reviewed by others, in order to gather ideas and suggestions for improvements in its content and structure.

1. If you haven't already done so, print out a draft of your entire essay—the introduction, body, and conclusion.
2. Depending upon your instructor's instructions, choose one of the following options for gathering feedback for your first draft: 1) Have your instructor review your essay and make suggestions for improvement. 2) Have one or more of your classmates review your essay. 3) Review your own essay. Place this copy in your Project Folder.
3. Write the second draft of your essay, making the improvements suggested in Step 2. Place this copy in your Project Folder.

LESSON FIVE—Editing Your Essay

The **editing phase** is the final phase of the writing process. You have written the first draft of your essay, received feedback on it, and revised it, producing a second draft. At this point you are ready to produce the final draft or document of your essay, and your primary goal is to produce a document that follows the required format, is neatly printed, and is error free.

Editing

Part of your responsibility for preparing your essay for presentation involves editing the sentences so that each one will communicate effectively with your readers. Each sentence must be clearly understood by you and by whoever is reading your essay. None of your sentences should wander from the topic, or your readers' minds may wander, too. Furthermore, the sentences within the paragraphs must tie together coherently so that your readers can easily follow your line of reasoning. Also, your choice of words should be appropriate, and the syntax of your sentences should not be awkward or confusing. (Syntax is the way words are put together to form sentences.) Finally, your sentences should be edited so they are concise and clear, enabling your readers to quickly comprehend each point you are making.

Proofreading

Because your final document must be free from errors in spelling, grammar, usage, punctuation, and other writing conventions, it must be carefully proofread. Proofreading is the process of reading and marking the corrections that need to be made. If you look at the insides of the front and back covers of *Survival* you will find correction symbols that are commonly used for this purpose. The computer you are using probably has a spell-check feature, and some even have a grammar- or style-check function. Most writers edit for content and structure several times during the drafting phase. Then in the editing phase, they read through the essay again, revising the sentences, and then one more time, proofreading for errors that need to be corrected.

Document Preparation

The document of your essay is the final copy that you submit to your instructor for evaluation. It is often referred to as the **final draft.** Its appearance is important because it is the final step in making your essay as easy as possible for your reader to follow and understand. Now your readers' response will be all important, particularly that of your most important reader—your instructor. Your writing during the drafting phase was expected to be less than perfect. Your final document, however, is like a publication. Therefore, you must spend the time and effort necessary to make it as nearly perfect as is possible.

The required format for your social problem essay is illustrated in Laura Burt's essay "Don't Follow the Leader." It shows how to write your heading, where to place the headers (author's last name and page numbers, and the essay's title). You will also notice that the entire document is double-spaced, that each paragraph is indented five spaces, and that it has one-inch margins. Of course, you will not number or label your sentences in your final document unless requested to do so by your instructor.

EXERCISE 1.17

Prepare the final document of your social problem essay to be handed in to your instructor for grading. Make all the revisions and corrections that are necessary to make your final document as effective and error-free as possible. Place it in your Project Folder.

FINAL DOCUMENT CHECKLIST

1. Does your essay have a strong, effective thesis sentence?
2. Are all topic sentences clearly stated?
3. Are there at least five or more sentences in every paragraph?
4. Have you used secondary support (details, facts, figures, and examples)?
5. Does your essay have an interesting opening?
6. Is the summary sentence precise and the conclusion effective?
7. Do your paragraphs have adequate sentence variety and smooth transitions?
8. Have you used third person throughout, except in anecdotes?
9. Is your essay free of awkward or grammatically incorrect sentences?
10. Is the first word of every paragraph indented?
11. Have you checked for fragments, run-ons, and comma splices?
12. Have you checked your spelling, punctuation, and capitalization?
13. Is your essay neatly typed in 12 point?
14. Is your essay double-spaced and on one side only?
15. Did you put the heading in the upper-left corner and center the title of the essay?
16. Are your page numbers and headers correct?

ORGANIZING YOUR PROJECT FOLDER

The following should be included in your Project Folder to be turned in to your instructor for grading. Organize your materials with the work you completed first on the bottom, with the final draft of the essay on the top.

1. Thesis-topic sentence outline (Exercise 1.8)
2. First draft (Exercise 1.16)
3. All research material copied and highlighted with the information used.
4. Second draft (Exercise 1.16)
5. Final draft (Exercise 1.17)

COMPUTER SAFETY TIPS

1. Keep your essay stored on your hard drive until you have received your grade for the course.
2. Back up your essay by copying it onto a disk.
3. File a photocopy of your essay.

Answers to Chapter One

Exercise 1.11

TS Aquatic life, especially the anadromous fish, has been adversely affected by the pumping stations at the southwest corner of the Great Delta. **PS** Pumping causes fast current flows. **SS** Thus, invertebrates on which the fish feed cannot grow properly because of the increase in water flow. **SS** In addition, small fish usually drift to their food supply, reaching it at the time their bodies need it. **SS** The increased flow often interferes with this cycle, and many of the small fish die. **PS** Pumping also changes the direction of the water flow in some Delta channels, causing confusion for migrating fish, especially salmon returning to their spawning grounds. **PS** To make matters worse, because the Southern Delta section is a nursery area for striped bass, fish are present there most of the year. **SS** The pumping action draws fish to the export pumps, and fish too small to be adequately screened, striped bass in particular, along with the organisms on which they feed, and fish eggs, are drawn through the pumps where they are either destroyed or transported south with water. **SS** Salmon and other large fish do not go through the pumps, but because they become trapped in the screens, they have to be literally picked out by hand and transported to the Western Delta. **SS** This handling is hard on the fish, causing many losses, and it is expensive.

Exercise 1.15

1. C
2. B
3. A
4. D
5. E
6. F
7. A
8. A
9. D
10. A
11. D
12. A
13. A
14. A
15. F

2

The Argumentative Essay

Objectives

When you have finished this chapter, you will have:

1. used the three-phase writing process.
2. selected a subject and narrowed it to a topic.
3. gathered information using the Internet and/or the library.
4. listed the pros and cons.
5. written and refined the thesis sentence.
6. planned an argumentative strategy.
7. written a thesis-topic sentence outline.
8. drafted a 750-1,000 word argumentative essay.
9. received feedback and revised the essay.
10. produced the final document in the required format.
11. compiled a Project Folder.

The Argumentative Essay 2

Life is filled with controversies—large and small. Nations make war; politicians debate; theorists argue; concerned citizens write letters to the editors; neighbors quarrel; customers complain. Violence may mark the failure of argumentative rhetoric, a civilized substitute. Persuasion and diplomacy lead to agreement, cooperation, peace, and other kinds of constructive behavior. Therefore, learning to deal with controversy in a reasoned way is important. You can learn to present your ideas in ways that offer you the best chance of persuading your audience to your point of view. The same basic rhetorical principles, once learned, will work well in both oral and written arguments. The persuasive strategies learned here will also help you develop critical thinking skills that will be useful in other courses and in many aspects of your life. In this chapter you will learn to write an argumentative essay, using variations of a time-proven strategy: the **pro-con argument**.

Of the different types of essays you will learn to write, the argument is one of the most useful. As William Hazlitt, the famous essayist wrote, "When a thing ceases to be a subject of controversy, it ceases to be a subject of interest." In general, instructors place a higher value on argumentative essays than they do on informative reports. They will appreciate the fact that you have the courage to venture a debatable position, even if they do not necessarily agree with your position. The argumentative strategy can be used for many writing assignments. Writing is rhetoric, and as Aristotle said, rhetoric is the art of choosing the most advantageous argument in a given situation.

The basic order of an argument is straightforward. First, you assert your position in the **thesis**, sometimes called the **claim**. Your thesis, or claim, is a single sentence summarizing what you are trying to prove. Second, you acknowledge viewpoints that are in disagreement with your thesis—the **opposition**. In these statements either you agree that some opposing viewpoints hold some merit or you simply summarize the opposing viewpoints. Third, you develop **reasons** and **evidence** that will persuade your readers to accept your thesis. These are statements that support your thesis—your **proof**. Fourth, you conclude your argument persuasively.

LESSON ONE–Discovering a Subject, Gathering Information, Narrowing It to a Topic

This lesson takes you through the first three steps of the Planning Phase as you prepare to write your argumentative essay.

Discovering a Subject

Use the techniques suggested in Chapter One's "Discovering a Subject" (pages 10-12) to find a **controversial subject** that will be interesting to both yourself and your readers. This subject will then be narrowed to the topic you will use for a 750-1,000 word argumentative essay (three to five typed pages).

Sources to Consider

Internet
Personal experiences
Differences of opinion among experts in your hobby
Issues in your chosen field or major
Class lecture notes and textbooks
Volunteer work or service-learning projects
Conversations with family, friends, classmates, co-workers
Local, national or international newspapers, such as the *New York Times*
Television and radio news and talk shows
National Public Radio's *Morning Edition* or *All Things Considered*
News magazines, such as *Newsweek*, *Time* or the *Economist*
Pamphlet files in library
Books and professional journals
Appendix D: Suggested Subjects (page 349)

EXERCISE 2.1

List three controversial subjects of interest and choose one that you will narrow to the topic of your argument. (Your instructor may select your subject from among the three you suggest.)

Possible Subjects:

1._____

2._____

3._____

Subject Chosen:_____

Gathering and Analyzing Information about Controversial Topics

In the process of narrowing your subject to a topic for your argumentative essay, you will need to do some background reading. A few hours spent reading about your subject will expand your knowledge, enabling you to see more clearly the possibilities for narrowing your subject.

Background reading will also help you see all of the issues involved in the controversy, helping you when you develop your list of pros and cons—the claims of the opposing sides.

After you have narrowed your subject to a topic, you will need to define the issues associated with the topic and read articles by authors who take opposing viewpoints. After developing this general background knowledge, you will then be well prepared to develop your own position on the topic and advocate it in an argumentative essay. Gathering and analyzing information from online sources, newspapers, magazines, books, and professional journals takes some time and effort, but it is essential preparation for you to write intelligently about a controversial topic.

This preliminary reading will prove useful again during the writing phase, providing the information you need to support the points you are making in your paragraphs. Your Internet printouts and library photocopies will be readily available in your Project Folder, making it easy to locate the examples, facts, and figures you need to prove your points.

Information gathering skills you must learn include searching the Internet and locating information in the library. Then once the information is gathered, you need to employ critical reading skills to paraphrase main ideas, to summarize paragraphs and whole articles, and to analyze information for credibility and bias. To accomplish these tasks, you will need to print pages from Internet sources, make photocopies of pages from books and articles in the library, and then spend time highlighting ideas with a colored marker, writing annotations in the margins, taking notes on note cards or in a notebook or on a computer. Learning how to give credit to your sources of information to avoid plagiarism is also essential.

What Needs To Be Done?

To complete your research you will need to do the following tasks:
- Locate and gather information about the topic.
- Print or photocopy information.
- Read and analyze the information.
- Paraphrase main ideas; summarize parts of and whole articles.
- Organize, highlight, make notes in margins and on note cards or the computer.
- Evaluate sources for credibility and bias.
- Identify each information source and keep all photocopies, printouts, and notes in a Project Folder.

Begin by Searching the Internet

The World Wide Web is a huge, seemingly endless source of information that grows even larger every day. If your school library with its collection of books and media is like a planet, the Web with its ever expanding number of Web sites and hundreds of thousands of pages on them is like a galaxy. Searching the World Wide Web is a good way to begin learning more about your topic, or even to find a topic. The problem is that unlike libraries with their predictable arrangements by either the Dewey Decimal or Library of Congress system, the Web is far less organized. The information you need is probably on the Web, but you must learn how to find it.

Surfing the Internet

Surfing the Internet is a popular, but somewhat haphazard way of locating information on the Internet. For example, while searching for a controversial topic you might go to a news site such as msn.com, cnn.com or bbc.com to find a story about human cloning. Then if you just start randomly clicking on the links that appear in conjunction with the news article, and they in turn lead to other links that you explore, you are surfing the Internet. If you are lucky with this random searching, you may find both a topic and enough information to write an argument, but your time will be better spent if you use one of the Internet search engines.

Search Engines

A search engine, like Alta Vista for example, constantly visits Web sites and creates up-to-date catalogs of their pages. Often changing, search results built by search engines are not permanent catalogs because the search engines continually "crawl" the Web, visiting and revisiting web sites in order to revise and update the catalogs.

Popular Search Engines

Alta Vista	(http://www.altavista.com)
Google	(http://www.google.com)
HotBot	(http://www.hotbot.com)
Yahoo	(http://www.yahoo.com)

Search Directories

Search directories are indexes of web sites that are more organized than the search sites built solely by the search engines. With search directories, employees of the directories categorize and organize the information found by the crawlers. Some of the search engines, such as *Yahoo* and *Google*, also list directories in which sites are organized by subject. For example, the home page of Yahoo, one of the most popular directories, lists categories such as "Arts and Humanities," "Government," and "News and Media." In turn, these categories are broken down into smaller divisions. "News and Media," for example, is broken down into "Current Events, Magazines, T.V., Newspapers." Although directories may seem more organized than search engine sites, they are often not as complete or up-to-date as the search engine sites whose crawlers constantly revise them.

Popular Search Directories

Infoseek	(http://www.infoseek.com)
Lycos	(http://www.lycos.com)
Magellan	(http://www.magellan.com)

How to Conduct a Simple Search

After first opening your **browser**, for example *Internet Explorer* or *Netscape Navigator*, access one of the popular **search engines** or **search directories** by typing in its Internet address, or URL, as it is commonly called.

After the page appears, locate the text box labeled "Search" and then type in one or two words or a short phrase that describes your topic. Use key words and do not include the words *a, an,* or *the.* You can limit your search by adding descriptive words. For example, instead of typing in just "cloning," you might type in "human cloning experiments" or "human cloning laws" or "human cloning laws United States." For best results, enclose your topic description in double quotation marks.

Example

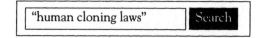

Then to begin the search either click on the Search button or press Enter (press Return on a Mac). The **search results** should then appear. A large number of results may appear, requiring you scroll through several pages. Some of the web sites listed, however, may be completely irrelevant to your topic. Browse through the Web site titles and open some of the more promising looking sites to see if you will be able to find the information you are seeking. You can also explore any **links** that are listed. If your search is unproductive, you may need to reword the search topic and try again. You might also try one of the other search engines or directories, for example, comparing the search sites located on both *Google* and *Alta Vista*. (See Chapter Three for how to conduct complex searches.)

EXERCISE 2.2

Using one of the Internet search engines or directories, locate and print at least one recent article that will provide useful information for your argumentative essay. Then do the following:

1. Print the article.
2. Using a colored marker, highlight the main ideas of the article.
3. Make notes in the margin about the important issues involved in this controversial subject. Also make marginal notes about which side of the controversy the author takes.
4. On your computer or on a note card, write a summary of the article.

Have your work checked.

Evaluating Internet Sources

Evaluating online sources for **credibility** is extremely important. You have heard the maxim, "Don't believe everything you read." The same advice holds true for the Internet. The fact that something is published on a Web site certainly doesn't mean that it should be believed in its entirety. Maintain a skeptical attitude as you examine online sources of information. Be on the look out for sites that represent both sides of the controversial issue you are researching. Ask yourself the following questions:

- Does the information seem accurate? Is the information up to date?
- Do you respect the expertise of the authors? What are their credentials? If there is a corporate author, what is the reputation of that organization? What are their vested interests?
- Does the information seem reliable because the ideas are well supported or because other articles seem to be saying more or less the same thing?
- Is there anything about the Web site that causes you to suspect a bias, either overt or hidden? If there is a bias, can you find other sources that present opposing points of view?

EXERCISE 2.3

Using the Internet, locate two more sources of information for your argument and print them out. Evaluate the credibility of each source, using the criteria on page 53 to write a short summary of each one. Have your evaluations checked.

1. Does the information seem accurate and up-to-date? Explain.

_____

_____

_____

2. Do you respect the expertise of the author(s)? Explain why or why not.

_____

_____

_____

3. Does the information seem reliable because the ideas are well supported or because other articles seem to be saying more or less the same thing? Explain.

_____

_____

_____

4. Does the article seem biased, or does it support one side or the other in the controversy you are studying? Explain.

_____

_____

_____

5. Do you think this is a useful article to refer to in your essay? Explain.

_____

_____

_____

Have your work checked.

Project Folder

Saving and organizing your information is important. Save any pages printed from the Internet, and make photocopies of any pertinent information located in the library. Keep your notes. You will be expected to show these supporting documents to your instructor, so organize everything in a **Project Folder**. All of your work for this assignment, including your rough draft and revisions will be kept in this folder.

EXERCISE 2.4

Conduct your background research and organize it in your Project Folder. Place materials in the folder in a way that will be useful, for example, paper clipping the articles that support one viewpoint and those that support another viewpoint together.

EXERCISE 2.5

After completing your background research, write a report answering the following questions and place it in the front of your Project Folder.

1. Why are you interested in this controversy?
2. What did you already know about the subject before you began your research?
3. Where did you find your information (Internet, library, books at home, newspapers, etc.)?
4. If you used the Internet, which search engines or directories did you use?
5. If you used a library, how did you go about locating information?
6. What information gathering techniques did you employ (paraphrasing, highlighting, annotating, note taking, summarizing)?
7. How did you evaluate the credibility of your sources of information?
8. Are you acquainted with the basic issues involved in the controversy now?
9. Are you satisfied now that you know enough about your topic to proceed?
10. Are you still firmly committed to writing about this topic?

Have your folder checked.

Narrowing the Subject to a Topic

Now that you have completed your background research, use one of the prewriting techniques discussed in Chapter One to a Topic to narrow your subject to the topic you will develop in your argument. When you feel you are ready, simply employ one of the prewriting techniques to choose your narrowed topic.

Prewriting Techniques

Brainstorming
Freewriting
Clustering
Analytical Questioning
Focused Questioning

Example

Controversial subject chosen: Genetic Engineering
Is there a controversial aspect that will allow you to write either for or against the subject?
Answer: Yes
Prewriting technique: Focused Questioning

Focused questions:	What are the possible health hazards of genetically altered food?
	Is it ethical to tamper with the reproductive process in humans?
	Do parents have the right to determine their child's characteristics?
	Is genetic therapy a breakthrough for curing life-threatening diseases like breast cancer?
	Should the government include preventative genetic technology in everyone's insurance coverage to ensure equal access?
	Is genetic predisposition a greater factor than environment for susceptibility to disease?
	Could there be abuse of genetic testing by health insurance companies? Is there well-planned regulation that will prevent accidental genetic disasters?
	Is the all-out ban on genetic engineering that many theologians are calling for necessary?
	Why are farmers and some scientists opposed to genetic alterations?
	Should genetic development be driven by profit motives?
	Should human functions be commercialized?
	What safety and security measures, if any, are in place in the United States and other countries to protect against genetic engineering disasters?
	What are the related issues? (To brainstorm, state them as questions.)
Possible Topics:	1. Ethical issues raised by genetic engineering
	2. Safety and security in biotech companies
	3. Government regulation of the biotech industry
Topic Chosen:	The moral dilemma of tampering with human nature

EXERCISE 2.6

On a separate sheet of paper, use one of the prewriting techniques to narrow your subject to the topic you will develop in your argument. Then write in the information requested below.

Subject chosen:_____

Prewriting technique:_____

Topic chosen:_____

Show your prewriting to your instructor, and have your topic approved. Place your prewriting in your Project Folder.

LESSON TWO—Listing Pros and Cons, Writing a Thesis

Listing the Pros and Cons

Any statement in your essay that raises arguments against the position you have taken in your thesis is con, or against your argument. Thus, if you are in favor of capital punishment, any statement against it is a con. But if you are opposed to capital punishment, any statement that favors it is a con. Any statement that supports the position you have taken is pro. Before writing your thesis, you must complete three preliminary steps that will help you organize your thoughts on what is pro and what is con.

First, pose your topic as a question, as you did in selecting your topic. This time, however, focus on your own opinions about the topic. Are you for or against building more nuclear power plants? Do you support or oppose the existing smoking ordinances in your community? Should a government agency be allowed to use potentially dangerous pesticides in residential areas to control insects harmful to agriculture? Should women be allowed (or required) to serve in combat roles? What measures should be taken to protect women from sexual harassment in the military? Should using a cell phone while driving be made illegal? Should the purchase of assault weapons be prohibited? In the battle against terrorism, should the government be able to detain non-citizens indefinitely? Any controversial issue can be stated as a question, and when you are able to answer that question, you will know what your basic position will be.

Second, compile a list of pros and cons that should be considered before answering your question. There are two good reasons for making a list of the pros and cons. The list will help you become more open-minded about the topic, seeing both sides of the issues. You might even change or modify your position as a result. The list will also enable you to anticipate opposition to your position. Therefore, you will see more clearly which points should be covered in your argument to counter that opposition.

Now, write down the main question to be decided.

Example

Should a person found guilty of first-degree murder be executed?

Next, list in two columns all of the pro and con reasons that come to mind. For instance, in the first column, the pro column, list reasons supporting capital punishment. In the second column, the con column, list reasons against capital punishment. Usually you can think of a con for each pro, but not always. At this point you are not concerned about your position, but rather you are trying to determine what in general are the pros and cons of the issue.

Capital Punishment

Pro	Con
1. The death penalty is a just punishment; victims' families have the right to revenge.	1. The death penalty constitutes cruel and unusual punishment.
2. The death penalty acts effectively as a deterrent to would-be murderers.	2. Statistics show that the death penalty is not an effective deterrent against murder.
3. Especially despicable and atrocious crimes warrant extreme punishment.	3. Especially horrible murders are committed by insane people, and insane people should be treated, not executed.

Pro	Con
4. Those who are against capital punishment are naive about the horror and savagery murderers perpetrate on their victims.	4. Opponents of the death penalty are well informed through the media.
5. The Old Testament supports the death penalty. "Who so sheddeth man's blood, by man shall his blood be shed: for in the image of God made he man." (Genesis 9:6)	5. The Bible opposes capital punishment: "Thou shalt not kill."
6. Hardened criminals cannot be rehabilitated.	6. Murderers can be rehabilitated.
7. Convicted murderers given life sentences may be paroled and murder again.	7. Convicted murderers are rarely paroled.
8. The death penalty deters potential armed robbers, rapists, and hijackers who realize that they might inadvertently murder their victims.	8. Armed robbers, rapists, and hijackers rarely anticipate murdering their victims.
9. Prison guards are not safe if convicts serving life sentences do not have the threat of the death penalty preventing them from murderous attacks on the guards.	9. The threat of the death penalty has not kept convicts from murdering guards and one another in the past.
10. A few innocent people may be executed, but most convicted murderers are guilty.	10. Many death-row inmates in Illinois have been shown to be wrongly convicted, leading to a moratorium on executions.
11. Use of DNA evidence reinforces other evidence proving accused murderers are guilty.	11. Use of DNA evidence proves that defendants wrongly accused of murder are innocent.
12. Convicted murderers deserve the death penalty regardless of race.	12. A disproportionate percentage of African Americans and Hispanics receive the death sentence.
13. People accused of murder who are innocent should not accept plea bargains, trusting that juries will find them innocent.	13. Lawyers may convince innocent people to take plea bargains out of fear of capital prosecution.

After you have compiled a list of the pros and cons, you will have to make up your mind which side is stronger—the pro or the con. If you decide you are on the pro side, the pro points will remain pros in your essay. If, on the other hand, you decide you are on the con side, the cons change to pros in your essay, and the list of pros change to cons. For example, if you were writing an essay on capital punishment, and you decided you are against capital punishment, the entire list of pros listed previously would change to cons. In your essay any viewpoint you support is a pro, and any viewpoint you oppose is a con.

EXERCISE 2.7

1. State the topic you have chosen for your argumentative paper as a question. (You may not use capital punishment as a topic.)

_____

_____

_____

_____

2. Make a list of the pros and cons. Number your list, and for every pro try to think of a corresponding con.

Pro	Con
_____	_____
_____	_____
_____	_____
_____	_____
_____	_____
_____	_____
_____	_____
_____	_____
_____	_____
_____	_____
_____	_____
_____	_____
_____	_____
_____	_____

_____   _____
_____   _____
_____   _____
_____   _____
_____   _____
_____   _____
_____   _____

3. Briefly answer the question posed at the beginning of this exercise. This answer is your basic position. From this point on, any statement that supports this position is a pro, and any statement against this position is a con.

_____

_____

_____

_____

Have your work checked.

Analyze Your Audience

Now take a few minutes to think about your audience. Who will read your argument? Obviously your instructor will read and grade your paper, but what about others in your class? How will they react to your argument during peer editing sessions or during discussion if you are asked to read your paper to the whole class?

One consideration is how much expertise your readers will have about your topic. What do they need to know? The less your readers know about your subject, the more carefully you will have to explain the basic issues related to your argument. Another consideration is just how controversial your argument will be with this particular group of readers. Will most of your readers probably agree with your argument, or should you anticipate some stiff opposition?

Your safest bet is to assume that your readers will react in a variety of ways. A few may know as much or more about your topic as you do, while others may be less informed. Some will be skeptical or outwardly opposed to your reasoning, but others will support your stand, either because they already agreed with you or because you have persuaded them. In any given English class you can expect a variety of viewpoints and beliefs. To be effective, the rhetorical strategy you use must be designed to deal with different levels of expertise and must anticipate differing opinions.

Your instructor may invite you to adopt a **persona** for this assignment. In other words, you may be asked to play a role of a writer that is not really you. You might, for example, take on the role of an irate taxpayer objecting to a proposed school bond issue, or you might pretend to be an investigative reporter for CNN or a parent who is concerned about an elementary school policy.

At some point you may realize that you have a broader intended audience than you first thought. You might, for instance, decide to send your argument to a newspaper as a letter to the editor or send it to a senator or city council representative.

All of these possibilities regarding your audience may affect the way you approach your argument. Anticipating who will be reading your essay and how they might react will help you strengthen your case and write the most persuasive argument possible.

EXERCISE 2.8

Determine who will be reading your essay and think about how they might react to it. Answer the following questions. (Write complete sentences.)

1. Will your instructor be evaluating your essay or including it in your portfolio? Has your instructor given you any feedback about your topic or the position you are taking that will cause you to make adjustments in your topic or your basic position?

_____

_____

_____

2. Will fellow class members be reading your essay, or will you be asked to read it aloud to the class? Will your essay be read in a peer editing session? Explain.

_____

_____

_____

3. How much expertise do your readers have about your subject? How will their knowledge or lack of knowledge affect the way you develop your argument? Explain.

_____

_____

_____

4. You can assume that your classmates will experience a variety of reactions to your argument, but do you anticipate that some class members may react strongly to your argument? If so, how can you strengthen your argument to make it more persuasive?

_____

_____

_____

5. Has your instructor asked you to adopt a persona for this assignment? If so, explain the role you will adopt and how that will affect your argumentative strategy.

_____

_____

_____

6. Is it possible that you might want others outside your class to read your argument, for instance, as a letter to the editor of a newspaper? How would that outside audience affect your argumentative strategy? Explain.

_____

_____

_____

Writing and Refining Your Thesis

Now that you have formulated a position and analyzed your potential audience, writing your working thesis is the next step. Look back at your statement of your basic position in Exercise 2.7. This statement is your thesis in its rudimentary form.

Examples

> The poor are not blessed.
>
> The electoral college is an outdated system.
>
> Not continuing affirmative action policies will lead to disaster.
>
> Affirmative action policies should be scrapped immediately.
>
> Income tax laws are unfair.
>
> Dams should be demolished to protect the ecosystem.

Each of these statements dogmatically asserts a debatable position. And your thesis must be a debatable declaration—a statement with which your reader can agree or disagree. But none of these statements is developed enough for a well-written argument. After having decided upon your basic position statement, you should transform it into a more refined thesis statement. This transformation can be accomplished easily in progressive stages.

Refinement #1—Add a phrase or clause summarizing the reasons you will use to support your basic position. The easiest way to connect this summary is to use the word *because*.

Examples

> Affirmative action hiring policies should be continued because without them organizations tend to continue racially exclusive hiring patterns and because we need to create a workforce that mirrors the ethnic mix of the community.

OR

> Because they are no longer needed, because they embarrass minority employees, and because they create reverse discrimination, affirmative action programs should be dismantled.

You do not have to use the word *because* in the summary of your reasons. The *because* can be implied, but not stated.

Example

> Banks should not be allowed to distribute unsolicited, pre-approved credit cards to college students because many students are already burdened with college loans, because the credit cards encourage them to live beyond their means, and because they don't realize how easy it is to fall into financial difficulty.

REVISED

> Banks should not be allowed to distribute unsolicited, pre-approved credit cards to college students, many of whom are already burdened with college loans, encouraging them to live beyond their means without understanding how easy it is to fall into financial difficulty.

If possible, revise your thesis so that it will have the same sequencing of the argument that follows it. Often the body of the argument will develop three to five reasons supporting your position. By listing these reasons in the same order they will appear in the argument, you make your line of reasoning easy to follow.

Refinement #2—Consider the advisability of softening your thesis statement. Your thesis assertion may be overstated, overgeneralized, illogical, too dogmatic, or inflammatory. As a result, readers may reject it immediately and refuse to read the rest of the argument. Although your thesis statement can be provocative, it needs to seem reasonable enough that readers will continue reading.

Examples

INFLAMMATORY

> All of the lawmakers who are attempting to impose ratings on hip-hop music are completely clueless about the lyrics and why hip-hop is so popular with its audience.

SOFTENED

> Critics who are attempting to impose ratings on hip-hop music should learn more about the lyrics and about the reasons for its popularity.

Refinement #3—After all of your dividing and refining, your thesis may be too long and too complicated, making it wordy and difficult to comprehend. If you think your thesis is long or awkward, ask your instructor if a shorter, simpler version would be more effective. Then revise your thesis, if necessary.

WORDY

When a student contemplating his or her first purchase of a computer considers cost, power and speed, screen size and clarity, keyboard size, ease of using the mouse, need for peripherals and batteries, and security from theft, the small notebook or laptop may not be the best choice compared to a desktop.

CONCISE

For a number of reasons, the small notebook or laptop computer may not be the best choice for a student buying his or her first computer.

EXERCISE 2.9

1. Repeat the basic position statement for your argument, the answer to the question that you wrote in Exercise 2.7.

_____

_____

_____

_____

2. Refinement #1—Add a clause or phrase that summarizes the reasons you will use to support your basic position. Select the reasons you want to use from those in the list of pros and cons you compiled in Exercise 2.7. As a general rule, use at least three but no more than five reasons.

_____

_____

_____

_____

3. Refinement #2—If necessary, write a softened version of your thesis.

_____

_____

_____

_____

4. Refinement #3—If your thesis seems too wordy, write a shorter version.

_____

_____

_____

Have your work checked.

LESSON THREE—Planning a Strategy, Writing an Outline

In academic writing, an argument on a controversial topic will generally be more effective if it shows that the author has a good grasp of the opposing viewpoints. Thus, a traditional argumentative strategy has evolved in which the writer summarizes opposing opinions—the **cons**—and counters them with his or her own opinions—the pros.

You can choose one of two organizational plans for the body of the essay when you write a **pro-con argument**. With the first plan, you summarize the opposing viewpoints first and analyze them later. With the second plan, you summarize each viewpoint one at a time and then discuss it before moving on to the next opposing viewpoint. Thus, the body of the argument alternates between the cons and the **pros**.

Plan One

The order in which you summarize and refute opposing viewpoints is important. Always summarize an opposing viewpoint first and then follow it with your rebuttal. In other words, put cons before pros. Your strategy, always, should be to end up on your own side. Do not weaken your position by following a statement supporting your thesis with a statement raising objections to the statement. Briefly summarize the point of opposition and then refute that point as persuasively as possible.

Example

Thesis:

Affirmative action in college admissions is a vital means of assuring that graduating classes reflect the diversity of the nation as a whole, and as such it should be retained.

Topic Sentence: *Con*

Critics argue that affirmative action in college admissions is no longer needed.

Topic Sentence: *Pro*

In spite of the critics' concerns, however, eliminating affirmative action in college admissions now would be premature.

When using Plan One to write an argument, you do not simply support your thesis with a series of body paragraphs explaining why your thesis should be believed. Instead, you insert a con paragraph before the pro paragraphs, just after the introductory paragraph, at the beginning of the body of the paper. In this con paragraph you summarize the arguments against your position. The idea is to anticipate the objections to your argument and show the reader that you are aware of them and that you can address them honestly and openly in the pro paragraphs that follow this con paragraph. This paragraph must be worded in such a way, however, that readers will make no mistake about which side you are on. They must realize immediately that you are merely summarizing the opposing point of view.

The way to signal clearly to your readers whether they are reading a con or pro paragraph is to use traditional argumentative transitions effectively. For example, *but* or *however* placed at the beginning of a sentence in an argument is a traditional signal that a writer is turning from the con to the pro side of the argument. If you use one of these transitional words to introduce a con point, you will confuse your readers.

Basically, there are two ways to lead into a con section in an argument. The first way is to acknowledge only that your opponents claim something is true. You do not concede that the opponents are right; you just show your readers that you are informed enough to know what your opponents think.

Examples

> Opponents of increased funding for space programs argue that the money would be better spent in programs providing more jobs for people.
>
> Those who argue against gun control like to quote slogans, such as "Guns don't kill, people do" and "Control criminals not guns."
>
> Some environmental scientists contend that the increased level of carbon dioxide in the earth's atmosphere will raise global temperatures until the mid-latitudinal regions become steaming jungles.

A second way to lead into a con section is to concede, or admit, that your opponents may have a valid point, or are at least partially correct, with some claim they make. You can make this admission knowing that by the end of the essay your line of reasoning will overcome that concession.

Examples

> Granted, air pollution in the area has increased noticeably in the last ten years.
>
> Opponents of the no eating or drinking in the classroom policy are correct in pointing out that the policy is widely ignored by both students and instructors.

Here are some commonly used **con** transitions:

CON

Opponents argue that	Doubtless,
Proponents claim that	To be sure,
Some people believe that	Granted,
One argument commonly raised is that	It would seem that
Although Jones and others found that	Apparently
One must admit	Jones and others are partially correct
Of course,	when they say that
No doubt,	

Your turnaround to the pro side should be bold and definite. Having made your concession to the opposing points of view, signal your readers that they are now seeing what you believe.

Examples

> But many of the technological advancements that will soon result in new commercial applications, and therefore more jobs, owe part or all of their development to previous space programs.
>
> Yet, the slogans of the pro-gun people, in spite of being catchy and popular, do not hold up under logical analysis.

However, in spite of the fears of these scientists, it is also quite possible that the increase in carbon dioxide will produce a new ice age.

But the proposal that automobile traffic can be cut 35 percent to combat this air pollution is unrealistic.

Nevertheless, any expense is worthwhile if it will prevent nonsmokers from risking serious health problems.

Here are some commonly used **pro** transitions:

PRO

But (no comma)	On the contrary,
However,	Surely
Yet,	Still
Nevertheless,	

By using the proper transition when you begin the concluding paragraph of your argument, you can reinforce the idea that your basic position is the logical culmination of your reasoning.

Examples

Therefore, increased funding for the space program is crucial.

Thus, handgun control is needed and can work.

Hence, the initial increase in the mean temperature of the earth will cause an eventual lowering of the mean temperature and, as a result, the return of the glaciers.

So one can only conclude that future proposals to curb automobile pollution will have to be more attractive to the general public.

Obviously, therefore, the anti-smoking regulations should be strictly enforced.

Here are some of the most often used concluding transitions:

Concluding Transitions

Therefore,	Hence,	Thus,
And,	Therefore,	Consequently,
Obviously,	So	

When using Plan One, your con paragraph can summarize more than one objection to your position. Try, however, to limit yourself to no more than two or three. Plan One works best when you have just one con point you want to develop thoroughly or when several con points can be summarized succinctly. Consider this plan when you want to summarize briefly the opposition's point of view before you go on to argue your position. (Note: Many variations of Plan One are possible. Check with your instructor if you want to adapt that basic plan.)

PLAN ONE (CON SECTION FIRST)

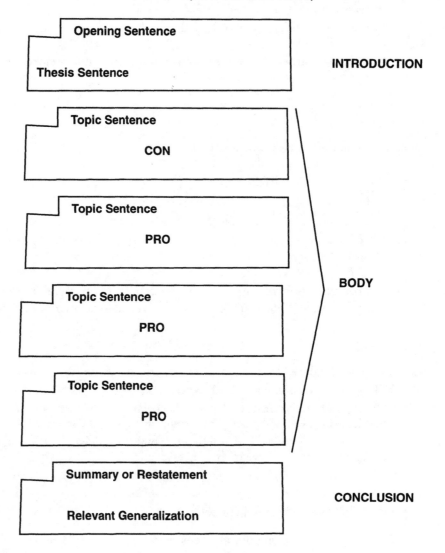

Read the sample paper that follows:

Sandra Huit

Professor Schneider

English 1-A

3 August 2001

Helmet Laws: Requiring Motorcyclists to Use Their Heads

INTRODUCTION "No brains to save," my husband murmurs whenever he sees a bareheaded motorcyclist. Carl has not come by this dictum naively or with rancor. After 22 years of safe and cautious "biking," his own helmet saved his life when he broadsided an automobile that was making an abrupt U-turn on a steep foothills road. Although he sustained a serious head injury that left him hemiplegic and subject to chronic motion sickness for the rest of his life, we know that without a helmet, he would have been killed, and his passenger, his 16-year-old son, would have suffered more than a light concussion. As a result, we have become fervent supporters of the legislation enacted in 1991 mandating that all motorcyclists wear helmets. Not all motor riders see things in the same light, however. A minority of riders has continued to lobby loudly to repeal the helmet law despite overwhelming statistical evidence to the contrary. Nevertheless, California should continue to require that all motorcyclists wear helmets because the law has been effective in reducing injuries and fatalities and medical costs, and the accompanying misery for the victims and their families.

CON Opponents of the helmet law present a litany of objections. They argue that the freedom of choice to ride a motorcycle without a helmet is a valuable personal freedom that has been lost.When asked why they prefer riding with their heads unprotected, they often respond that helmets are hot and uncomfortable and they enjoy feeling the wind blowing through their hair. They argue that helmet laws are unconstitutional. Opponents express concern that wearing helmets may actually increase the chance of motorcyclists crashing. Helmets, many of them contend, impair visibility by limiting peripheral vision. Some also argue that helmets muffle sound and prevent riders from hearing traffic noise, which may be a critical factor in avoiding some accidents. Others, citing a study by J. P. Goldstein, claim that helmets cause neck injuries in accidents ("Q&A: Motorcycle Helmet Use Laws as of December 2000." Insurance Institute for Highway Safety, Highway Loss Data Institute. 30 May 2001. <http://www.hwysafety.org/safety_facts/qanda/helmet_use.htm>). They argue, further, that motorcycle helmets are often hot and uncomfortable. Frequently, opponents of the helmet law state that they don't expect to have an accident because they are expert and cautious riders, so for them helmets are unnecessary.

PRO   These protestations, however, are not valid. Motorcycle helmet laws do not violate individual rights. Simple logic dictates that any feelings of lost personal freedom need to be weighed against the possibility of years of being seriously disabled, physically, mentally, and emotionally, or even death. Moreover, comparable legal restrictions are placed on automobile drivers and passengers, habitually obeyed and strictly enforced with few complaints from the public. Local and state laws requiring that seatbelts be worn and that babies and small children be properly strapped into certified car seats are examples. Nor are helmet laws unconstitutional. The constitutionality of motorcycle helmet laws has been affirmed in more than 25 states. In Simon V-8. Governor of the Commonwealth of Massachusetts the court wrote:

> From the moment of the injury, society picks the person up off
> the highway; delivers him to a municipal hospital and municipal
> doctors; provides him with unemployment compensation; after
> recovery, he cannot replace his lost job, and if the injury causes
> permanent disability, may assume the responsibility for his and
> his family's continued subsistence. We do not understand a state
> of mind that permits plaintiff to think that only he is
> concerned." ("Common Myths about Motorcycle Helmets and

Motorcycle Helmet Laws." 26 July 2001. <http://

www.nhtsa.dot.gov/people/injury/pedbimot/safebike/myths.html>)

PRO   Furthermore, opponents' arguments that helmets are dangerously

restrictive are not defensible. Their arguments that helmets reduce peripheral

vision and the ability to hear traffic are not borne out by research. In 1994

A. James McKnight and A. Scott McKnight conducted traffic tests with 50

motorcyclists to study the effect of helmets on their vision and hearing. The

researchers' two objectives were to test the effect of helmets on the ability

of riders to hear traffic noise at highway speeds and to visually detect the

presence of vehicles in adjacent lanes prior to lane changes. The researchers

concluded that their ability to hear traffic noise, specifically horn noise,

was not reduced. The noise created by the motorcycle, which increases as speed

increases, is loud enough that any reductions in the ability to hear caused

by wearing a helmet is not statistically significant. Thus, if a sound is loud

enough to be heard above the noise of the motorcycle's engine, it can be heard

by a driver wearing a helmet. The researchers also concluded that the effect

on the riders' lateral vision was insignificant. They found that the test

subjects could compensate the slight restriction of peripheral vision by

turning their heads further, which 76 percent of the tests subjects did

automatically without being told to ("The Effects of Motorcycle Helmets Upon

Seeing and Hearing." 4 Mar. 2001. National Highway Traffic Safety

Administration. 26 July 01. <http://nickolson.net/helmet1.htm >). In

addition, more than 12 studies have found that helmets do not cause neck

injuries. The Insurance Institute for Highway Safety states that "A study

reported in the Annals of Emergency Medicine in 1994 analyzed 1,153 motorcycle

crashes in four midwestern states and determined that 'helmets reduce head

injuries without an increased occurrence of spinal injuries in motorcycle

trauma'" ("Q&A: Motorcycle Helmet Use Laws as of December 2000." Insurance

Institute for Highway Safety, Highway Loss Data Institute. 30 July 2001.

<http://www.hwysafety.org/safety_facts/qanda/helmet_use.htm.>). Finally, the inability of some opponents to conceive that they could possibly be involved in an accident is patently illogical. My husband is a surviving example. After 20 years of careful riding, his luck ran out in a few seconds the day of his accident.

PRO   Whether opponents believe helmets are dangerous or not, it is difficult to understand how they can ignore statistics gathered since the helmet law went into effect. California Highway Patrol Integrated Traffic Records Systems statistics show that a sharp decline resulted almost immediately after the law became effective on January 1, 1992, and continued on a downward trend. Motorcyclist fatalities in California declined from 512 in 1991 to 230 in 1998, a reduction of 55 percent. Motorcyclist injuries were reduced from 16,910 in 1991 to 6,833 in 1998, a reduction of 60 percent ("California Helmet Law – 2001." Trauma Foundation. 23 July 2001. <http://www.tf.org/tf/ injuries/ mc2001.html>). California Office of Statewide Health Planning and Development: Hospital Discharge Data show that between 1991 and 1998 the number of brain injured motorcyclists dropped from 1,254 to 316, a reduction of 75 percent ("California Helmet Law - 2001." Trauma Foundation. 23 July 2001. <http://www.tf.org/tf/injuries/mc2001.html>). Statistics show that California's experience has been reflected nationwide. According to a report published by the National Highway Traffic Safety Administration in 2000, for motorcyclists wearing helmets the chances of fatalities in an accident are reduced 29 percent, and in 67 percent of the accidents the helmets prevent brain injuries ("California Helmet Law - 2001." Trauma Foundation. 23 July 2001. <http://www.tf.org/tf/injuries/mc2001.html>).

PRO   Critics of the helmet law also ignore statistics showing that the helmet law has had a huge economic impact. According to a 1998 University of California, San Francisco study, in 1993 medical costs for motorcycle injuries were 35 million dollars less than in 1991, dropping from 98 million dollars to 63 million dollars, a 35 percent decrease ("California Motorcycle Helmet Law Saves Money, UCSF Study Shows." UCSF'S Electronic Daily Daybreak News. 11 May 1999. University of California. 23 July 2001. <http://www.ucsf.edu/daybreak/1998/09/16_helm.html>). UCSF Professor Wendy Max, the study's main researcher, stated, "'The helmet law has definitely saved the state quite a bit of money. For economic reasons, the helmet law is a success'" ("California Motorcycle Helmet Law Saves Money, UCSF Study Shows." UCSF'S Electronic Daily Daybreak News. 11 May 1999. University of California. 23 July 2001. <http://www.ucsf.edu/daybreak/1998/09/16_helm.html>). The UCSF study found that both state and private insurance companies saved significant amounts of money, as did California taxpayers, since only one of every two hospitalized motorcycle riders has private medical insurance. According to Professor Max, the study concluded that approximately 60 percent of the savings can be attributed to the mandatory helmet law rather than other factors such as driver's education ("California Motorcycle Helmet Law Saves Money, UCSF Study Shows." UCSF's Electronic Daily Daybreak News. 11 May 1999. University of California. 23 July 2001. <http://www.ucsf.edu/daybreak/1998/09/16_helm.html>).

PRO   For every motorcyclist killed in vehicular accidents, many more are injured. Although broken bones and crushed spleens are painful, head injuries are the most devastating result of motorcycle accidents. The brain-damaged frequently linger in comas for hours, days, or months. When they awaken, if they awaken, the very qualities of mind and personality that made up their unique personhood may be altered, perhaps permanently. Brain injury can impair motor skills and cause paralysis that limits walking or even use of hands, just as in stroke victims. Speech impairment is another noticeable result, as head trauma victims often must entirely rebuild their vocabularies and search for appropriate words. The search can be hampered by a stalling in the thought processes, making it impossible to process thoughts quickly or even to handle simultaneous thoughts. Questions, if even understood, may require 10 to 20 minutes for the brain to send a reply to the mouth. Occupational therapy is often required to relearn the sequencing of mundane tasks, like dressing (socks first, then slacks, and then the shoes).

PRO   Short-term memory loss interferes with everything; the sequence can become interminable. In the worst instances, bright, urbane men and women become cheerful dullards, with rare interests beyond their present needs, with logical thinking frustratingly scrambled, but with a memory of who they used to be. Although the frustration can indirectly lead to depression or other personality disorders, major personality changes, including violent temper, are often a direct result of head injury. Wives find themselves married to strangers; young children are more mature than their brain-damaged parents. Understandably, 90 percent of marriages end when one partner suffers brain damage. Even the most accommodating employers cannot find any position suitable for formerly competent workers. The consequences are more than disabling.

CONCLUSION   As the statistics show, it would be foolish not to retain the helmet law. My husband and I were lucky because his intelligence and wonderful sense of humor survived his head trauma. But while we were in the "survivor" community, we witnessed families destroyed and lives wasted by the head injuries sustained by unhelmeted motorcyclists. Whenever I see a bumper sticker proclaiming "Helmet Laws Suck," I am reminded of the alternative. Whenever I hear a rider bemoaning his loss of freedom to choose, I wonder what choices his loved ones would have if he were to become another unhelmeted motorcycle injury statistic. To reduce that possibility, California should retain its current helmet law and even consider sentencing violators to community service with head-trauma families and organizations.

Plan Two

When using Plan Two, alternate cons and pros. Argue back and forth, admitting that arguments against your position do exist, but always turn around to refute these opposing points. Do not weaken your position by following a statement supporting your thesis with a statement raising objections. You may devote an entire paragraph to a con point and a separate paragraph to the pro point refuting it, or include both the con and pro in a single paragraph. An easy way to organize the body of an argument using this plan is to write a con paragraph and its corresponding pro paragraph, then another con paragraph and its accompanying pro paragraph, and then at least one strictly pro paragraph a full body of five paragraphs. Ideally, the paragraphs should be ordered so the essay becomes more convincing as it progresses from argument to argument. Plan Two works best when your opposing points are formidable, complex, and difficult to refute.

PLAN TWO (CON SECTION FIRST)

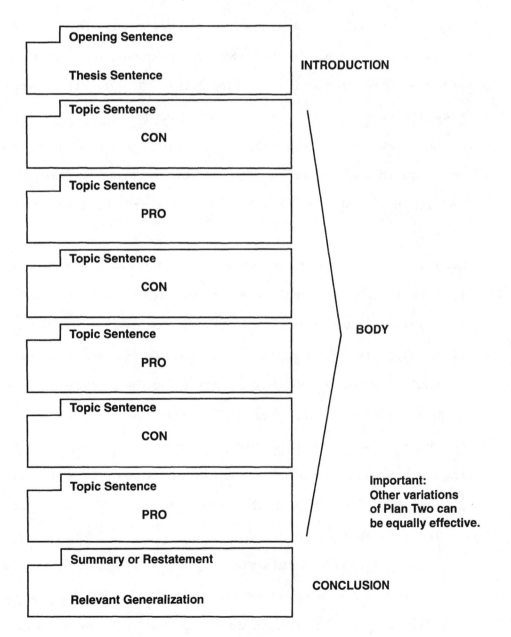

Daniel Nota

Mrs. Sessano

English 1A

21 February 2003

Computers: Will the Real Frog Please Stand Up

INTRODUCTION In the 1960's Marshall McLuhan proclaimed that television would revolutionize communications in the modern world, driving print into obscurity and eventual obsolescence. Now, similar predictions are being made for computers: they are expected to revolutionize business, entertainment, medicine, and education, boosting power and efficiency in these and many other areas of our lives. In many ways, computers have satisfied these expectations and show even greater promise for the future. In education, vast financial resources are expended in hopes that computers will fulfill a variety of educational needs. It is important to recognize, however, what computers can and cannot do in the classroom. In teaching critical thinking, reading and writing, and social skills, they have definite and sometimes little-realized limitations.

CON Many parents and teachers bemoan the fact that television is a passive activity; it usually does not encourage critical thinking and often induces a sort of waking sleep as mindless images flicker across the screen. Computers are different. Some computer games, such as Tetris and SimCity, encourage critical and creative thinking to identify problems, propose solutions, and create new worlds within the parameters of the game. Many schools are offering such software to students as a means of developing analytical and creative thinking skills. Other kinds of educational software claim to help elementary or high school students master challenges such as the rigors of scientific method. Nicholas Negroponte claims:

> Since computer simulation of just about anything is now possible, one need not learn about a frog by dissecting it. Instead children can be asked to design frogs, to build an animal with frog-like

behavior, to simulate the muscles, to play with the frog.

(Negroponte, Nicholas. <u>Being Digital</u>, 1996. 199).

This computerized way of learning about frogs suggests dazzling benefits to educational software: it can help students master scientific methods, think creatively, and learn about the world all through an exciting, interactive engagement with computers.

PRO   However, we should be skeptical about attempts to elevate computer software to the status of an all-powerful teaching tool enabling students to learn critical and creative thinking. Any computer user must work within the limitations of the program he or she is using; student writers using word processing programs often find that the spell-check systems give them a "right" answer that is not right at all within the context of the particular sentence they are writing. Although computers have many scientific applications, the rigors of scientific method are best taught by engagement with the real, not the virtual, world. Negroponte's celebration of learning science by software suggests the limitations of the software. Exploring frogs in this way may be entertaining and of some benefit, but it is difficult to see how such a "computer simulation" will help students discover the characteristics of the real frog lying ignored on the dissecting table. Students and teachers should be aware that software can constrain rather than encourage critical and creative thought; students may be harmed by squeezing imagination and free-ranging critical thinking into the limiting demands of a computer simulation guiding them through a programmed world.

CON   Every year there is a growing drumbeat of concern that reading and writing skills are declining among the student population. It is conceivable that the trend to teach reading through hypertext (linking text with pictures) will aid slow readers or those with certain learning disabilities. Certainly reading through software and CD-ROMs, immersed in a flashing kaleidoscope of music, pictures and words, can be more engaging than struggling with the unadorned printed word. Furthermore, some software may be of use in teaching some writing skills, such as basic grammar and sentence writing. A growing number of teachers also believe that students can enhance their research and writing skills on the Internet, an interactive medium that helps students communicate with others through the written word.

PRO   Nevertheless, educators should view the entertaining, audio-visual enhanced reading and writing software as just that: entertainment that can actually have an adverse effect on learning. Clifford Stoll quotes a high school English teacher in California: "Computers are lollipops that rot your teeth. The students love them. But when they get hooked, they get bored with all the whoopee stuff. It makes reading a book seem tedious. Books don't have sound effects and their brains have to do all the work" (Stoll, Clifford. <u>Silicon Snake Oil: Second Thoughts on the Information Highway</u>. Anchor 1996. 140).

CON   Granted, computers can be used to teach social skills such as cooperation and communication between students. Schools have always been important places to develop social skills; the daily, face-to-face contacts in the classroom are a vital training ground for communicating and working cooperatively. Computers are touted as an exciting means of promoting communication between students. Some programs allow students to edit or review one another's written work online. The Internet and software programs may help promote learning and communication within a school, or even between cities and other countries.

PRO   However, computers are a very expensive means of accomplishing what can be done using more traditional methods. Student team projects (co-writing and editing, peer review) can be pursued face-to-face in small groups, or by letter writing campaigns between schools. Also, one of the most important social skills, conflict resolution, is not aided by computer enhancement. Software can teach students to overcome programmed obstacles or chat online, but computer programs cannot help with the messy, unpredictable tensions and frustrations of everyday social interaction. Indeed, someone isolated behind a computer may be learning how not to deal with social life.

CONCLUSION Should computers be used in the classroom setting? Absolutely. Students should know how to handle a word-processing program and, depending on grade level, use a spreadsheet or some of the other information systems computers do so well. But computers are not an educational panacea. Edutainment software is not the only or best means for teaching students to think, to read and write, or to develop social skills. Computer technology is a part of the learning experience, but we should not forget that there are real frogs in a real world demanding attention.

Other Strategies

Not all writers follow Plan One or Plan Two when they write arguments. Many professional magazine and newspaper writers, for example, seem to violate advice given in *Survival*, and yet their arguments are interesting and persuasive. Employing the journalistic style, they often do not include explicit thesis statements; they frequently write very short paragraphs; they often use first and second person; they sometimes use unorthodox punctuation. But they do usually follow basic argumentative rules, for instance, that a con always be followed by a pro and that an organized line of reasoning be used. These writers are using different strategies than you are asked to use in this course, and they are doing so much like musicians who play extemporaneous jazz piano only after they have mastered the basics of classical or traditional piano style.

EXERCISE 2.10

The following argumentative essay was printed in the "Opinion" section of a newspaper, the *San Francisco Chronicle*. It was written by Jeff Jacoby of the *Boston Globe*. After reading the essay carefully, you will notice some obvious differences in its structure and style compared to the arguments you have studied thus far. As you read and reread the argument, make marginal notes. Your instructor may ask you to discuss your notes with classmates or in a class discussion.

Catch-and-Release Fishing Is Inhumane

By Jeff Jacoby

I'M NOT A VEGETARIAN. I eat fish and fowl. I don't oppose experimenting on animals when necessary for medical research. I like zoos. I have no moral objection to wearing fur or leather. I think it's OK to keep pet dogs on a leash and birds in a cage. And I am no supporter of PETA (People for the Ethical Treatment of Animals) or its fanatic agenda.

But I do think fishing is cruel.

By sport fishing I mean catch-and-release fishing by a barbed hook in its mouth, or that there is pleasure in making it struggle frantically, or that it is exciting to force a wild creature to exhaust itself in a desperate effort to get free. I don't deny the allure of it all. But finding gratification in the suffering of another isn't sport. It's sadism.

One of PETA's billboards shows a dog with a hook through its lip, and asks: "If you wouldn't do this to a dog, why do it to a fish?" PETA'S analogies are frequently tasteless and morally repugnant, but this one is exactly right.

Writing a few years ago in *Orion*, a magazine about nature and culture, essayist and outdoorsman Ted Kerasote opened a piece about the ethics of catch-and-release fishing with a quote from a fellow outdoorsman, "the philosopher, mountaineer, and former angler Jack Turner."

"Imagine using worms and flies to catch mountain bluebirds," Turner told him, "or maybe eagles and ospreys, and hauling them around on 50 feet of line while they tried to get away. Then, when you landed them, you'd release them. No one would tolerate that sort of thing with birds. But we will for fish because they're underwater and out of sight."

I can hear the indignant reply of countless anglers. Fish are different. Fish don't feel pain. The hook doesn't hurt them.

But there is mounting evidence that fish do feel pain. A team of biologists a Edinburgh's Roslin Institute make the case in a paper just published by the Royal Society, one of Britain's leading scientific institutes. Their experiments with rainbow trout prove the presence of pain receptors in fish, and show that fish undergoing a "potentially painful experience" react with "profound behavioral and physiological changes . . . comparable to those observed in higher mammals."

Other studies have demonstrated the responses of fish to painful conditions, from rapid respiration to color changes to the secretion of stress hormones. Does this mean that a fish feels pain in the way we do, or that its small brain can "understand" the painful event? No. It does mean that the ordeal of being hooked through the mouth, yanked at the end of a fishing line and prevented from breathing each time its body leaves the water is intensely unpleasant and distressing.

Anglers tell themselves that catch-and-release fishing is more humane and nature friendly than catching fish and killing them. That strikes me as a conscience-salving fib.

"We angle because we like to fight," Kerasote writes. "Otherwise all of us would be using hookless (flies) and not one angler in 10,000 does. The hook allows us to control and exert power over fish, over one of the most beautiful and seductive forms of nature, and then, because we're nice to the fish, releasing them 'unharmed,' we can receive both psychic dispensation and blessing. Needless to say, if you think about this relationship carefully, it's not a comforting one, for it is a game of dominance followed by cathartic pardons, which . . . is one of the hallmarks of an abusive relationship."

I'm not blind to the beauty of fishing. But any sport that depends for its enjoyability on forcing an animal to fight for its life is wrong. Wrong for what it does to the fish. Even more wrong for what it does.

DISCUSSION QUESTIONS

1. Where is the thesis sentence, and why did the author place it there?

2. What is the author's strategy—how are the pros and cons arranged?

3. Is the author's use of evidence, examples, and quotations compelling?

4. Do you think that the variety of sentence and paragraph lengths makes the essay effective? Why or why not?

5. Has the author made a good argument for his point of view?

EXERCISE 2.11

Which strategy seems best for your argumentative essay? (Circle one)

PLAN ONE   PLAN TWO   OTHER STRATEGY

Briefly explain your decision:

_____

_____

_____

_____

Outlining Your Argument

After the preliminary planning work you have already completed, writing a thesis-topic sentence outline will be relatively easy. The exercise that follows will guide you through the process.

EXERCISE 2.12

Using your list of pros and cons in Exercise 2.7, select the two or three points against your position that you will include in your argument.

(1) _____

_____

_____

(2) _____

_____

_____

(3) _____

_____

_____

List the three to five points you will use to support your position.

(1) _____

_____

_____

(2) _____

_____

_____

(3) _____

_____

_____

(4) _____

_____

_____

(5) _____

_____

_____

Using the strategy you decided on in 2.11 (Plan One, Two, or Other Strategies), convert the con and pro points listed earlier in this exercise into the topic sentences you will use for the body paragraphs in your argument.

Move the thesis you have developed from Exercise 2.9, and write your thesis-topic sentence outline. Double-check your thesis first. Does it cover the points you plan to include, or do you need to revise it in light of the work you have done in this exercise?

Thesis:_____

_____

_____

_____

_____

1. _____

_____

_____

_____

_____

2. _____

_____

_____

_____

_____

3. _____

_____

_____

_____

_____

4. _____

_____

_____

_____

5. _____

_____

_____

_____

_____

6. _____

_____

_____

_____

_____

7. _____

_____

_____

_____

8. _____

_____

_____

_____

Have your work approved. Place your thesis-topic sentence outline in your Project Folder.

LESSON FOUR—*Writing Your Argument*

First Draft

Writing a first draft of your argument is your first attempt to expand your thesis statement and integrate topic sentences in a detailed discussion. Although every writer develops an approach to first-draft writing unique in some respects, two general techniques seem to be used most frequently. Some writers develop their first drafts slowly, painstakingly writing and rewriting almost every sentence. They cannot begin a new sentence until the previous one is as perfect as they can make it. For these writers first-draft writing is an exhausting ordeal. Most writers, however, work as rapidly as possible, revising very little as they write their first drafts. They need the satisfaction of immediately putting their most important thoughts down on paper, reorganizing, refining, and correcting their paragraphs in subsequent drafts. Try to use the rapid-write method when you write your first draft, but if that does not work, develop a method that does.

The Introductory Paragraph

You have a choice. You can begin by writing the introductory paragraph, or you can begin by writing the body paragraphs. You have that choice because you have already written the most important sentence in the introductory paragraph—the thesis. By beginning with the body paragraphs, you will avoid the problem of saying something in the introduction and then having to repeat it in the body paragraphs. Furthermore, after writing the body paragraphs, your mind will be better primed to write an interesting, creative opening for your essay.

Begin your introductory paragraph with an interesting statement. Then add three or four sentences building up to your thesis, which should be placed at the end of the paragraph. See that the sentence leading into your thesis makes a smooth transition. You may need to add a sentence to prevent the connection from being awkward. But spend as little time as possible on this paragraph for now. Unless you are a compulsive reviser, try to be content with your first or second version temporarily. Return to your introductory paragraph later; you will find it much easier to revise the paragraph after you have written the rest of the essay.

SUGGESTION:

Print your thesis and list of topic sentences on a poster and
tape it to your desk or wall.

The Body Paragraphs

Follow your outline, and stay on the subject in each body paragraph. Every sentence should flow smoothly into the next. Think ahead. Plan the sequence of sentences—this forethought takes only seconds when your writing faculties are working well. Of course, writing is not entirely a mechanical process: it is also a creative, evolving process. Planning does not always work. Writing one idea often inspires another, an idea not thought of before and therefore not in your plan. Adapt your paragraph plan and use these ideas if they will help the paragraph and the paper. Then double-check the topic sentence for two problems. It should still cover the content of the entire paragraph, and any modifications in the topic sentence must not prevent the smooth progression of ideas from topic sentence to topic sentence. The paragraph must make the thesis of the argument clearer.

Paragraph Length

How long should a body paragraph be? Any body paragraph in your argument that does not have five or more sentences should be expanded. As pointed out in Chapter One, very short paragraphs belong in newspapers and magazines, where the columns are narrow, not in academic essays. Occasionally in a long essay you can use a very short paragraph for transitional purposes when you are linking major sections within the body of the essay. But short transitional paragraphs are not needed in your argument and other essays you will write in *Survival*.

In general, longer paragraphs are better than very short ones, but paragraphs can be too long. For example, a paragraph more than a page long in a typed essay can be hard to follow. If a paragraph seems too long, you can usually find a natural break where it can be divided into two paragraphs or places where it can be divided into three paragraphs if it is extremely long. After dividing a long paragraph, you may have to rewrite the original topic sentence and reword the first sentence of each new paragraph to ensure that each one begins with a strong topic sentence. You also may have to add sentences to extend any new paragraph that as a result of the dividing may be too short.

Paragraph Development

More than anything else, every body paragraph needs pertinent details. Your instructor expects detailed discussion, not a series of unsupported ideas and aphorisms. You may know what you mean when you make a generalization, but you cannot be sure your reader will know what you are thinking unless you explain your ideas thoroughly. Of course, easy-to-follow organization helps.

Begin each body paragraph with a topic sentence, and support it with a clearly organized pattern of primary and secondary support sentences. To write detailed paragraphs, you must make a special effort to include enough secondary support sentences. When you add examples, explanations, quotations, statistics, anecdotes, and other kinds of specifics, you make it easier for your reader to understand what you are trying to say.

Where do you go to find these specifics? You have already conducted background research and included it in your Project Folder (Exercise 2.4). Review that material for specific information you can use. You can find additional information on the Internet, in books, magazines, pamphlets, lecture notes, television programs, movies, interviews, and discussions. However, the best source of supporting information may be your own experiences. You have read; you have listened to others; you have lived and worked. Through all of this experience you have been gathering ideas, opinions, and facts about controversial issues. If you take the time to think, you can probably come up with most of the specifics you need to support your argument without consulting other sources. Many appropriate examples and other supporting details will occur to you as you write your first draft. Write them in your essay or on your outline before you forget them. In subsequent revisions you can examine your paragraphs closely in a more organized effort to add specific secondary support.

The Conclusion

When you have written your body paragraphs, begin your concluding paragraph with a restatement of your thesis or a summary of the major points developed. Whatever you write, avoid the same wording used in your thesis or body paragraphs. If you do not change the wording of your reiteration, you will likely bore the reader, and your instructor may comment that your conclusion seems redundant. Also remember not to end your essay with your restatement or summary. Add two or three sentences, wise generalizations, perhaps an apt quote, affirming the relevance and importance of what you have argued. Take time with these statements because the wrong thing written at the end of an essay can invalidate the effect of everything written previously.

Documentation—Avoiding Plagiarism

Plagiarism is academic theft. Using someone else's ideas or information in your writing without giving proper credit is stealing—theft—whether it is intentional or unintentional. If you incorporate researched material in your paper, you must give credit to your sources of information. This procedure of referencing your sources is called **documenting your sources**. You must tell your readers where you found your ideas unless you thought of them yourself. Also, you must state the source of any information that you use in your essay whether you quote it exactly, paraphrase it in your own words, or summarize it. Material that must be documented includes that from the Internet, books, newspapers, encyclopedias, magazines, journals, pamphlets, essays, CDS, films, speeches, interviews, and e-mail. Plagiarism can be avoided if you follow some simple procedures:

1. Make printouts or photocopies of any sources of your ideas and information.

2. Underline, highlight, or note the specific passages used in your essay. If you summarize an entire article, clip your summary to the copy.

3. Keep all of your research material together in your Project Folder.

4. In this essay, list your sources in parentheses at the end of whatever is quoted, paraphrased, or summarized. (Place a period after the last parenthesis.)

5. As much as is possible, include the information about your source in the following order:

Online Sources

1. Last name, first name, middle initial of author(s) or editor(s), The author may be an organization. (Place a period at end of author's name.)

2. Title of the document. (Enclose in quotation marks, and place period inside last quotation mark.)

3. Title of the Web site. (Underline and place period at end.)

4. Date of the Web site. If any updates are listed, use the latest one. First, list the day, then the month, then the year. (Place a period at end.)

5. Name of the organization sponsoring the Web site. (Place a period at end.)

6. The date you accessed the web site. (Place a period at the end.)

7. The URL (online address). Enclose in angle brackets (< >). (Place a period after last bracket.)

Printed Sources

1. Name of author(s) or editor(s), last name first. (Place a period at end.)

2. Title of article (if in a newspaper, magazine, or journal. (Enclose in quotation marks. Place a period at end, inside last quotation mark.)

3. Title of book or publication. (Underline and place period after title.)

4. List the date of the newspaper, magazine, or journal. (Day, followed by month, followed by year. Place colon at end.)

5. List the publisher of a book. (Place period at end.)

6. List latest copyright date of book. (Place period at end.)

7. List exact pages referred to. (Place period at end.)

Lead-Ins

If you mention the author or title of a reference in a lead-in, the author or title does not have to be repeated in your parenthetical documentation.

Example

Joseph B. Verrengia, citing a recently released World Wildlife Fund report, writes, "Nearly 1,000 whales, dolphins and porpoises drown every day after becoming tangled in fishing nets and other equipment, scientists say, in what appears to be the first global estimate of the problem" ("308,000 Mammals Die in Fish Nets Each Year." San Francisco Chronicle. 16 June 2003: A2).

EXERCISE 2.13

Write the first draft of your argument.

LESSON FIVE— Critical Thinking: Evaluating the Reasoning of Your Argument

During the writing phase, you have been concentrating on the structural aspects of the argument. A large part of your effort has been spent organizing your argument, writing a thesis, listing the pros and cons, writing topic sentences and supporting them. At this point you need to spend some time evaluating the reasoning of your argument. You have already engaged in this kind of evaluation when you evaluated the credibility of your sources during the information-gathering stage. Your argument must stand up to the following tests of critical thinking:

- Does your argument distinguish between facts, inferences, opinions, beliefs, values, and assumptions?

- Does it summarize disagreements about them and make your position on alternative views clear?

- Are your assertions supported by either evidence or a list of reasons?

- Is your essay free from argumentative fallacies?

Distinguishing Between Facts, Inferences, Opinions, Beliefs, and Assumptions

FACTS

Facts are thoughts that can be verified by observation–especially by measuring, weighing, and counting–or by the expertise of authorities generally regarded as reliable. Most facts are non-controversial. You must gather facts to support your argument, meaning you must present information that has an objective reality as its basis.

Examples

Each parking spot in the center section of the Stadium Lot measures 8' x 15'.

Four of the six county supervisors voted against the sales tax increase proposal.

Calculations by Orrin Pilkey, Jr., a marine geologist at Duke University, show that for every foot of ocean rise there will be a 10-1,000-foot submergence of the coastline area. This submergence is due to the land's tendency to warp downward as the ocean's level increases, due to the increased weight of water on the continental shelf. "The beaches along North Carolina, for example, are already retreating an average of four or five feet a year" ("Antarctic Meltdown?" 19).

Whereas the previous examples seem very clear, facts are often much more difficult to discern or are even controversial. Often the problem is that when we begin to research a topic, we are overwhelmed by the amount of information available that purports to be factual, and new research constantly throws earlier research into doubt. Sometimes the "facts" are contradictory or open to different interpretations, so as a result we don't know what to believe. A good example is the current controversy about which diets are best for losing weight and improving our health. Some diet experts advocate low-fat, high-carbohydrate diets, whereas others tout high-protein, low-carbohydrate diets. Each side uses medical facts to back up their claims.

When this kind of confusion occurs, what should you do? One thing you can do is to summarize both sides of the conflicting facts, showing that you are aware of the differing views. Another thing you can do is look for the most recent information. Has some recent research invalidated previously published facts? The third thing you can do is look for general agreement among experts about the facts, or for supporting examples that seem typical rather than isolated or extreme. Eventually, of course, you will need to pick a side. You may decide to support the side advocated by the majority of the experts, or you may decide on a more daring course, supporting the side advocated by only a few experts. Keep in mind, too, that you may be able to strengthen your case against the opposition by arguing that it is using old information or by criticizing its interpretation of the facts.

INFERENCES

Whereas facts are more apt to be non-controversial, inferences may be doubted. That is because an inference is someone's interpretation of the facts. We make inferences when we "read between the lines," based on what is said or not said. Thus, we reach a conclusion that is not actually stated. For example, reading in the newspaper that the state faces a severe budget shortfall next year, you might infer that your college tuition and fees will be raised next year even though nothing was actually said in the newspaper article about raising them. Until next year arrives and everyone knows for sure, your conclusion is an inference, not a fact, and may be doubted by your readers. In your argument an inference must be presented as an inference, not a fact. Nevertheless, an intelligent inference supported by a list of reasons can be very persuasive.

Example

> The governor's budget proposes cutting community college budgets $279 million this year and $249 million more next year for a total of $528 million in cuts this year and next. Although tuition increases are not yet proposed, it is very likely that either the governor or the legislature will propose tuition increases for next year, possibly doubling the current tuition. During the last budget crisis in 1990 and 1991, community college tuition was increased 100 percent and tuitions and fees were raised sharply in the state universities. Since the current budget crisis is far more severe than the previous one, it is reasonable to predict that the state budget cutters, desperate to find new revenues, will implement increased tuitions and fees. It is too late in the school year to implement increases this year, but increases next year are likely.

You may be able to strengthen your argument by criticizing the inferences of your opposition. In the following excerpt, the writer argues against a scientist's conclusion that plant life would benefit from a 100 percent increase in the amount of carbon dioxide in the atmosphere and that global temperatures would increase only slightly. The writer does this by citing authorities who have questioned the scientist's findings.

Example

> . . . Sherwood Idso's 12-year study of the greenhouse effect revealed that doubling atmospheric carbon dioxide would not only be beneficial to plant life, but would cause a global temperature increase of only 0.26 degrees Celsius, far less than the natural variation in climate of approximately two degrees Celsius (Meredith 64).

> Most researchers in this field, however, disagree. They believe that a doubling of atmospheric carbon dioxide would raise the global temperature by about three degrees Celsius. Richard Kerr reports that a National Research Council panel sided with the majority and stated that Idso's conclusions were based on imprecise models. . . .

OPINIONS

Opinions are beliefs, appraisals, conclusions, or judgments formed in people's minds about particular matters. Opinions should not be confused with preferences, such as preferring the taste of chicken over beef or preferring the basketball over hockey as a spectator sport. Because opinions are not yet or cannot be verified by evidence or outcomes, they are different from facts. Examples can be seen every day in the newspaper on the editorial page where a journalist expresses his or her opinion on an issue or in the letters to the editor.

Examples

> SUVs are dangerous.
> Women are better communicators than men.
> Palestinians should have their own national state.
> Baseball is a boring game compared to basketball.

A problem in reasoning develops if a writer presents an opinion as if it is a fact. In your argument you must not mistake fact and opinion, and you must back up any opinions you state with supporting discussion and evidence.

Example

> Male teachers should wear suits or sport coats and ties in class. By wearing business attire, teachers present a professional image appropriate to their profession. They also show respect for their students, caring enough to dress up for them. By dressing professionally, they also gain more respect from their students, who take what the teachers say more seriously. Even as a student I have noticed that I get more respect and better service at the grocery store after work when I am wearing my suit. One teacher told me that dressing casually makes it easier for students to relate to him because he is a less threatening authority figure. But I don't buy that line of reasoning. Teachers shouldn't come to class looking like they are dressed for a beach party.

BELIEFS

Beliefs are ideas held to be true that are beyond proof or verification. Belief in God is an obvious example. Some beliefs are proven right or wrong after time. Before Columbus's voyage to the New World, for example, the widespread belief was that the world was flat, but Columbus proved that belief to be wrong. Although beliefs are opinions, beliefs are more firmly planted in people's minds than opinions. Belief systems, such as religions, are complex integrated collections of principles, practices, and beliefs. Opposing strong beliefs or belief systems in your arguments is a formidable task requiring careful reasoning, convincing evidence, and persuasive language.

ASSUMPTIONS

Assumptions are ideas that we accept as being true without proof or qualification. For example, your friend failed to show up at the downtown Starbucks because you assumed she would know you meant the downtown location whereas she assumed you meant the midtown Starbucks. Assumptions play a part in arguments because we often assert ideas that we assume are true and easily verifiable or ideas that are generally acknowledged to be true.

Checking the Validity of Underlying Assumptions in Your Thesis

Up to this point your major concern with your thesis has been to construct a statement that clearly states your main idea and fits with the organization of your argument. At this point you should check the logic of your thesis sentence. Understanding the assumptions upon which your thesis is based is the first step. Suppose, for example, you have written the following thesis:

Thesis

> To solve the campus parking problem, the college should build a multistory parking garage in the Stadium Lot because no land is available for expanding the current parking lots or for building new lots.

For every thesis statement there is one or more underlying assumptions. These assumptions may be either stated or unstated. With this thesis an unstated assumption you are making is the idea that ample parking should be available for all students, staff, and visitors who drive to the campus. Furthermore, you believe that most of your readers who include your instructor and fellow students will agree with this assumption. The section on parking fees in the class schedule implies that anyone should be able to park on campus. Possibly some of your readers might argue that for environmental reasons students should not drive to school, that they should take public transportation or ride bicycles instead. Nevertheless, the chances are good that most readers will agree with you that parking spaces should be available on campus at all times.

Another assumption you are making with this thesis, a stated assumption, is that a serious parking problem exists. Probably this is a safe assumption to make although you realize that only a systematic survey of each parking lot every hour the college is open would confirm your personal experience with the parking. Your experience has been that whenever you arrive for classes, day or evening, the parking lots usually are full, causing you to wait up to ten minutes or more before finding a parking spot, and many of your friends and a few of your instructors have also complained about the lack of parking. Furthermore, the campus newspaper recently ran an article about the parking problem on campus. Consequently, you feel confident in stating that there is a campus parking problem.

Next look at the stated reason in your thesis. In this thesis the stated reason is connected with the word *because*.

Example of Stated Reason

No land is available for expanding the current parking lots or for building new lots.

Either you need evidence or a related list of reasons to validate this stated reason. How confident are you about stating that no land is available for more parking spaces? Suppose that the Vice President of Administration was quoted in the newspaper article, saying a study conducted by an engineering consulting firm concluded that it is not possible to expand the lots or build any new ones on campus. Based on this information, you came to the conclusion that the solution to the parking problem is to build a multistory parking lot, which would not require more land to build. You have visited the state university nearby and have parked in its multi-story garage and noticed that you have never had a problem finding a parking place. Although the vice president has warned that a multistory garage would be extremely expensive, perhaps costing $10,000 per parking space, you are still convinced that it is the best solution, and you are prepared to justify the cost in your argument. Thus, you believe that your stated reason is sound.

At this point you have a much better understanding of your thesis sentence in terms of its logic, and you are better prepared to check the logic of your reasoning in the body of the argument.

Example of Logical Components of Thesis

Main idea:	The college should build a multi-story parking garage.
Stated reason:	No land is available for expanding the current parking lots or for building new lots.
Stated assumption:	A campus parking problem exists.
Unstated assumption:	Parking should be available to all students, staff, and visitors.

EXERCISE 2.14

Copy the thesis of your argument in the spaces provided, and then analyze its logic by answering the questions that follow.

_____

_____

_____

1. What is the main idea of your thesis?

_____

_____

2. What is the stated reason?

_____

_____

3. What is the stated assumption, if there is one?

_____

_____

4. What is the unstated assumption?

_____

_____

5. Explain which readers are or are not likely to agree with your assumptions and why.

_____

_____

_____

6. What evidence or list of reasons have you presented to convince your reader that the stated reason is sound?

_____

_____

_____

7. Are there any revisions you want to make in your thesis to make it more logical?

_____

_____

_____

Have your work checked.

EXERCISE 2.15

Study the body of your argument, giving examples as directed.

1. Give an example of a sentence that states a fact.

_____

_____

2. Give an example of a sentence that states an opinion.

_____

_____

3. Copy a section of your argument in which you summarize disagreement over the facts about your topic.

_____

_____

_____

_____

_____

4. Copy a section of your argument in which you take a position regarding the alternative views about the facts.

_____

_____

_____

_____

_____

5. Give an example of a belief, value, or assumption basic to your argument, and explain why the majority of your readers will accept or reject it.

_____

_____

_____

_____

_____

Have your work checked.

Reasons Supported by Evidence

The thesis of your argument is an assertion—a positive statement or declaration. But you also make assertions in the body of the essay. When supporting one of your assertions with **evidence**, the evidence must be convincing. Each **example, fact, statistic, or reference to an authoritative source of information** presented is a piece of evidence that helps convince your readers of the validity of your assertion. Whereas one piece of evidence is not likely to be very convincing, three or four pieces will probably be sufficient. If you write that the plum tree in your backyard bloomed last spring and therefore it will bloom next spring, your readers may not be convinced. If, however, you write that the plum tree in your back yard has bloomed every year for the past 17 years that you have lived at this house, and that, furthermore, the next-door-neighbor says hers has bloomed every year that she can remember, and your aunt who lives on the next block says hers has never failed to bloom in 34 years, your readers are more likely to be persuaded when you predict that your plum tree will bloom next spring. Because of the argumentative structure you have chosen for your argument, providing enough evidence should not be a problem. You have supported your thesis with three or more pro points, each of which should include its accompanying evidence.

References to Authority

References to authority can be cited as evidence if you are careful to avoid problems that commonly arise. First, you must not cite an authority outside of his or her field of expertise. For example, although a sports star doing commercials to promote reading among young children is performing a worthwhile community service, he or she is probably not an expert authority on reading. Second, you must present what the authority says accurately, not misrepresenting what the authority actually says. If a highly respected law professor has written that she is against capital punishment except in two kinds of cases, you cannot write that she supports capital punishment without exception. Third, what the authority says should not be non-typical of the authority's views–not an isolated instance of the authority saying what he or she said. And fourth, what the authority says should not be outdated. More recent events and new research may have discounted the validity of an authority.

List of Reasons

You can also support your thesis with a list of reasons. With this approach, you are relying on your ability to explain to your readers why they should accept your thesis. You are giving reasons as support rather than evidence.

Example

Thesis: College students should be required to complete all of their remedial classes before they are allowed to take regular college classes because otherwise they lack the skills to be successful.

Reasons: 1. Students not reading at college level cannot read the textbooks assigned in history, English, mathematics, economics, psychology, electronics, and other courses, so some instructors have to outline the texts for the students.

2. Students writing at the remedial level are not able to write the reports, research papers, and essay exams in the more advanced classes.

3. Students who need basic mathematics classes cannot do the calculations required in college-level science and technology classes.

4. These students lack the study skills necessary to succeed in regular college classes.

EXERCISE 2.16

Answer the following questions about your argument:

1. Has your primary strategy been to support your assertions with evidence or with reasons? Explain and copy an example.

_____

_____

_____

_____

_____

2. If you have used evidence, how many pieces of evidence have you presented? Do you think you have presented enough evidence to be convincing? Explain.

_____

_____

_____

_____

_____

3. If you have used references to an authority as evidence, explain how it meets the three requirements explained in that section.

_____

_____

_____

_____

_____

4. If you have employed a list of reasons, write an outline of the list.

_____

_____

_____

_____

Have your work checked.

Avoiding Logical Fallacies

Faulty logic should be avoided in your writing, so you must develop the ability to detect it both in your own writing and in the writing of others. Although faulty logic sometimes may seem to be effective at first, once your readers think more carefully about your reasoning, they will be turned off about your argument. Furthermore, you have an ethical responsibility to present your argument in a straightforward, honest manner. Logical fallacies are types of errors in reasoning that appear in argumentative writing so often that they have been labeled.

MISLEADING THE READER

As a writer you should be leading your reader toward the truth, not leading them away from it. Misleading arguments should be avoided.

IGNORING THE QUESTION

Also known as the red herring fallacy, this logical fallacy occurs when the writer introduces an issue that distracts the readers away from the real issue that is being discussed. You may be aware of the phrase "dodging the question," which means the same thing.

Example

When challenged about his country's repeated human rights violations, the country's spokesperson replied, "How can you make such accusations when we have made such tremendous strides in combating the AIDS epidemic?"

BEGGING THE QUESTION

This logical fallacy results when the writer argues in a circle. The writer treats a question as if it has already been answered or makes a statement that assumes that the very issue he or she is supposed to be proving is already proven.

Example

It is doubtful that SUVs are prone to rollover accidents because major auto manufacturers have defended their safety on numerous occasions.

SLIPPERY SLOPE

This fallacy is the result of the writer erroneously predicting a series of undesirable events will occur if something happens first.

Example

If we pass laws restricting handguns, it won't be long until we ban all weapons, and then we will take away other freedoms, and within a decade we will be a totalitarian state.

POST HOC

Also known as the coincidental correlation fallacy, this fallacy is named from the Latin phrase *post hoc, ergo propter hoc* which means that because something happens after something else that that something else caused it to happen. In other words, the fallacy occurs when the writer assumes that because event A happens first, the following event, event B, is caused by A.

Example

Ever since you have been dating that girl, your grades have been bad.

NON SEQUITUR

This fallacy, Latin for "it does not follow," is the result of the writer linking two or more unrelated ideas as if they are really related.

Example

If you can get elected class president, you should be able to earn an A in organic chemistry.

OVERSIMPLIFICATION

Another type of faulty cause-and-effect reasoning occurs when the writer oversimplifies the link between the cause and its effect.

Example

If drugs are legalized, we will no longer have a problem with drug addicts.

HASTY GENERALIZATION

This logical fallacy occurs often in student essays. It occurs when the writer arrives at a conclusion that is based on insufficient evidence, inaccurate evidence, or misunderstood evidence.

Example

After ten minutes the Kings are behind 18 to 12, so they don't have a chance of winning this game.

IRRELEVANT CONCLUSION

This fallacy is the result of the writer claiming to prove one thing but actually proving a different conclusion.

Example

The number of homeless downtown keeps increasing because police don't crack down on the dope dealers and prostitutes.

Unfairly Attacking Opponent's Credibility

When dealing with opposition in your argument, it is almost always better to attack the reasoning of an opponent rather than the character of the opponent. As a general rule, you should concentrate on the issue at hand. However, you may be forced to question the credibility of an opponent in some situations if the authority is biased, dishonest, or using his or her stature and reputation rather than valid evidence and sound reasoning.

ATTACKING THE PERSON

This fallacy is also known as *argumentum ad hominem*, Latin for "argument to the man." This logical fallacy is the result of the writer distracting the reader from the issue by attacking the character of one or more people involved in the issue instead of discussing the issue itself.

Example

We shouldn't support this tax legislation because how can we trust a man who has been divorced three times?

GUILT BY ASSOCIATION

This fallacy is the result of the writer attempting to discredit an opponent by associating that person with other people, organizations, or activities considered undesirable, dishonest, disloyal, immoral, or unethical.

Example

The senator should not be allowed to chair such an important committee because he was an Eagle Scout, and everyone knows that the Boy Scouts discriminate against gays.

NAME CALLING

As a child you may have heard the chant, "Sticks and stones can break my bones, but names can never hurt me." In fact, name calling can badly, and unfairly, damage an opponent's reputation. In your argument, name calling should not be substituted for reasoning.

Example

The author of that legislation is a liberal, Communist, kook.

Unfairly Appealing to the Emotions of Readers

Beware of arguments that attempt to sway readers emotionally rather than logically. Appealing to your readers' emotions is legitimate if you are using such appeals to add to or intensify the appeal of your logic. However, using emotional appeals as a substitute for evidence or solid reasons or to confuse or lead readers away from the true substance of an argument is not legitimate.

FALSE AUTHORITY

An appeal to authority normally should be to the expertise or experience of the authority. A fallacy of reasoning occurs when a writer employs the testimony of a person on the basis of his or her popularity when the celebrity is not a true authority on the subject of the testimony. This happens often in advertising. A sports star appears in an ad for vacation real estate or life insurance, but the athlete actually has no expert knowledge of either. The advertiser intends for readers to make a positive emotional attachment to the celebrity and thereby be influenced to inquire about the product.

FALSE DILEMMA

Often called the either/or fallacy, this type of faulty reasoning occurs when the writer presents only two sides of an issue when in fact there are more that should be considered. The writer is hoping that his or her readers won't realize this and make an emotional decision to agree with the author's argument.

Example

Anyone who doesn't eat red meat regularly doesn't support American agriculture.

APPEAL TO POPULARITY

This fallacy occurs when the writer assumes that an idea is true because many people believe it is true.

Example

If I win this week's lottery, I will be happy and problem-free.

BANDWAGON APPEAL

This fallacy occurs when the writer asserts that a huge national or worldwide movement involving thousands or millions of people is happening and that the readers would be foolish or even disloyal not to join the movement.

Example

"Don't miss out. Everyone is buying stock in that dot.com company. The price is skyrocketing."

POWERFUL SYMBOLS APPEAL

This fallacy employs powerful symbols to affect people emotionally instead of using logical reasoning. The writer attempts to appeal to deep felt beliefs or prejudices rather than evidence or reasons. Recently, for example the Supreme Court of the United States ruled that burning crosses of the type used in Klu Klux Klan rallies invokes fear in African Americans and others to the point that the practice can be banned without violating freedom of speech. Another example would be a car dealer draping the dealership with American flags for a Fourth of July sale and running television ads implying that it is patriotic to buy a new car during the holiday.

EXERCISE 2.17

Examine your argument for logical fallacies, and make any revisions that are necessary to correct them.

LESSON SIX—Editing Phase: Revising

Feedback about Your First Draft Suggestions for Revision

By the time you finish your first draft, you will be ready for some feedback about its content and organization, either from your instructor or from your classmates. Most important, you will want to know if the points you are making are clear and whether your arguments seem logical and are affecting your readers the way that you thought they would. Through this feedback you will learn what works well and what could be improved. Your readers will probably also comment about sentence construction problems, punctuation, and spelling errors. But, most likely, these concerns won't be addressed in earnest until the Editing Phase when you proofread and correct your essay for formal presentation and evaluation.

Time may not permit your instructor to read and comment on everyone's draft or to set aside a class period for peer editing by your classmates. If that is the case, you will have to look elsewhere for constructive criticism. After laying the draft aside for awhile, you will find upon rereading it that you will see a number of improvements that can be made. The Checklist that follows has been provided to guide you through the feedback process.

EXERCISE 2.18

After you have completed your first draft, use the following checklist to find improvements you can make in the next draft. Your instructor may want you to have a fellow class member check your essay and make suggestions for improvements. Include this draft in your Project Folder.

CHECKLIST

INTRODUCTORY PARAGRAPH

1. Does your introductory paragraph begin with an effective opening sentence? (See Chapter One.)

2. Is your introductory paragraph at least five sentences long?

3. Is your thesis a debatable statement located at the end of your introductory paragraph?

4. Is your thesis a miniature outline of your argument? Would your thesis be more effective if it were divided, or if it is divided, would a shorter, undivided version work better?

BODY PARAGRAPHS

5. Have you successfully employed Plan One, Plan Two, or Other Strategies, or an adaptation of one of those plans?

6. Does each body paragraph begin with a topic sentence that covers the content of the entire paragraph and supports the thesis?

7. Does each body paragraph contain all of the primary and secondary support sentences it needs? (At least five sentences in each paragraph?) Is each paragraph free from irrelevant sentences? Have you included enough examples? Are they interesting?

8. Have you used enough transitional words and phrases, especially to signal pro and con sections? Have you used the pro and con words correctly? Does each sentence flow smoothly into the next?

CONCLUDING PARAGRAPH

9. Does your concluding paragraph begin with a summary or restatement of the thesis? Have you rephrased to avoid redundancy?

10. Have you added a thought-provoking generalization to your summary or restatement?

11. Is the concluding paragraph at least five sentences in length?

OVERALL CONSIDERATIONS

12. Have you successfully supported your thesis? Is your argument logical and persuasive?

13. Have you given credit to other sources of information correctly (parenthetical documentation)?

14. Will your paper hold your reader's interest? If not, how can it be improved?

As an example of how the basic structure of your paper can be improved, read question 7 on the checklist. Perhaps you did not include enough detail in your first draft. Search for places where generalizations can be made clearer by adding specifics more secondary support. Add details! Add facts and figures; include comparisons; rely on personal observations and anecdotes you have heard or read about; use common sense and logic to develop your arguments. Most important, add examples—too many are better than too few.

USE EXAMPLES

Example

For example, clothing construction is a valuable endeavor. It is obviously creative and productive in and of itself, yet as an activity from which boys are diverted. Conceivably, background in working with fabrics could give boys a familiarity with textures, colors, and patterns that would give them advantages in artistic design.

USE FACTS

Example

For every motorcyclist killed in vehicular accidents, many more are injured [. . .]. The brain-damaged frequently linger in comas for hours, days, or months. When they awaken, if they awaken, the very qualities of mind and personality which make up their unique personhood may be altered, perhaps permanently. Brain injury can impair motor skills and cause paralysis that limits walking or even use of hands, just as in stroke victims. Speech impairment is another noticeable result, as head trauma victims often must entirely rebuild their vocabularies and search for thought processes, making it impossible to process thoughts quickly or require 10 to 20 minutes for the brain to send a reply to the mouth. Occupational therapy is often required to relearn the sequencing of mundane tasks, like dressing (socks first, then slacks, and then the shoes). Short-term memory loss interferes with everything; the sequence of dressing is lost when someone forgets he or she is dressing. . . .

USE FIGURES (NUMBERS)

Example

According to a report published by the National Highway Traffic Safety Administration in 2000, for motorcyclists wearing helmets, the chances of fatalities in an accident are reduced 29 percent, and in 67 percent of the accidents the helmets prevent brain injuries ("California Helmet Law – 2001." Trauma Foundation. 23 July 2001.

USE COMPARISONS

Example

According to a 1998 University of California, San Francisco study, in 1993 medical costs for motorcycle injuries were 35 million dollars less than in 1991, dropping from 98 million dollars to 63 million dollars, a 35 percent decrease ("California Motorcycle Helmet Law Saves Money, UCSF Study Shows," UCSF'S Electronic News Daily News. 11 May 1999. University of California. 23 July 2001. (<http://www.ucsf.edu.edu/daybreak/1998/09/16helm.html>).

INCLUDE PERSONAL OBSERVATIONS AS GENERALIZATIONS

Examples

Short-term memory loss interferes with everything; the sequence of dressing is lost when we forget that we are dressing, so the process can become interminable.

Any computer user must work within the limitations of the program he or she is using; student writers using word processing programs often find that spell-check systems give them a right answer that is not right at all within the context of the particular sentence they are writing.

INCLUDE NARRATIONS YOU HAVE HEARD OR READ ABOUT

Example

No brains to save, my husband would murmur whenever he saw a bareheaded motorcyclist. Carl did not come by this dictum naively or with rancor. After 22 years of safe and cautious biking, his own helmet saved his life when he broadsided an automobile that was making and abrupt U-turn on a steep foothills road. Although he sustained a serious head injury which left him hemiplegic and subject to chronic motion sickness for the rest of his life, we know that without a helmet, he would have been killed, and his passenger, his sixteen-year-old son, would have suffered more than a light concussion.

USE COMMON SENSE TO DEVELOP YOUR ARGUMENTS

Example

As the nation's population grows more ethnically diverse, common sense dictates that the makeup of its college graduating classes should mirror those changing demographics.

Revising Your Draft

Begin work rewriting your argument as soon as you have received suggestions from your readers or as soon as you have completed your self-check. It is important to work on the revisions while the suggestions are fresh in your mind. Of course, you will need to consider each suggestion carefully before you decide to make the change. You will find, too, that you may need further clarification about a suggested change. If so, check further with the reader who made the suggestion to better understand that person's perception of the problem and how a revision might improve the essay.

EXERCISE 2.19

Rewrite your argumentative essay, making all of the changes that you think will improve it. It is highly unlikely that your instructor will provide feedback about this revised draft. As soon as this second draft is completed, you will be moving into the editing phase. (If required, have your revision approved.) Include this draft in your Project Folder.

LESSON SEVEN—Editing Phase: Preparing the Final Document

Stylistic Improvements

Your argument, perhaps after considerable struggle, is down on paper. You have asserted a thesis and supported it with an organized line of reasoning (Plan One, Two, or Other). Furthermore, you have made improvements in the basic structure of your argument. But you still must make the revisions and corrections that will make your writing more articulate, persuasive, and easier to read.

For suggestions, turn to Appendix C: A Guide to Stylistic Revision at the back of the book. Study each section, attempting to find stylistic improvements you can make in your argument. You may discover, for example, that some sentences lack parallel construction or that many of your sentences are unnecessarily wordy; you may find a few sentences lack energy because they are built around passive verbs.

Even if you do not consider yourself to be a skillful writer, at least not this early in the course, you can learn to make desired improvements in your writing. You can practice these new skills in your argument and perfect them as you write other essays both for this course and for your other courses.

While evaluating your argument, your instructor may make comments referring you to specific sections in Appendix C. These comments will be of great help to you in rewriting your essay.

Final Proofreading and Format

Before you submit your argument for evaluation, give your sentences some last-minute attention. Slowly proofread your essay for errors. If you need help, ask for it. Correct mistakes in agreement, pronoun reference, tense, and person; check for sentence variety and proper use of coordinating conjunctions and transitions; repair all run-ons, comma splices, and fragments. Double-check your punctuation.

REMINDER:
Never use the phrases *In my opinion,*
I believe, I think, or *It seems to me.*

Finally, correct any misspelled words. (Check for capitalization errors, too.) Use the spell-check on your computer or consult a dictionary for the preferred spelling of any words that might be misspelled. Your instructor expects only an occasional misspelling and no uncorrected typographical errors. Allow time to proofread your essay carefully.

FORMAT FOR FINAL DOCUMENT

1. Type your argument, double-spacing the entire document.

2. Print or type on one side of the page only, using a 12 point font.

3. Make corrections right up until you print your final document.

4. Use the sample essays in this chapter as a guide in format matters: heading, headers, title, spacing, margins, and page numbers.

5. If you are including a graphic, such as a chart, a table, or an illustration, ask your instructor for advice regarding its acknowledgment and placement.

EXERCISE 2.20

Prepare the final document of your argumentative essay. Place it in your Project Folder.

Project Folder

Place the following materials in your Project Folder in the order indicated:

1. Final document (on top)

2. Second draft

3. First draft

4. Thesis-topic sentence outline

5. All research materials and notes (on bottom)

COMPUTER SAFETY TIPS

1. Keep your argumentative paper stored on your hard drive until you have received your grade for the course.

2. Back up your work by copying your essay onto a disk or other media.

3. File a photocopy of the hard copy of your essay.

4. Print out and keep all Internet source material in case your instructor is concerned about possible plagiarism.

3

The Library Research Essay

Objectives

When you have finished this chapter, you will have completed

    1. a library orientation

    2. a Project Folder, including

        a. a topic proposal

        b. a working bibliography

        c. research notes

        d. a thesis and an outline

        e. a first draft of the essay

        f. works cited

        g. the final document

        h. copies of all research materials

        i. a revision, if necessary

The Library Research Essay 3

In this chapter you will learn a step-by-step approach to writing a **library research essay**. The skills you practice will be useful when you write other essays for this course and future courses. This systematic approach to gathering information, shaping it into an essay, documenting your references, and preparing a document can be used now and on through graduate school. Being organized and attentive to details will reduce your chances of encountering problems that often bewilder and frustrate students working on research projects.

STEPS IN WRITING THE RESEARCH ESSAY

1. Proposing the topic
2. Familiarizing yourself with the library you will be using
3. Compiling a working bibliography
4. Evaluating your sources
5. Taking research notes
6. Writing a final thesis and outline
7. Composing the first draft of the essay
8. Documenting your sources
9. Compiling a Works Cited
10. Preparing the final document
11. Organizing the Project Folder
12. Revising the essay, if required

To make certain you have mastered the skills being taught, you are required to have your work for each step approved before you proceed to the next. By the time you have completed all five lessons in this chapter, your library research essay will be written and ready for evaluation.

LESSON ONE—*Proposing a Topic*

Unless instructed otherwise, you will be allowed to propose your own topic for your library research essay. Choose your topic thoughtfully, and do not hesitate to consult with your instructor and others about the advisability of pursuing a particular subject.

FACTORS TO CONSIDER

Your interests
A proper-sized topic
Availability of material
Time limitations
Minimum requirements
Your instructor's advice

Your Interests

Select a general topic that interests you. Consider the assignment an opportunity to study an issue that concerns you, to reach a conclusion about the issue, and to communicate your findings in an essay. Being interested in your topic is of paramount importance.

> See the comprehensive list of general topics in Appendix D.
> Mark those topics that spark your interest.

EXERCISE 3.1

Indicate three or four of the topics from Appendix D that interested you.

_____

_____

_____

_____

Choosing a Topic

Other sources are available to help you in your search for a suitable essay topic. Study recent newspapers, both local and national, such as the *New York Times*, the *Wall Street Journal*, and the *Christian Science Monitor*; many libraries keep current newspaper copies for the last thirty days on the shelves. Be sure to look through all of the sections of the paper as well. Furthermore, look through current magazines that appeal to you. Listen to talk radio shows and watch TV documentary and news shows. Many libraries have lists of appropriate research topics and have even compiled bibliographies that will help you identify some preliminary sources. Another source to investigate would be one of the Internet directories, but because of the vast resources on the World Wide Web, make sure you narrow your topic sufficiently before you attempt to search.

A Proper-Sized Topic

Working with your general topic until it is the proper size is of utmost importance. You have already spent considerable time in previous chapters learning to narrow topics. However, the problems that can arise if the topic is too large become especially frustrating while you are writing a library research essay. If the topic is too large, you will probably not be able to gather all of the information needed in the time allocated; you will also encounter difficulty when it comes time to organize an outline. Thus, by narrowing your topic before beginning your research, you can avoid being swamped by an unwieldy mass of information. Also, if your topic is not narrow enough, your essay may end up being too long. One way to help narrow your topic is to state it in a question form; for example, should the Supreme Court overturn Roe v. Wade?

Most electronic indexes are programmed to help you narrow the field of your research, but some are not. Consequently, if you attempt to research a topic that is too broad, like abortion, you might find yourself faced with a list of several thousand sources. Such a long list would require you to spend an excessive amount of time eliminating irrelevant sources. A long list would indicate from the start that your topic should be further narrowed before you proceed.

A topic that is too broad will almost certainly lead to a superficial essay, lacking detail and in-depth discussion. The library essay that reads as if it is from an encyclopedia is generally a poor idea. Instructors do not want essays that summarize everything there is to know about a topic. Likewise, they do not want a biography essay that deals with the entire life of a person. Keep in mind, too, that the older a topic is and the more that has been published about it, the more specific and creative you have to be in choosing some particular aspect about which to write.

Availability of Material

Narrowing your topic too much can lead to serious problems also. You must consider whether or not sufficient material will be available in the library or on the Internet. The most common problem that students encounter when their topics are too narrow is that they are unable to find enough source material to write their essays. Watch out for topics that have just become big news, too. A brand-new controversy may be prominently featured in the media when it breaks, catching your interest, but it takes several months for most libraries to accumulate and index materials on new subjects. Beware of local issues also; many topics dealing with your own community may be best left for Chapter Six, where you will write an investigative essay.

Do not abandon an interesting topic too hastily. The fear that the library does not contain enough information may be unfounded. Perhaps the information is there, and you simply have not figured out how to find it. For instance, you may be looking in an index under Weapons when the articles are actually listed under Nuclear Weapons. Talking to your librarian and instructor is important before deciding whether or not a topic will work.

Time Limitations

Time is another important consideration. In a 16–18 week class, you should spend no more than four weeks gathering your information, planning, and writing your library research essay.

Length—1,500 Word Minimum

The minimum requirements of the research paper will influence your choice of topic, too. For this essay you need to write at least 1,500–2,000 words of text, or approximately six to seven typed pages of text.

Required References—A Minimum of Ten Sources Cited

At the end of your library research essay, you will include a Works Cited page. In the Works Cited you will list in alphabetical order all of the research sources referred to in your essay . To fulfill the requirements for this chapter, your Works Cited must contain at least ten research sources actually cited in the final version of your essay. You may include more than ten sources, but you must obtain your instructor's permission to include fewer than ten. As you prepare your research essay, you will use the Modern Language Association (MLA) format .

Your Instructor's Advice

Be positive and creative in approaching your instructor with a proposed topic. Sometimes an instructor experiences renewed interest in a worn-out topic if the student proposes a fresh approach. An instructor who has read too many essays on the pros and cons of nuclear power may be interested in an essay on the risks involved in transporting nuclear wastes. An essay outlining the causes of divorce would be dull, whereas one explaining the unique problems of divorced male parents might be interesting. Discuss your topic with your instructor before you commit yourself to it.

Writing the Topic Proposal

The topic proposal is a very brief report explaining what you hope to accomplish in your research essay and your research strategy. Although research essay proposals can be very formal in nature, yours will be informal. Thus, you may use first person (*I* and *my*) in your proposal, and there is no required format. You should, however, try to include the following information:

TOPIC PROPOSAL

1. Your narrowed topic
2. Why did you select this topic
3. Any tentative thesis, research questions, or working outline you have developed, including the type of organization (comparison or contrast, cause/effect, etc.)
4. An assessment of the availability of materials
5. An assurance that the topic can be researched in one week

Sample Proposal

My general topic is Diabetes. I will concentrate on Diabetes Type 2. My document will focus on a definition of Diabetes, some of the symptoms, who is most likely to get Diabetes Type 2, and some possible treatments for this disease.

I am interested in this topic because this disease has recently been featured in the newspaper and some national magazines that I read. Also, my father has Diabetes Type 2, and my cousin died from complications of this disease a few months ago; therefore, I'd like to know if I could develop this disease or if my children could.

Some research questions include: How does a person contract Diabetes 2? How would a person know if he or she had the disease? How can a person live with Diabetes 2? What are some of the treatments available to a diabetic? What new research is being conducted on this disease? How much of a problem is this disease?

A check of electronic and printed sources shows a number of recent articles on the topic are available in the library and on the Internet. I also hope to get an interview with my father's doctor, the school nurse, and to contact the National Diabetes Society for current pamphlets. I believe my topic is limited enough to allow me to complete my note taking in three days.

> If you are unfamiliar with the library you will be using, you may want to read
> Lesson Two before you visit the library to look for a topic.

EXERCISE 3.2

List three potential topics for your library research essay. Then after making a preliminary investigation in the library or the Internet—skim through the next lesson if necessary—consult with your instructor and the librarian.

Finally, choose the topic that seems best for your topic proposal (to be written in Exercise 3.3).

Potential Topic #1

_____

_____

_____

Potential Topic #2

_____

_____

_____

Potential Topic #3

_____

_____

_____

Have one of your topics approved.

EXERCISE 3.3

After having one of the potential topics in Exercise 3.2 approved, type a topic proposal for your library research essay. Prepare your proposal on a computer. Submit the final, edited copy to your instructor. Remember to save a copy to disk. Once the topic proposal is approved, place the approved proposal in your Project Folder.

LESSON TWO—Library Areas

For you to be successful at research essay writing, you need to develop the knack of rapidly finding your source material and taking notes, leaving plenty of time to write your essay. Become familiar with the areas and services provided by the library. Think of the library as an information bank made up of a number of areas, each specializing in certain types of materials and services. Most libraries have at least seven areas:

1. **Online Catalog**—Most libraries have their card catalogs (index of their books) on computers. When you work in a library that has a computerized catalog, it will probably be referred to as an online catalog. Generally, online catalogs are given a name, such as *LOIS, MELVYL,* or *EUREKA.* These names are usually acronyms that stand for the company that developed the system or the school district that owns the system.

   Online catalogs now contain not only a listing of books but also Internet sources (which allow you to communicate electronically with other institutions) and indexes for many videos, audio tapes, newspapers, magazines, and journals stored in your library.

2. **Stacks**—Books are kept on shelves called stacks. After you find the call number of a book that you would like to examine, go to the stacks to find the volume. If the library does not allow you access to the stacks, that means it has closed stacks and you simply ask a librarian to obtain the book for you. Many libraries that have open stack areas have some closed areas, such as the reserve stacks, where instructors place special materials to which students have controlled access.

3. **Checkout Counter**—Information, reserve books and materials, library cards, and checkout services are available at this counter.

4. **Reference**—Encyclopedias, almanacs, maps, biographical indexes, dictionaries, and other reference materials are kept in the reference area or room. Often these materials can be used only in the library.

5. **Serials**—Commonly referred to as the periodicals area, the serials area contains all of the magazines and professional journals in the library. Most libraries use a combination of stacks and microfilm and microfiche for their periodicals. Newspapers are also found in this area, in piles and on microfilm. Indexes for the periodicals may be computer programs such as *EBSCO* (full-text periodicals database), *InfoTrac* (full-text periodicals database), *Newsbank* (index for newspapers, such as the *San Francisco Chronicle*), and *Pro-Quest* (index for newspapers such as the *New York Times* and the *Washington Post*).

6. **Pamphlet File**—Often referred to as the vertical file, the pamphlet file is normally found in or near the reference area. It has pamphlets, newspaper clippings, government bulletins, and reprints on most current topics.

7. **Microforms**—Almost every library has a collection of microfilm and microfiche materials. Back issues of national newspapers such as *New York Times*, *Wall Street Journal*, and *Christian Science Monitor* are commonly stored on microforms; newer issues are more commonly found on the Internet. As you familiarize yourself with the library, take the time to learn what is available on microforms and whether indexes for those materials are available.

Library Services

LIBRARIANS

You will sometimes need help locating materials. The librarian who specializes in the area where you are working will be your best source of information. If you need general orientation, inquire about scheduled library orientation tours or any orientation packets that may be available to assist students unfamiliar with the library or some of its materials.

INTERLIBRARY LOAN

You will often find that the library you are using does not have a particular book you need. Through the librarian, Interlibrary Loan may be able to borrow the book from another library for you. (Allow a week or two for transit time; the failure of a book to arrive on schedule is not a valid excuse for handing in a late paper.)

Libraries also keep lists of the magazines and journals located in other libraries in your area. If your library does not have a periodical you need, ask your librarian for the serials lists from other libraries. To read these periodicals, however, will require you to obtain them through Interlibrary Loan or to visit the libraries where they are housed.

MICROFILM AND MICROFICHE READERS

Most libraries have at least one microfilm—and one microfiche—reading machine. Although directions for their use are usually displayed, a librarian will show you how to operate any machine you may wish to use if you have difficulty.

PHOTOCOPY MACHINES

Modern libraries also provide equipment that can assist you with the task of collecting the information you will need to write your essay. To save time, you can make photocopies of periodical articles, portions of books, and other materials. These photocopies can then be studied more carefully at home. You can use the photocopy machine for a small fee. Most larger libraries also have coin-operated copiers that will produce copies of articles on microfilm or microfiche.

ELECTRONIC AIDS: MEDIA MATERIALS

Many libraries lend students record and tape players, film viewers, and other audiovisual equipment. More and more libraries are providing computers and word processors for student use. Ask at the checkout counter for the equipment you need. (Make it a point to inquire about recordings, films, computer software, and other media materials housed in the library.)

COMPUTER DATABASE SEARCHES

Most libraries have replaced or will be replacing their traditional volumes of indexes with computers that are connected to mainframe systems or CD-ROM readers. These computer software programs enable you to find the same information you were able to find previously in the printed volumes. These computers are often connected to printers that provide you with a printout telling you where to get a copy of the book or article you need. This makes your research much faster. Some of these programs also offer you the option of a computer printout of the newspaper or magazine article you wish to read.

Computers also enable you to conduct research electronically, connecting you to an online database. Such online research can be remarkably helpful when investigating some topics. However, you can quickly run up a bill of many dollars on such searches if you copy every page of every article you find. Another cost and time-saving technique is to e-mail the database information to yourself if you have a computer available to you.

Another online database that you may find useful as you research your topic is the Internet, and it may not be necessary to go to the library to use this source. More and more students have access to the Internet at home, in the dorm, or at work. Thousands of live databases offer information on virtually every subject on which you may wish to write. Before you invest too much time into online research, however, you should check with your instructor to find out what your school's policy is on the use of online sources in research essays. Some schools limit the number of online sources students may use.

If you do use online sources in your essay, remember that it is just as important to document electronic sources as printed sources. Your reader must be able to find every source you refer to in your essay from the information you provide. If your reference is to a book, your reader must be able to find the book on the shelf; if your reference is to an online source, your reader must be able to find it as well. You are required, therefore, to provide documentation that will allow your reader to go directly to that source and read the entire original document. In order to allow your reader to find an electronic source you must, therefore, give an exact path that will lead your reader to each electronic source without fail. If you are not confident that a source can be found, don't include it in your essay.

EXERCISE 3.4

To familiarize yourself with the library you will be using during your library research project, choose one or more of the following options:

1. Attend a library orientation arranged by your instructor.
2. Complete a library orientation exercise distributed by the library staff.
3. Arrange for someone familiar with the library to give you a walking tour.
4. Conduct your own library orientation. Explore the library you will use, locating the areas mentioned in this lesson and inquiring about the services offered.

Answer the following questions:

1. Which of the above options did you complete? _____

2. Have you obtained a library card? _____

3. What are the library hours?_____

LESSON THREE—Compiling the Working Bibliography

After completing your library orientation, the next major step in your library research essay project is to compile a **working bibliography**, a preliminary listing of the sources you find in the library, on the Internet or in person, such as interviews. This list will help keep you organized and you will know which material you have seen and which material you still need to see.

Little time is needed to compile the working bibliography as you do not stop to read each promising source; you merely list the source, recording all the important identification information, and then return to the source when you are ready to begin taking notes. Being careful at this point by recording the appropriate author, title, date, publisher, editor, and page numbers will save you from having to go back to the library and research this information at a future time.

Because some sources you want may be checked out of the library or you are unable to find a source for some reason or the source doesn't offer any valuable information, it is important to list three times as many sources as you think you will need. Since you will need to include a minimum of 10 sources in the Works Cited in your final document, you will need 30 working bibliography sources.

How to Compile the Working Bibliography

Choose a method that is best for you or is recommended by your instructor, one that seems the easiest for you and the one that will help you write your essay the most effectively:

- Library database printout (check with your librarian to see if your library has one of these programs)
- Bibliography cards, listing one source per card
- Copies of articles and a listing of potential interviews
- Self-generated computer notes

Whichever method works best for you, remember that all sources must be included in the Project Folder, which will be turned in with your final document.

To make certain you have conducted a thorough investigation of the library, use at least **five** of the following kinds of sources:

1. Magazine articles in the *Reader's Guide to Periodical Literature, InfoTrac,* and *EBSCO* (the last two being full-text periodical databases)
2. Newspaper articles listed in *Newsbank* and *ProQuest*
3. Books
4. Newspaper articles listed in the indexes to the *New York Times* and *Wall Street Journal*
5. Books shelved in the reference area of the library
6. Materials from the pamphlet files/vertical files

7. Recordings, videos, and CD-ROMs
8. Information gathered from electronic sources
9. Journal articles listed in the *Education Index, Nursing Index,* etc.
10. Interviews

Computer-Generated Working Bibliography

Many libraries now have software that enables you to create a customized list of selected library sources and print out the list. For example, imagine you selected the research topic "Diabetes 2 in Adults." When you go to the library, you find that your library has twenty-five books on this topic, but only five have been written in the last four years, so these may be the only ones you want to consider for your working bibliography. The software allows you to select these four entries initially and then investigate other sources for your research, such as periodicals, videos and reference materials. Again, each time you find a source you want to investigate further, you add the citation to your list, until you have your 30 required. When you have researched all possible areas, you print out the list and show it to your instructor.

One of the problems with compiling the working bibliography this way is that the citations will not be in MLA format. But one of the advantages to this system is that it is fairly quick, and since the source is not in front of you, you can resist the urge to read the document.

Working Bibliography Cards

If you are using bibliography cards, use one 3x5-inch index card for each source. Separate cards are better than a single list for a working bibliography because they can be shuffled, sorted, and matched to your note cards, outline, and Works Cited as you write your essay. Each time you discover a potential source of information, fill out a card, listing all of the information you will need to identify and locate the source. Although you may include a brief note about the content of the source on a working bibliography card, these cards should not be confused with note cards. The main purpose of the working bibliography cards is to guide you to the sources.

Every time you locate a new source, take the time to create a working bibliography card, even later in the project. You will need your working bibliography cards to assemble your Works Cited, which will be placed at the end of your final document. The format used for your working bibliography cards is the one you will use for the entries in your Works Cited. Samples of the most common kinds of entries are included in this lesson. For examples of other types, study the sample entries in Appendix B.

Some students enter working bibliographies on computers so they can organize all of their information in one place. These students worry about losing their stack of 3x5-inch cards if they write them out and carry them with them. This is a realistic concern, but putting the working bibliography on a computer takes more time and creates other problems. When you have completed your working bibliography, if you keep it on a computer, you will need to print out and cut the working bibliography into separate entries in order to proceed. The time-tested practice of writing out working bibliography cards will most likely save you time.

Photocopied Working Bibliography

The most informal way to compile a working bibliography is to make copies of all the printed material, organize them alphabetically and show them to your instructor. The major advantage of this system is that you will have ready the copies of the research material that you will need to include in your Project Folder.

However, there are some major disadvantages: 1) you will pay for copying material you will probably never use for the final document; 2) you may forget to copy down all the necessary information needed for the Works Cited; 3) unless you are very careful about clipping all the pages together, you could lose pages or clip pages together that don't belong together; and 4) you will need to highlight or underline key information and also make notes in the margins of the printouts in order to easily refer back to the information you want to use.

BEGIN YOUR WORKING BIBLIOGRAPHY

> **NOTE!** Resist the temptation to start finding and reading the articles and books as you assemble your working bibliography. If your essay must have a minimum of 10 sources listed in the Works Cited, you should collect at least 30 working bibliography cards before you begin locating and reading the sources. If you can't find enough sources for your working bibliography, you will need to change your topic. If you have begun finding and reading articles and then have to change your topic, you will have wasted considerable time.

The working bibliography should include all the information necessary for you to find the source again and to be able to compile the Works Cited page. Most of the sources you will use will be books, periodicals and Internet sources. The following guide contains the information you will need to include for these different types of sources, together with examples for you to copy for your own working bibliography.

Guide For Recording Working Bibliography

BOOKS

Format: Call number, author's last name, first name. Title of the book. Place of publication: Publisher, publishing date.

Example: QC 912.3
G 69
1992
C.1
Kraljic, Matthew. The Greenhouse Effect. New York: Wilson, 1992.

While you are searching for useful books, you may have to think of synonyms for your subject or subcategories that may be listed. Often you will be unable to find a book devoted entirely to your topic. Therefore, be a good detective. You may find information in a book that only generally relates to your topic. For example, there are entire books about vitamins, but each book on nutrition has information about vitamins as well.

ENCYCLOPEDIA/DICTIONARY

Format: Author's last name, first name (if given). "Title of article." Title of the Encyclopedia/Dictionary. Edition. Publishing date. Page.

Example: Mast, Gerald. "Motion Pictures, History of." The New Encyclopedia Britannica Macropedia. 1981. 515-516.

The most frequently used encyclopedias are the general encyclopedias, which are often good sources of background information for library research papers. These encyclopedias are usually found in the reference section of the library. There are also an increased number of specialized encyclopedias, such as *Encyclopedia of Psychology* and *Encyclopedia of Educational Research*, that can cover your topic in depth. Agriculture, art, education, history, religion, science, social science, biography, and literature all have one or more specialized encyclopedias.

A number of encyclopedias are currently available on CD-ROM. If you have access to a computer with CD-ROM, you should check to see if an encyclopedia is installed.

PERIODICALS

Journal: Author's last name, first name. "Title of the article." Journal title volume number (year of publication): page numbers.

Example: Kerr, R. A. "Iron Fertilization: Atomic, but No Cure for the Greenhouse." Science 263 (1994): 1089-90. (**Note:** the pages are numbered continuously through the year.)

Example: Miner, Thomas. "You Never Hear the One That Hits You." The Forum (1994): 10-11. (**Note:** the pages are numbered separately in each issue, so the volume number is omitted.)

Magazine: Author's last name, first name. "Title of the article." Title of the magazine date: page numbers.

Example: Quindlen, Anna. "Doing Something Is Something." Newsweek 13 May 2002: 76.

Newspaper: Author's last name, first name. "Title of the article." Title of the newspaper date: page numbers.

Example: Pender, Kathleen. "Investors Are Sick of Tech." San Francisco Chronicle 14 June 2002: B1.

Most libraries have electronic indexes to help you locate periodicals more effectively than searching through the stacks of magazines and newspapers. All of these indexes serve the same purpose: to provide you with the information needed to locate articles and books that will help you write your essay. These will reduce your research time considerably, so ask the librarian which indexes your library has. These might include *InfoTrac*, *Newsbank*, and *ProQuest*.

Pamphlets: Title of the pamphlet. Place of publication: Publisher. Date.

Example: Lilley, John and Calvin Webb. Climate Warming? Exploring the Answers. Alberta, Canada: Environmental Council of Alberta. 1990.

Don't forget to investigate the pamphlet file, sometimes called vertical files. These files are usually filled with pamphlets, news clippings, bulletins, government printings and a variety of other types of materials on frequently researched subjects. You may also find pamphlets on your own at medical facilities, government offices or agencies.

Pamphlets are sometimes difficult to list in standard working bibliography format as often the date and/or publisher may not be indicated. On your working bibliography cards use **N.p.** to indicate that no place of publication is given, **n.p.** to show that the publisher is not listed, **n.d.** to indicate that the date is not given, and **N.pag.** to indicate that the page number is missing. Remember, you can't give information if it isn't given to you.

WEB SOURCES

Periodical: Author's last name, first name. "Title of the article." <u>Title of the source</u>. Volume number or any other identifying numbers (Date of Publication). Page numbers or number of paragraphs. Date of access and URL address. If not all of this information is given in the web site, include what information you can.

Example: Zetter, Kim. "New Technologies, Laws Threatening Privacy." <u>PC World</u> Mar. 2002. 20 Oct. 2002 <http://proquest.umi.com/pqdweb?TS=1035180084>.

See Appendix B for more samples of what information is required for the working bibliography and Works Cited.

As you learned in Chapter Two, the World Wide Web is an excellent source of information, if used efficiently. You can spend too much time researching a subject if you don't know some of the tools available to you.

Use your browser to access some of the most powerful search engines on the web:

Yahoo	(http://www.yhoo.com)
Google	(http://www.google.com)
Lycos	(http://www.lycos.com)
Webcrawler	(http://webcrawler.com)
Librarians' Index to the Internet	(http://www.lii.org)

Once you become comfortable using these search engines, you are ready to narrow your search, using specific strategies.

Using Quotation Marks

One way to narrow your search is to put the topic in quotation marks indicating that you want to search for that exact wording. Without the quotation marks the search engine is looking for all the words in any order. For example, if your topic is funding for elementary schools and you don't use quote marks, the search results would include any document using the words "funding," "elementary," and/or "schools." Putting the topic in quotation marks "funding for elementary schools" is indicating you want those exact words, in that exact order to be researched.

Boolean Searches

A Boolean search allows you to narrow your search by showing the relationship of ideas. The most common Boolean searches use the terms *NOT, OR, AND*. For instance, going back to the previous topic example, "funding for elementary schools," these are how the Boolean searches would be worded:

NOT *example*—

Funding for elementary schools **NOT** Alaska and Hawaii would give you funding for elementary schools on the mainland and would exclude both Alaska and Hawaii.

OR *example*—

Funding for elementary schools **OR** middle schools would give you both funding for elementary schools or middle schools.

AND *example*—

Funding for elementary schools **AND** Hawaii would give you funding for elementary schools and Hawaii.

See Appendix B for more samples of what information is required for the working bibliography and **Works Cited**.

EXERCISE 3.5

Keeping in mind the subject for your topic proposal, complete the following questions.

1. Select one of the suggested search engines and use quotation marks around your topic; what are the results?

_____

_____

2. Select another search engine and use quotation marks around your topic; what are the results?

_____

_____

3. Using your topic, go into a search engine and use a Boolean search with **NOT**; what are the results?

_____

_____

4. Using your topic, go into a search engine and use a Boolean search with **OR**; what are the results?

_____

_____

5. Using your topic, go into a search engine and use a Boolean search with **AND**; what are the results?

_____

_____

6. Which narrowing strategy worked best for your topic? Why?

_____

_____

Have your work checked.

EXERCISE 3.6

Compile your working bibliography; use at least five different types of sources and have thirty sources total. Consult with your instructor or librarian whenever problems arise. When your working bibliography is finished, have it checked by your instructor. Also, remember to include it in your Project Folder.

EVALUATING SOURCES

Before you begin taking your notes for your research essay, you need to be aware of how to evaluate your Internet sources. As you probably know by now, anyone who can create a web page can put information on the World Wide Web. Therefore, as a researcher, you have to be able to separate the credible sources from the not so credible sources. The following are strategies for you to use to access the credibility of your Internet sources.

Authority/Source
- Is it clear who the author/publisher is of the site?
- Are the author's credentials available?
- Is there an organization that is sponsoring the site? What is its reputation?
- Is there a phone number or address to contact someone for more information?
- Are there footnotes or endnotes that the writer used to substantiate the information?

Content
- Are there typographical errors? Grammatical errors?
- Is the information primary? (based on firsthand research, such as a study, conducting surveys, visitations, observations)
- Is the information secondary? (based on library research)
- What is the depth of the information? Can you verify the information in other sources you've read?
- Do other sources you've read refer back to the information on the web site? (A study, for example)?
- What is the purpose of the site? To inform? To persuade? To explain?

Bias
- All writing is biased in some way. What is this author's bias?

Timeliness
- Is the information up to date?
- What is the publishing date?
- Given the publishing date, is the information still valid for your purposes?
- Is the site updated in a timely fashion?

You should scrutinize all of your web sites based on the previous criteria. If you are in doubt about any of your sources, the best rule of thumb is to not use the source; find another one, a more credible one. Your instructor or librarian can also help you evaluate sources about which you are in doubt.

EXERCISE 3.7

Answer the following questions for at least three of your web sources. Type up your responses. Then have them checked by your instructor and place them in your Project Folder.

1. What is the complete citation for your selected source?
2. Who is the author and/or organization sponsoring the web site? Is the sponsor reputable?
3. How is the information relevant to your topic?
4. Does the source provide contact information?
5. Is this source current enough for your essay?

LESSON FOUR—*Taking Notes*

Note Card Format

As a researcher you have a choice of the format for your notes: the formal 4x6 index cards or typing the notes into the computer. The disadvantages of using the index cards are 1) they are bulky to carry around; and 2) you could lose one or more of them. The advantages of using the index card system are 1) they are easy to stack in piles to match your outline; 2) it is visually apparent if you need to research a specific area of your topic because you might have a small stack of a given paragraph idea; and 3) you can carry the cards around with you and work on your essay almost anywhere.

The disadvantages of typing the notes into the computer and not using cards are 1) you can only work on your essay when you have access to your computer files; and 2) the typed information is harder to match to the outline unless you cut up the notes. The advantages of typing your notes directly into the computer are 1) the notes can be easily edited; 2) the notes are easily incorporated into the essay as they are already typed; and 3) if you save them both to a disk and your hard drive, you have an excellent chance of not losing them.

Keep Your Research Guide Handy

When you are ready to begin taking notes, use your research proposal to develop a **research guide**. On an index card, write your tentative thesis, research questions, or working outline. You may want to combine two types, for example, a tentative thesis and a working outline. Since you should avoid compulsively taking notes on everything you read, you can use the research guide to help you make decisions about when to take notes.

TENTATIVE THESIS

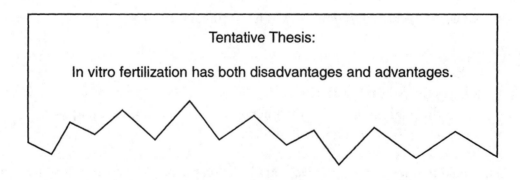

Tentative Thesis:

In vitro fertilization has both disadvantages and advantages.

RESEARCH QUESTIONS

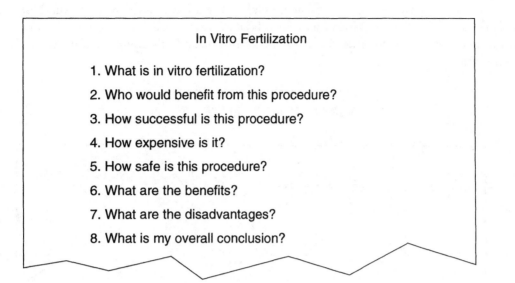

In Vitro Fertilization

1. What is in vitro fertilization?

2. Who would benefit from this procedure?

3. How successful is this procedure?

4. How expensive is it?

5. How safe is this procedure?

6. What are the benefits?

7. What are the disadvantages?

8. What is my overall conclusion?

WORKING OUTLINE

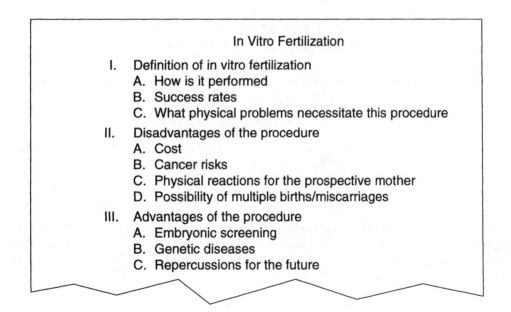

In Vitro Fertilization

I.   Definition of in vitro fertilization
     A. How is it performed
     B. Success rates
     C. What physical problems necessitate this procedure

II. Disadvantages of the procedure
     A. Cost
     B. Cancer risks
     C. Physical reactions for the prospective mother
     D. Possibility of multiple births/miscarriages

III. Advantages of the procedure
     A. Embryonic screening
     B. Genetic diseases
     C. Repercussions for the future

EXERCISE 3.8

Develop your research guide—tentative thesis, research questions or working outline (see above examples)—and type it; then have it checked by your instructor. Keep a copy for yourself and remember to put the approved copy that your instructor has seen in your Project Folder.

NOTE CARD HEADINGS

Regardless of the type of notes you are taking, the information contained on them is exactly the same. If you are taking notes from a book, write the following information at the top of the first note taken for that book: 1) the author or author's complete names and 2) the book's title.

SAMPLE NOTE CARD HEADING
FOR FIRST REFERENCE—BOOK

PROULX, E. ANNIE. THE SHIPPING NEWS.

If you need more than one note card for a book, abbreviate the heading on subsequent cards. Repeat the author's or authors' last names and the title of the book in case you later take notes from another book by the same author(s).

SAMPLE NOTE CARD HEADING
FOR SUBSEQUENT CARD—BOOK

PROULX.   SHIPPING NEWS.

If you are taking notes from a periodical, for example, a magazine, write the following information at the top of the first note card you use for that particular source: (1) the author's or authors' complete names and (2) the article title and subtitle. If no author is given for an article, write just the article title and subtitle.

SAMPLE NOTE CARD HEADING FOR
FIRST REFERENCE—PERIODICAL

On any additional note cards for the same article, abbreviate the original heading, taking care not to abbreviate so completely that confusion could arise if you later take notes from another article by the same author or another article with a similar title.

Check Your Working Bibliography Cards

As soon as you actually have a source in your hands, recheck to make certain that your working bibliography card for the source contains all of the information you will need later when you write your Works Cited. Your working bibliography cards must be legible, accurate, and complete. You may, for example, have to replace authors' initials with full names, which may be listed in the actual magazine article but not on your original working bibliography entry. Or you may discover that a book is a reprint of an older edition and you need to add the reprint information. Furthermore, you may not have been able to list the exact page numbers of an article when you first wrote the bibliography card.

LIMIT YOURSELF TO ONE POINT PER CARD

As you take notes, limit yourself to one point per card so that the cards can easily be put into the order they will be used for the paper. While you read and take notes, refer to your research guide (thesis, questions, or outline) frequently. If you find that the source you are reading includes information that can be used in a section of your essay, write a note card and label it in the upper-right corner with the appropriate outline or research question number. Make sure you write on one side of the note card only so as not to overlook important information.

SUMMARIZING, PARAPHRASING, QUOTING

Summary Cards

In your notes you may summarize, paraphrase, or quote from your sources. When you summarize, condense what you are summarizing, stating the essential ideas in your own words. You may include specifics statistics, details, and examples, but the basic idea is to detail briefly what the author has said. Summaries are always shorter than the original passage.

SAMPLE NOTE CARD—SUMMARY

Authors and Title →

Morison, Samuel Eliot, and Henry Steele Commager. <u>Growth of the American Republic</u>, vol. 1.

I. B. ← Outline Item

Summary of Passage →

Jefferson and Hamilton disagreed with Washington's means for securing foreign policy that would allow for period of peace. Hamilton wanted United States to cooperate with Great Britain, but Jefferson advocated an alliance with France. Jefferson feared that Hamilton and his friends planned to make the United States a copy of Great Britain (345-346).

← Pages of Summary

(S) ← Summary Symbol

This sample note card succinctly summarizes six paragraphs from Morison and Commager's history of early America. Note that the exact page numbers are stated in parentheses at the end of the summary. This information is necessary for preparing the parenthetical references in your essay. Also note the (S) in the lower-right corner of the note card. This symbol will remind you that the note is a summary and that it will require a lead-in when integrated in the text of the research essay. The "I.B." in the upper-right corner keys the note card to your working outline.

Paraphrase Cards

When paraphrasing, you must rewrite the original passage in your own words. More is required than just changing the order of the words a bit and inserting several synonyms. If you decide to keep some of the key words or phrases, be sure to enclose them in quotation marks. Paraphrases are frequently longer than the original passage. Note how the following statement is paraphrased on the card.

> Epcot designers have focused on a series of themes that are intended, through example, to inspire people to apply modern technology responsibly to develop solutions to human kind's problems.

SAMPLE NOTE CARD—PARAPHRASE

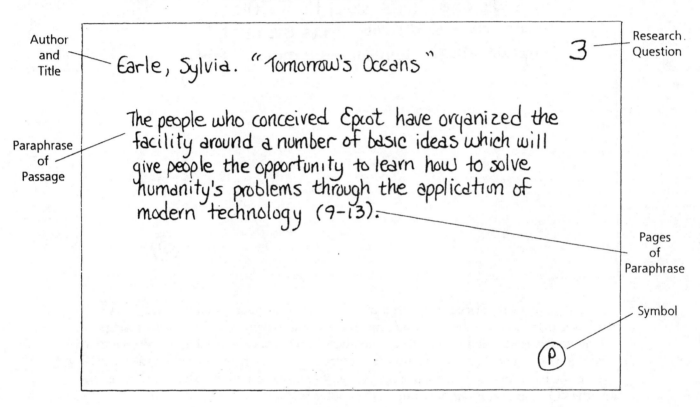

Note again that the exact page numbers of the reference are cited in the parentheses after the paraphrase. This information is needed for the parenthetical references in your essay. The symbol (P) in the lower-right corner of the card is to remind you that the material is paraphrased and will need a lead-in when used in the essay. The "3" in the upper-right corner keys the card to one of your research questions.

Quotation Cards

When you use quoted material, copy the passage exactly as it is written word for word. Note the following example:

SAMPLE NOTE CARD—QUOTE

Author and Title

Quotation Marks

Skinner, B. F.   Beyond Freedom and Dignity.   6

Research Question

"Those who object most violently to the manipulation of behavior make the most vigorous efforts to manipulate minds" (54).

Quotation Marks and Page of Quotation

Ⓠ

Quotation Symbol

Quotation marks placed at the beginning and end of the quoted material and the Ⓠ in the lower-right corner of the note card remind the writer to write a lead-in for the passage, to use quotation marks, and to include a parenthetical reference. Forgetting to use quotation marks around a quoted passage creates the appearance that you have plagiarized the material even if you have documented the passage. Recheck to make certain that the quotation marks and the Ⓠ appear on your note card of the quoted passage.

Idea Cards

As you take notes, ideas will occur that you want to remember for your essay. Possibly you will react to something you have read, or you will see a connection among what several sources have to say. Or you may have an idea for changing the organization of your paper, or perhaps you will realize suddenly what your final thesis should be. You will not want to lose these thoughts, so record them on idea cards. Each time such an idea occurs, simply fill out a note card and label it appropriately with a short reminder. Place an (I) in the lower-right corner of the card.

SAMPLE IDEA CARD

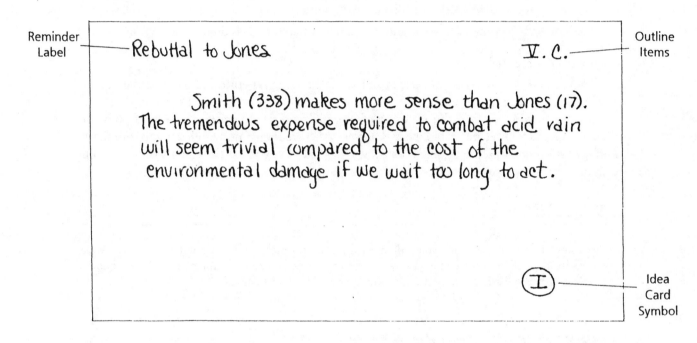

Reminder Label

Rebuttal to Jones   V. C.   Outline Items

Smith (338) makes more sense than Jones (17). The tremendous expense required to combat acid rain will seem trivial compared to the cost of the environmental damage if we wait too long to act.

(I)   Idea Card Symbol

Photocopies

By photocopying library materials, you can spend less time in the library, but later you must take notes from the photocopies. When you write your essay, you should be working from your note cards, not directly from your photocopies. Make sure that the photocopied material is accurately identified, and keep it all together in your Project Folder.

A Warning about Plagiarism

If you intentionally take another person's thoughts, ideas, words, or data and use them as your own, you are plagiarizing. Plagiarism is absolutely not condoned, and being caught plagiarizing may result in your failing the essay, the course, or worse. Anything summarized, paraphrased, or quoted must be properly acknowledged with a lead-in, quotation marks around a quote, properly used ellipsis marks, and accurate documentation. Study the following example of plagiarism.

Here are two sentences from an article by Wally Wyss, "Rotary Round-Up, Part 1," in *Motor Trend* magazine:

> For every booster, however, there's a detractor, among them [sic] environmentalists who won't settle for anything but complete obliteration of the internal combustion engine. . . . The announcements of "breakthroughs" will continue . . . in gas turbines, Stirling engines, steam hybrid/electrics, or—SHAZAM—even atomic power.

Now read the last two sentences of a student's paper:

> For every booster, however, there is a detractor, among them environmentalists who won't settle for anything less than the complete obliteration of the internal combustion monster. The announcement of "breakthroughs" will continue . . . gas turbines, steam, hybrid/electronics, or even—SHAZAM—atomic-powered engines.

Be honest! Do your own work, and give credit where credit is due.

Accuracy Is Essential

Accurate note taking is your responsibility. Clear comprehension of what you are reading and clear communication of that meaning in your notes is a must. Be aware that it is highly unethical to change the meaning of original material to achieve a certain point of view when you summarize, paraphrase, or quote. Also, you must not carelessly mix summary and quotation or paraphrasing and quotation. Anytime that you use the exact wording of the original passage, you must enclose the original wording in quotation marks.

EXERCISE 3.9

Complete all of the notes you will need for your research essay. Remember to follow your research guide, and include a variety of different kinds of cards—summary, paraphrase, quotation, and idea cards. Have your note cards approved by your instructor.

LESSON FIVE—Writing the Essay

Now that you have finished your research notes, the task of completing your library research essay can be broken down into the following steps:

1. Title page or heading
2. Final outline
3. First draft of essay, including parenthetical documentation
4. Notes (if needed)
5. Works Cited
6. Final document

Read the sample library research essay that begins on the page 135. On left-hand facing pages accompanying the essay, you will find detailed advice explaining the steps listed above.

Study these explanations so you will know what is expected as you write your own essay. After you have studied the sample essay and the facing pages, complete the exercises at the end of the lesson. Then your library research essay will be completed.

Appearance of the Document

The appearance of the document is especially important. You need to use a computer, with a clear font, 12 point, in black ink, double-spaced, on one side of the page. If you discover errors, you need only edit with the computer to correct them. You should also run a spell-check, but a couple of final read throughs is also essential to find errors that spell-check will not, such as "their" for "there" which is a usage error rather than a misspelling. You also need to make sure that the document is accurately paginated, according to MLA specifications.

> **NOTE:** Make sure you save your document to a disk and on your hard drive in case the document is lost or misplaced. Protect yourself by making a photocopy of your final document.

Title Page

Your instructor may require a title page. If the instructor provides no format to follow, set up the title page according to the following directions:

1. Center the title four inches from the top of the page. Use standard capitalization rules for titles; do not place your title in quotation marks or underline it.
2. After the title, quadruple-space and center the word *by*.
3. Then quadruple-space and type your name, centering it.
4. Center the course title and number two and one-half inches (approximately fifteen spaces) below your name.
5. Skip two spaces and center the meeting time for the course.
6. After double-spacing, key in the instructor's name. Use the appropriate title, for example, Professor, Dr., Ms., or Mr.
7. The name of the school may be included (double-space after the instructor's name).
8. Last, after double-spacing, include the date of submission either with the month first and a comma after the day or with the day first and no comma (e.g., May 11, 1995 or 11 May 1995).
9. Do not place a page number on the title page.

Controlling Our Reproductive Destiny

by

Crystle Hodgson

English 1A

TTh 11:00

Professor Monsen

American River College

11 April 2003

Outline (Thesis and Topic Sentence)

Many instructors require an outline page listing the thesis and either the topic sentences for the paper or the topics and subtopics that are covered in the paper. A sample thesis-topic sentence outline is presented on the facing pages.

1. In the upper-right corner, one-half inch from the top (approximately four spaces) and one inch from the right edge of the page, set a header in your computer. The header consists of your last name, the page number, and the lowercase Roman numeral **i**. Subsequent pages of the outline would be numbered **ii**, **iii**, **iv**, and so on. You must put your last name in front of the page number, leaving one space before the number.

2. Center the word *Outline* one inch (approximately six spaces) from the top of the page.

3. Then double-space and type in the title of your paper, centering it and capitalizing properly.

4. Quadruple-space after the title and type in your *thesis*. Precede your thesis sentence with the word Thesis: (including a colon and followed by a single space). If your thesis is more than a single line, use double-spacing.

5. Next, quadruple-space and write a topic-sentence outline: a consecutively numbered list of all the topic sentences that will appear in your paper. Be sure to list the first sentence of the introductory and concluding paragraphs. Remember to make changes in your outline if you make any revisions in the topic sentences as you write your paper. Double-space the entire outline.

Outline

Controlling Our Reproductive Destiny

Thesis: A future where there are no limits on in vitro fertilization raises some frightening prospects along with remarkable benefits for the treatment of infertile couples.

1. In vitro fertilization is a process whereby eggs are retrieved from the ovaries of the woman with a small needle passed through the top of the vagina and combined with prepared semen in a laboratory dish.

2. The conception rates for in vitro fertilization are very comparable to the conception rates of that of a fertile couple trying to conceive the natural way.

3. Physicians initially developed IVF in the early 1970s in hopes of treating infertility caused by blocked, severely damaged or absent fallopian tubes (Ingram 67).

4. Unfortunately, most infertile couples do not have the extra money to pay for the entire process, and the majority of insurance companies do not cover it.

5. As with most medical procedures, there are risks associated with IVF.

6. Another complication when using fertility drugs is the chance of multiple births.

7. Embryonic screening is another step that scientists have added onto the IVF procedure in hopes of being able to give couples a better chance of being able to conceive the child they want.

8. Couples where one or both of the partners carry some kind of genetic disease have only a 1 in 12 chance of having a healthy baby, void of any diseases or disorders the parents may have passed along (Fischer 60).

9. Nine months later the mother gave birth to a healthy baby boy.

10. Furthermore, embryo screening may be to aid sick siblings or even let couples with genetic disorders have healthy children, but what are the possible repercussions of this new technology?

11. Another way to look at embryonic screening is to see it as a way to increase the success rates of in vitro fertilization.

12. There will always be an ongoing search for new procedures and techniques to help couples overcome what they have been dealt naturally.

Heading (No Title Page)

The *MLA Handbook for Writers of Research Papers* recommends that a heading be used rather than a title page. (With this format no outline page would be included either.) The format for the first page of a research paper with a heading is as follows:

1. **Header:** Beginning with page two, key in a header that will identify you as the author. In the upper-right corner, one-half inch (approximately four spaces) from the top of the page, place your name, leave a space, and then insert the page number. Never place any punctuation after the page number; do not place the word *page* in between your name and the page number, and don't underline the page number, enclose it in hyphens, or parentheses. Most computer software packages will help you create a header, automatically inserting your name and the appropriate page number on each page of your paper. This header should be located in the upper-right corner, one-half inch (approximately four spaces) from the top of the page; it should also be one inch from the right side of the paper. (The margin default on your computer may make it necessary to place this header one inch from the top of the page.) Be aware that the *MLA Handbook for Writers of Research Papers* suggests that you should also have a header at the top right of page one. Some instructors, however, prefer that you not put the header on page one, because the complete heading of your paper is at the top left of the page. Check with your instructor.

2. **Heading:** Begin your heading in the upper-left corner, one inch from the top of the page and one inch from the left edge of the page (the normal margin). Double-space the entire heading—your name, then your instructor's name, on the next line the course name and number, and the date submitted on the last line.

3. **Title:** After the heading, double-space and center the title. Use the standard conventions for capitalizing titles. Always capitalize the first and last words of the title and any word after a hyphen or colon. Capitalize the first letter of all words in the title except for articles (*a, an, the*), coordinating conjunctions (*and, nor, but, for, or, yet, so*), prepositions (e.g., *in, on, with, before, to*) and to in infinitives (e.g., *to Learn*). Do not capitalize the entire title, place it in quotation marks or underline it. However, any portion of the title that would be placed in quotation marks or underlined if it were in the essay (e.g., the title of a poem or book) would be an exception and should be punctuated appropriately.

   If more than one line is needed for the title, use double-spacing. To separate a subtitle from the main title, place a colon after the main title, followed by a single space.

4. **Spacing:** Double-space before beginning the first line of the text, and double-space between each line of text. Use the same double spacing between paragraphs in your essay.

Crystle Hodgson

Professor Monsen

English 1A

13 April 2001

Controlling Our Reproductive Destiny

Every day more and more people find out that they may never get the chance to have a child of their own, but with new assisted reproductive technologies, new hope is being given to these unlucky couples. "Infertility affects 6.1 million American women and their partners, about 10 percent of the reproductive age population" ("FACT SHEET"). For the percentage of those people whose only hope and dream in life is to have a family of their own, this kind of problem is a major setback in their lives. Up until 1978, there was no hope or cure for these infertile couples to conceive a baby on their own. It was believed that there was no way around this heartbreaking obstacle. But on July 27, 1978 with the birth of Louise Brown, a new medical procedure opened new doors and created a promising outlook for those couples that had problems conceiving children on their own. This new procedure was called in vitro fertilization (IVF), and it was the beginning of a whole new world of advancements in assisted reproductive technologies; however, some ethical concerns have arisen because of these advancements (Tyckson 3-5). A future where there are no limits on in vitro fertilization raises some frightening prospects along with remarkable benefits for the treatment of infertile couples.

In vitro fertilization is a process whereby eggs are retrieved from the ovaries of the woman with a small needle passed through the top of

Margins and Spacing

All margins—top, bottom, and both sides—should be as close to one inch as possible. Your instructor will not expect you to adhere to this rule without exception, however, because some computer programs may not allow you to change the margin settings. Therefore, if they are a little too wide or narrow, you might ignore the margins, but if they are noticeably different, discuss the problem with your instructor. The heading on the first page, subsequent pages of the document, the Notes, and the Works Cited all begin one inch from the top of the page. If you prepare your document using a computer, use a ragged right margin; do not use a justified right margin. Justified right margins are fine in magazine articles, but they make student essays difficult to read.

Double-space all lines in the essay, including long quotations. Never leave additional space between paragraphs as is customary in some business writing. Indent each new paragraph five spaces or one tab.

Documentation

When you borrow ideas or quotes from other sources, you must show your reader where you found that information. The notes you place in the text of your essay that show the origin of those ideas or quotes are called **documentation**.

the vagina and combined with prepared semen in a laboratory dish. Egg retrieval is a non-surgical procedure performed under light sedation. By putting the sperm and the eggs in a laboratory dish, the likelihood of fertilization is positively enhanced. Upon fertilization, one or more embryos are retrieved via a small catheter passed through the cervix into the uterus. This is where the embryo implants and develops. Usually two to four embryos are transferred with each cycle to heighten conception chances. This technique achieves pregnancy in 20-40% of the attempts. Within a few hours after the initial procedure is complete, the woman is free to go home and rest, hoping that it will be successful ("ART: IVF").

The conception rates for in vitro fertilization are very comparable to the conception rates of that of a fertile couple trying to conceive the natural way. According to the latest statistics, the success rate of IVF is 22.8% live births per egg retrieval. This success rate can be compared to the 20% chance that a healthy, reproductively normal couple has of achieving a pregnancy that results in a live birth baby in any given month ("FACT SHEET"). This comparison shows just what a miracle IVF scan be to an infertile couple, who without this procedure would have a 0% chance of conceiving on their own. When most IVF clinics try to explain success rates to the patients, it is rather confusing and a majority of the patients do not comprehend the odds. The odds are measured by clinical pregnancy and live birth rates per egg retrieval. Many different factors affect the rates of success, and every couple is different. The most universal factor in lessening the success rate is the woman's age. Because women are born with all of the eggs their body will ever produce, as they

What Must Be Documented?

Whenever you include information in your essay from another source, you must give credit to that source in a reference in the text of your essay and in the Works Cited. Information that is "general knowledge" may not need to be documented. Note, however, that instructors' opinions differ as to what is "general knowledge." So check with your instructor in case you are in doubt.

DOCUMENT THE FOLLOWING

1. All quoted material
2. All paraphrased sentences
3. Most summarized information

Lead-Ins

Integrate the researched information from your cards smoothly and concisely. Because anyone reading your paper should be able to tell where a quotation, paraphrase, or summary begins, you should use **lead-ins** to signal that you are including borrowed material.

Examples

Researchers found that

According to Richard D. Smith,

Bertrand Russell argues that

In *Civilization and Its Discontents*, Sigmund Freud writes,

Brenner found the opposite to be true:

In an interview with Doris Jones, historian Kenneth Ramirez learned that

A 1984 study conducted by University of Iowa psychologists shows that

Roueche explains further that

Morris, Suber, and Bijou note that

A few critics of the proposal (e.g., Margery Gumper and Wilson Worley) have disputed the figures.

Computers and word processors, writes Alan Toffler, will revolutionize the office (202-09).

Tables

A table is labeled Table with an Arabic number and titled. Both the label and the title are flush to the left margin on separate lines. Use normal capitalization. Double-space throughout the table. Indicate the source of the table and any explanatory notes immediately below the table.

age, their eggs age as well. As a result, the chances of achieving pregnancy are much greater when the woman is still of a young age (see Table below).

Table 1

Conception Rates According to the Woman's Age

Woman's Age	Alta Bates (1997-1998)	National (1998)
Under 35 years	43%	35%
35-37 years	37%	30%
38-40 years	23%	22%
41 and older	12%	11%

Alta Bates: an individual IVF clinic. National: the national conception rate. "Alta Bates In Vitro Fertilization Program." The Alta Bates IVF Program: Results & Pricing. 2000. 20 Mar. 2001 <http://www.abvif.com/program>.

Physicians initially developed IVF in the early 1970s in hopes of treating infertility caused by blocked, severely damaged or absent fallopian tubes ("ART: IVF"). Through IVF, the fallopian tubes are bypassed and the fertilization, which usually occurs in the fallopian tubes, is now performed in the human embryo culture laboratory. In vitro fertilization has also been considered for couples where the woman suffers from endometriosis. From that point forward, new reasons for couples to participate in IVF continually emerged. In the present, IVF is also used to circumvent infertility caused by male factors, such as oligozoospermia, more commonly known as low sperm count. It is also used to help treat couples that have been experiencing unexplained infertility for a long duration, who have failed with other infertility treatments (Kearney 13-14).

Parenthetical References

At the end of any quotation, paraphrase, or summary, use a **parenthetical reference** to indicate the exact source of the material. In the parentheses include any part of the reference that has not been made in the lead-in that introduces the researched material (see "Lead-Ins"). Since readers will learn the complete information needed to locate one of your sources by turning to your Works Cited, you need only to cite the author(s) and page number(s) of the reference or, if no author is given, a shortened title of the article or book and the page number(s). Refer only to the exact page number(s) of the reference.

Examples

As Andrew Sinclair points out, "It was one of the first cases in the American market of scandal being used to push the sales of a book" (102).

[The above example shows a quotation with a lead-in and page number separated.]

Jack London's separation from his first wife, Bess, became a great help to him in an unexpected way. "It was one of the first cases in the American market of scandal being used to push the sales of a book" (Sinclair 102).

[In the example above, the author's name and page number are placed together in the parentheses.]

According to Claudia Caruna, years of photographic experience and expensive equipment are not required to take good photographs (69-71).

[In the above example, several pages are summarized.]

Smith doubts that nuclear missiles could destroy a large incoming meteorite in time to spare the earth from catastrophic damage (Henick 328).

[Note that in the above example the article was written by Henick who reports what Smith thought.]

Sociologist John B. Purnell believes that children who grow up in suburban neighborhoods mature more slowly than children raised in urban and rural environments (78-80, 93-95).

[The above summary came from the pages listed; the *Works Cited* entry would read 78-80+.]

However, it is also possible that the earth will encounter an ice age. The controlling factors are the following: continental drift into warmer or cooler latitudes as suggested by Miller and Thompson (210); solar radiation, the movement of solar systems through interstellar dust as proposed by Fodor (111); or mountain building processes that lift land masses to higher elevations that are cooler, as explained by Strahler (350).

[By using multiple references a great deal of information can be condensed in a short space as shown in the above example.]

Recent studies on the effect of marijuana on driving skill (Brooks 9; Conrad, Elmore, and Stodetz 123; Klonoff 317) have linked overestimation of the passage of time to the deterioration of driving ability.

[Each of the sources above is separated with a semicolon.]

Researchers have found that people between the ages of twenty and fifty are most likely to become victims of rheumatoid arthritis ("How to Cope" 16).

[No author is listed in Consumers Research magazine, so a shortened version of the article title has been used. The complete title for the article is "How to Cope with Arthritis."]

Through these procedures, dedicated partners get the chance to fill the empty void in their lives with the child or children they have always wanted.

Unfortunately, most infertile couples do not have the extra money to pay for the entire process, and the majority of insurance companies do not cover it. How much does the average IVF process cost? It is estimated that it can cost an average of $7,800 a cycle ("FACT SHEET"). The price is different for each couple, depending on their individual success and how many cycles they go through. But what if the couple wants to use the new technology for embryo screening to make sure their baby will not have any genetic diseases? Adding on to the final tab would give the couple a grand total of around $20,000 ("Infertility Information"). "We've been able to perform embryonic testing since March 1992, and more than 100 couples have asked about it. But we haven't had a single patient who can manage the cost" (Cecchin 113). So for a couple just starting their life together, that cannot conceive naturally, it is almost as if they have to make a choice to use their money to invest in their future or spend thousands of dollars on a procedure that is not 100 percent guaranteed to produce a child.

As with most medical procedures, there are risks associated with IVF. During the in vitro cycle, the woman often chooses to take fertility drugs to accompany the process in hopes of getting more positive results. While these drugs, such as clomiphene and Perogonal, increases the couple's odds by making the woman release up to six eggs per month, they also have some serious side effects (Salzer 217). A woman's chance of getting ovarian cancer is heightened to as much as three times, compared to the average woman not taking any kind of fertility drugs (Kearney 267). Twenty percent of the women using these drugs will suffer from ovarian hyper stimulation (OHS). OHS causes the women's ovaries to enlarge and fluid accumulates in the abdomen. This causes the women

Alan Toffler observes that the meaning of punctuality is changing. As the country moves out of the industrial age and into the computer age, strict punctuality is giving way to situational punctuality (<u>Third Wave</u> 270-71).

[If more than one work by an author is listed in the Works Cited, refer to the title, as in the example of the book cited above.]

Electronic Sources

Just as in a traditional parenthetical citation, the citations for electronic sources need a sufficient amount of information for the reader to find it on the Works Cited page. Usually you will include the author's name or the title of the source if there is no author given. Additionally, if the pages are numbered, include the page(s) used; otherwise, if the section or paragraphs are numbered, use those in the citation, using the marker "par." or "sec." preceding the number. Often, for these types of citations, you will just use the author's name or the title in the parenthetical citation. See "FACT SHEET" in the student essay on the previous page.

Quoted Passage Enclosed in Quotation Marks

When you copy the exact words someone has spoken or written, you are quoting, and you must copy the passage precisely as it appears in your source. You must use the same spelling, inside punctuation, and capitalization as in the original, even if it contains errors.

When you are quoting fewer than five lines, connect the quoted portion to its lead-in with quotation marks (" "). Capitalize the first word of the quoted passage if it starts a complete sentence, and continue the double-spacing you are using for the rest of the text. Signal the end of the quoted passage with the proper punctuation—commas and periods are placed inside quotation marks. However, if the quotation marks are followed by a parenthetical reference, the period follows the parentheses, as in the previous examples.

[*Sic*]

Errors within quotations may be designated by the word *sic* in square brackets, i.e., [*sic*]. Any error found in quoted material will be considered yours unless you designate it. Never correct an error in a quotation; instead use [*sic*], placing it immediately after the error.

Brackets

Brackets [   ] are used to insert additional information in quoted material; for example, after an ambiguous pronoun you may want to clarify the pronoun antecedent or ellipsis.

Slash Marks

When quoting poetry or song lyrics in your text, use slash marks (/) to indicate where one line ends and another starts.

to feel constant discomfort and pain in her lower regions. In serious cases, massive loss of fluid in the blood may result, leading to accumulation of fluid around the abdomen, lungs and heart. This extra pressure on these critical organs causes extreme distress, and there is difficulty in breathing and excessive vomiting. When the blood loses fluid, it thickens, leading to kidney damage and blood clots that can be carried over to the heart, lungs and even the brain. When the damage reaches this phase, it is often fatal (264-265).

Another complication when using fertility drugs is the chance of multiple births. Because these drugs stimulate the release of more eggs, there is a 20-30 percent chance of having twins or triplets. "Of the 78% of pregnancies as a result of IVF that result in a live birth, about 50% are singles, 24% are twins, and 5% are triplets or more" ("FACT SHEET"). Multiple-birth rates increased as high as 45.7% for women aged 20 to 29 years and 39.8% for women aged 30 to 34 years if three embryos were transferred (Schieve 1832). Though many couples may consider this to be a blessing, multiple fetuses increase the risk of miscarriage. Every time a woman miscarries, scar tissue is left behind. The more this tissue accumulates, the less likely the woman will be able to carry a child to full term. This condition can lead to even more complications and make it even harder to conceive, making the entire process a complete failure.

To try to alleviate some of these problems, embryonic screening is a step that scientists have added onto the IVF procedure in hopes of being able to give couples a better chance of being able to conceive the child they want. Before scientists developed embryonic screening, IVF specialists primarily used visual inspection to choose which embryo to implant. Then it was discovered that embryos that look healthy when viewed through a microscope can have severe chromosome abnormalities and would have little chance of producing a viable pregnancy. Further screening of the cells of the embryos

Use Good Judgment: Do Not Over-Quote

Train yourself not to quote frequently. Instead, develop the habit of taking the time to skillfully summarize and paraphrase your researched information. When should you quote? Although no definite answer can be given to this question, the general guidelines are (1) select passages for quoting that seem to be especially well written, and (2) consider quoting passages that are very difficult to summarize or paraphrase. Never quote material that is badly written, for example, sentences containing grammatical errors. Remember that almost all material can be reworded if you take the time.

As a general rule, avoid long quotations whenever possible. One or two long quotations in the block format look good and enhance the readability of a document. But readers resent having to slow down to plow through a long quotation every few paragraphs. They especially resent long quotations when they suspect the writers have quoted without good reason or that writers have padded their documents to make them long enough.

can give the scientists more insight as to whether the embryo could lead to a successful pregnancy (Sivitz 276). Because many embryos naturally have chromosome abnormalities, implantation of the embryos without screening them could lead to added exertion, more of an emotional upheaval, and also a bigger bill for the couple.

Couples where one or both of the partners carry some kind of genetic disease have a 1 in 4 chance of having a healthy baby, void of any diseases or disorders the parents may have passed along (Norton 115). But through embryonic screening, the physician can retrieve numerous embryos from the woman and find the healthy one that had not been affected by any disease. Recently, the first baby was born from a genetically selected embryo in order to save a sibling's life. A young girl was born with a fatal case of anemia that was passed to her genetically from both of her parents. The only way for her to be cured was to get a bone marrow transplant from a person whose bone marrow was a perfect match to her own. The parents of the sick girl realized that the only way to save her was to have another child and hope that he or she was a perfect match. But through normal conception there was too high a chance that their next child would be born with anemia also (Fischer 60). When they found out they could pre-select the embryo to make sure that the new baby would not be born with the same disorder, they jumped at the chance to save their daughter.

Nine months later the mother gave birth to a healthy baby boy. By using the blood from the new baby's umbilical cord, which was rich in "blood stem cells," they were able to give their daughter the transplant she needed. By using the new technology of embryonic scanning, doctors were able to save one girl's life, and they were able to bring another healthy child into the world. By screening the DNA of fertilized eggs before implanting them in the mother's

Blocked Quotations

For long quotations, those of more than four lines, a special blocked technique is used. Whereas shorter quotations are integrated by using the normal left and right margins of the paper, a blocked quotation is indented ten spaces or two tabs from the left margin and then carried to the normal one-inch right margin.

When blocking a single paragraph or a portion of a paragraph, do not indent the first line more than ten spaces. If, however, two or more complete paragraphs are quoted, indent the first line of each paragraph three extra spaces (thirteen spaces from the left margin). Double-space the blocked portion like the rest of the essay, and double-space both before and after the quotation. The lead-in for a blocked quotation is normally punctuated with a colon.

Example

Patricia Kingston describes the procedure:

The reader will know automatically that your indented passage is quoted. Therefore, do not enclose the blocked passage in quotation marks. Quotations within the blocked quote (quotations within quotations), however, should be set off at beginning and end with double quotation marks (see page 153).

A parenthetical citation placed at the end of a blocked quotation is placed outside of the sentence end (two spaces to the right of the period).

Note, too, that short passages and lines of verse, fewer than five lines in length, can be blocked to give them special emphasis or to retain their original layout.

Quotation within a Quotation

Use single quotation marks (' ') to indicate where a quotation within a quotation begins and ends. You will recognize the need to use this punctuation when the passage you want to quote is already enclosed in double quotation marks.

If both the quotation within a quotation and the main quotation in your essay end together at the end of the sentence, the period should be placed inside the single quotation mark, and the double quotation marks should be placed outside the single quotation mark.

Example

"Upon later being asked about his observations of flying saucers, pilot Kenneth Arnold explained, 'By no stretch of the imagination did I observe balloons, mock suns, ice crystals, or clouds, and I certainly would not classify my observations in the categories of illusions, hallucinations, apparitions, temperature inversions, or mirages' " (Reese 6).

womb, doctors can now help cure such dire disorders. In the near future they expect to have the knowledge and technology available in order to select embryos with the marking for a higher IQ, and improved physical traits.

Furthermore, embryo screening may be able to aid sick siblings or even let couples with genetic disorders have healthy children, but what are the possible repercussions of this new technology? Are all the people with disorders, young and old, going to be seen as a waste of life? Through IVF, parents who would otherwise have avoided conception, to avoid the stress of fetal diagnosis and abortion, would be conceiving and rejecting multiple offspring. Of course, whatever the process of selection there is no guarantee that the embryos selected will be born healthy, much less that they will not acquire some kind of disability at some time after birth. The more parents are encouraged to reject those of their offspring who fall below a certain standard, the harder they will find it to reverse their attitudes after their children have been born (Watt). Helen Watt makes a good point concerning this idea:

> It is not only the parents and children who will be affected by the practice of pre-implantation selection. Older disabled people will be living in a society that sees their condition as a fate worse than death—or at least the grounds for 'selecting out' before a certain stage of development. With more and more conditions being diagnosed prenatally—conditions now including late-onset disorders such as certain cancers—more and more people will receive the message that life with such conditions is intolerable for the individual and/or for the family. (Watt)

Ellipsis Marks

An ellipsis denotes an omission. You may shorten quotations by using ellipsis marks to indicate where the omissions occur. According to MLA standards, you enclose the ellipsis in brackets, before and after the ellipsis, i.e. [. . .] .

Example

> Ayensu explains, "All the Earth's [. . .] great ecological realms [. . .] have evolved and continue to maintain themselves by the power of the sun" (34).

If you omit the end of a sentence, use three spaced periods before the final period, for a total of four periods.

Example

> Ayensu continues, "Atmospheric water vapor absorbs the infrared rays, and the sun's energy is transformed into long-wave energy [. . .] ."

If the ellipsis falls at the end of the sentence and the ellipsis is accompanied by a parenthetical reference, type an opening bracket, three spaced periods, a closing bracket, the quotation marks, then the citation, and finally the fourth period.

Example

> "Atmospheric water vapor absorbs the infrared rays, and the sun's energy is transformed into long-wave energy [. . .]" (Ayensu 34).

Use a lead-in to take the place of ellipsis marks when beginning a quotation in the middle of a sentence.

Example

> Janet Brown found that "twenty-two of the thirty-five mice had severe birth defects caused by the drug."

Never use ellipsis marks to alter the meaning of a passage, and make sure the ellipsis does not create an awkward or incorrectly punctuated sentence.

Another way to look at embryonic screening is to see it as a way to increase the success rates of in vitro fertilization. When scientists Dagan Wells and D.A. Delhanty, of the University College London Medical School, inspected embryos donated by their IVF patients, they found that only 3 of the 12 embryos had the normal 23 pairs of chromosomes in every cell examined (Sivitz 278). Most embryos start out with a bad deck of chromosomes, but through embryonic screening, IVF can be more successful because the doctors can make sure the embryos that they are implanting will have a good chance of survival. Using the new technique to examine the chromosomes of IVF embryos at the same time they are implanted in the womb, researchers are now reporting abnormalities never seen later in development. Some of these newly observed flaws might explain why in vitro fertilization has been so hit or miss. "It has been a mystery why about two-thirds of early embryos fail to implant and develop. [. . .] These data help solve this riddle by confirming that many embryos already have major chromosome abnormalities as early as the eight-cell stage," stated geneticist Lucille Voullaire (278). Every day more and more findings are leading scientists and geneticists to new ways in order to help infertile couples overcome their infertility and create the family they have always dreamed of having.

Therefore, the ongoing search for new procedures and techniques to help couples overcome what they have been dealt naturally will continue. In vitro fertilization has gone through many stages of development. First, it was used to help people who could not conceive children naturally. It was considered a godsend; however, that was not considered good enough. From that point, IVF progressed more into a new technique that let doctors screen the embryos that had a greater chance of carrying

Subsequent References

Most subsequent references—references to previously cited sources—are simply variations of the lead-in/parenthetical citation combinations used in the initial references. Repeating all of the information in each subsequent reference is not always necessary, however,
depending on the situation. If the context of the paragraph makes it quite clear that you are
still referring to the same author or article, all that may be needed is a parenthetical reference
to the page number(s) of the material. Or, if the subsequent material is in the same paragraph
and comes from the same page or pages of the earlier material, a brief reference such as "Jones
states further that" or "The study results also show that" may suffice.

Raised Note Numerals (Superscript)

To mark the place where readers should turn to the Notes page for supplemental information or additional references, type or key in the appropriate numeral, raising it one-half
space above the line (superscript). Although you will probably have very few note numerals,
perhaps none, make certain that the numerals are consecutive throughout the paper: 1, 2, 3,
and so on. These raised note numerals should not be confused with "footnote numbers,"
which were formerly used in the place of parenthetical references.

Notes

Supplementary information, additional references, and comments about references can
be made on a Notes page. Raised numerals in the text alert readers to turn to the Notes. The
general directions for the Notes page are as follows:

1. Place your last name and page number in the upper-right corner of the page one-half
   inch from the top, as in preceding pages.
2. Center the title, Notes, one inch from the top of the page.
3. Skip two spaces after the title, and double-space the rest of the page.
4. To begin each entry, indent five spaces, type or key in the appropriate note numeral
   one-half space above the entry line, return back to the original line, skip one space,
   and begin the note.
5. Indent only the first line of each entry; do not indent any subsequent lines.
6. Any references cited in the Notes must be listed in the Works Cited.

> **NOTE:** Notes are not mandatory. In fact, they may not be needed. Avoid
> long explanatory notes that should be either integrated in the text of the doc-
> ument or omitted because they are not relevant or relate trivial information.
> Also avoid the temptation to update your document at the last minute by add-
> ing information or references discovered too late to be included in the first
> draft. If you want to include this information, revise the entire document.

a genetic disease or disorder from one of the parents. This way the parents were almost guaranteed a healthy child, which probably would not have been possible had they conceived the child the natural way. When embryo screening came into play, scientists decided to push it even further. Why not let people design their own child? They are still trying to figure out the chromosome signature for different characteristics, such as hair color and IQ. With new technologies such as these emerging, there seems to be no end to the many ways in which humans can choose their own destiny and that of their children as well.

Works Cited

The Works Cited lists all of the materials referred to in your paper and Notes. The Works Cited is arranged alphabetically so readers can easily locate more information about your sources than is given in the lead-ins and parenthetical references in the paper. Each type of entry—book, magazine, journal, newspaper, pamphlet, recording, computer service, interview, and so on—has a correct format to be used.

Read the general guidelines below, study the Works Cited on the facing page, and for additional directions and a more comprehensive list of sample entries, turn to Appendix B.

1. Place your last name and the page number in the upper-right corner as on previous pages in the paper.

2. Center the title, **Works Cited**, one inch from the top of the page. Capitalize as shown, and do not underline.

3. Skip two spaces after the title, and double-space the rest of the page. In other words, double space the lines within each entry, and double-space between entries.

4. The first line of each entry begins at the left margin, but any other lines in the same entry are indented five spaces from the left margin.

5. The author's last name is listed first. When more than one author is given for a source, only the first author's name is listed in reverse order.

6. If a source does not have an author listed, alphabetize it by its title, ignoring *A, An, The, La,* and other articles when used as the first word.

7. The prescribed punctuation must be used consistently. Note, for example, that article titles are enclosed in quotation marks whereas magazine and book titles are underlined. Note that periods are used to separate different parts of the entry and that a period is placed at the end of each entry. Notice that no punctuation is used to separate the title of a magazine and the date of issue.

8. The names of publishers should be shortened (e.g., Prentice-Hall to Prentice, Cambridge University Press to Cambridge UP, and Alfred A. Knopf, Inc. to Knopf).

9. Page numbers are not needed when listing a book unless the book is a collection of poems, plays, stories, or essays. In such cases, list the total pages covered by the selection being referred to (e.g., 30-36). Precede the page numbers with a colon but not p. or pp.

10. Note that weekly and monthly magazine entries do not include volume and issue numbers whereas some professional journals do, in front of the year in parentheses.

11. For articles in periodicals, list the pages covered by the article (e.g., 23-27), but when the article begins on one page and skips to other pages, merely signify and other pages by placing a + immediately after the first page number (e.g., 17+).

12. Instead of repeating an author's name when more than one work by the author is listed, use three hyphens followed by a period (---.) in place of the author's name for the second and any other entries by that author.

13. For a list of commonly used abbreviations, see page 329. For instance, use n.d. for "no date" and N. pag. or n. pag. for "no page numbers."

14. Use capitals for names of most computer and information services (e.g., DIALOG, ERIC, NewsBank ENV).

15. See the web site <www.mla.org> for any questions you still may have, in the online version of the *MLA Handbook for Writers of Research Papers.*

Works Cited

"Alta Bates In Vitro Fertilization Program." <u>The Alta Bates IVF</u>
   <u>Program: Results & Pricing</u>. 2000. 20 Mar. 2001 <<u>http://</u>
   <u>www.abvif.com/program.html</u>>.

"ART: IVF." <u>ART Fertility Treatment:IVF</u>. 2000. ProCare Pharmacy. 31
   Mar. 2001 <<u>http://www.fertilttext.org/p2_doctor/ivf.html</u>>.

Cecchin, Anita. "Genetic Screening of Embryos: An Overview."
   <u>Reproductive Technologies</u>. Ed. Carol Wekesser. San Diego: Green
   Haven Press, 1996. 111-114.

"FACT SHEET: In Vitro Fertilization (IVF)." <u>ASRM: FACT SHEET: In Vitro</u>
   <u>Fertilization (IVF)</u>. American Society of Reproductive Medicine.
   20 Mar. 2001 <<u>http://www.asrm.org/patients/factsheet/</u>
   <u>invitro.html</u>>.

Fischer, Joannie. "A Brotherly Donation." <u>U.S. News & World Report</u>.
   16 Oct. 2000: 60.

"Infertility Information: Treatments." <u>Infertility Treatments--ARC</u>.
   2002. Advanced Reproduction Care Inc. 31 Mar. 2001 <http://
   www.arcfertility.cvom/treatments.html>.

Kearney, Brian. <u>High-Tech Conception</u>. New York: Bantam Book: 1992.

Norton, Vicki. "Allowing Parents to Genetically Screen Embryos Is
   Unethical." <u>Reproductive Technologies</u>. Ed. Carol Wekesser. San
   Diego: Green Haven Press, 1996. 115-120.

Salzer, Linda. <u>Infertility: How Couples Can Cope</u>. Boston: G.K. Hall
   & Co., 1986.

Schieve, Laura. "Live Birth Rates and Multiple-Birth Risk Using IVF."
   <u>JAMA</u>. Vol. 282. Nov. 1999: 1832-1838.

Sivitz, L. "It's a Boy! It's a Girl! It's a Mosiac Embryo." <u>Science News</u>. Vol.

    158. 28 Oct. 2000: 276.

Tyckson, David. <u>Test Tube Babies</u>. Arizona: The Onyx Press. 1986.

Watt, Helen. "Pre-Implantation Diagnosis." 6 Mar. 2001 <<u>http://</u>

    <u>www.linacre.org/preimp.html</u>>.

EXERCISE 3.10

After reviewing your notes and thinking about what you want to say in your essay, formulate a thesis sentence.

_____

_____

_____

_____

Make a list of the topic sentences you imagine you will need in your essay. Put them in the same order they will appear in the essay, and number them 1, 2, 3, and so on. Keep in mind that you may find it necessary to revise your outline as you write the first draft of your essay.

_____

_____

_____

_____

_____

_____

_____

_____

_____

_____

_____

_____

_____

_____

_____

_____

_____

_____

_____

_____

_____

_____

_____

_____

_____

_____

_____

Have your thesis and outline approved. Place the approved thesis and outline in your Project Folder.

First Draft

By now you have probably developed an approach to writing preliminary drafts of your essays, either completing an entire draft and then returning to revise and correct it or perfecting it as you proceed from paragraph to paragraph.

Two suggestions will help you write the first and any subsequent preliminary drafts of a library research essay:

1. Work from an outline that has evolved in conjunction with your research notes. Above all, your thesis should be composed along with the outline before you begin writing the first draft of the essay.

2. Integrate your research material as you write the first draft. Be very careful to use appropriate lead-ins (see page 144) and to include parenthetical references wherever needed (see pages 146, 148). Never plan to insert the parenthetical citations and lead-ins later! Always insert your documentation as you proceed through the first draft. Furthermore, you must be aware of whether you are using summaries, paraphrases, or quotations; otherwise, your essay may end up with quoted portions but no quotation marks (see pages 128 and 148).

Following the above advice may save you hours of revision later if your documentation turns out to be faulty or if your citations are mixed up. Always assume that the documentation in your essay will be checked by the instructor for accuracy and correct format. More important, if you are going to be proud of what you write, you want your documentation to be meticulously correct.

Certainly you want to avoid being guilty of having conducted "sloppy research." Before you begin writing the first draft, arrange your notes in piles that correspond with the categories in your outline. Evaluate your notes, selecting those that seem best for inclusion and putting the others aside. Make some preliminary decisions as to which information will be included as quotations and which will be paraphrased or summarized. See if there are any gaps in your research that will require additional trips to the library for more information.

EXERCISE 3.11

Write the first draft of your essay. Work from your notes, referring frequently to your thesis and outline. Integrate your documentation as you work.

This is not to be a rough draft! When your first draft is completed, you should have an essay that is as close as you can make it to the final version you will submit for grading. Use the same heading, title, and format that you will use for the final copy. Include all documentation, Notes, and Works Cited, observing all format conventions. Edit and proofread your first draft until it represents the best work you can possibly accomplish within the time limits of the assignment. Your instructor will be happy to assist you during the drafting process. (See the Research Essay Checklist, below, and do not forget the explanations and directions accompanying the sample research paper; also, refer to Appendix B: Documentation and Appendix C: A Guide to Stylistic Revision whenever necessary.) Place your first draft in your Project Folder.

Research Essay Checklist

1. Have all of the preliminary steps been approved before you begin writing the first draft?

2. Does the introductory paragraph open with an interesting statement and proceed smoothly to the thesis?

3. Does each body paragraph begin with a topic sentence? Is each topic sentence thoroughly supported by a network of primary and secondary support sentences? At least five sentences in each body paragraph? Smooth transitions connecting ideas, sentences, and other paragraphs?

4. Is research material smoothly integrated by using a combination of summary, paraphrase, and quotation? Quotations not used excessively? Quotation marks at the beginning and end of each quotation or long quotations blocked properly? Quotations double-checked for accuracy? Lead-ins and parenthetical references skillfully combined?

5. Does the concluding paragraph begin with a summary statement and end with an appropriate generalization?

6. Check all sentences for clarity, structure, punctuation, grammar, capitalization, and spelling.

7. Title page and outline pages in correct format (if required)? Heading, title, headers and page numbers completed correctly?

8. Cross-check each reference in the essay and Notes with the corresponding Works Cited entry. Notes included only when information is really worth adding? Note numerals in essay are raised one-half space? Entire Works Cited checked for alphabetical order, format, punctuation, and spelling?

EXERCISE 3.12

After your first draft has been completed, begin working immediately on the final document. If necessary, confer with your instructor about the improvements and corrections that have been recommended. When you have completed your final document, check it over, using the Research Essay Checklist, just as you did after completing the first draft. Place your final draft in your Project Folder.

The Project Folder

Most instructors want you to fasten the final document together with a paperclip or a single staple at a 45-degree angle in the upper-left hand corner. The outline should be on the top, followed by the final draft of the document (with the Works Cited as the final page of the document). Also included in your Project Folder is the Working Bibliography, the Topic Proposal, the Research Guide (with the research questions, tentative thesis statement and working outline) all notes taken, all preliminary drafts of your essay with the peer review sheets and all photocopies of the information you have used.

EXERCISE 3.13

If assigned by your instructor, write a revision of your final draft, being sure to ask when the revised essay is due.

4

The Critical Review Essay

Objectives

When you have completed this chapter, you will have:

1. read and evaluated a professional movie review.

2. evaluated a student critical review.

3. viewed a film or television program, read a story or poem, or attended an event for a critical review.

4. identified, classified, described and evaluated the topic for critical review.

5. developed a thesis and list of main points for a critical review.

6. written a 750–1000 word critical review.

7. compiled a Project Folder.

The Critical Review Essay 4

A **critical review essay** introduces and assesses the worth of a subject that is unfamiliar to the reader. It may be about a book, a movie, an event, or a social phenomenon. You might, for example, familiarize your readers with the setting, plot, characters, and theme (thesis) of a novel and let them know whether or not, in your opinion, the book is worth reading. Your basic goal should be to introduce readers to something—not to analyze every detail and every shade of meaning. In reviewing a movie, for instance, you cannot reveal how the story ends because you will be destroying the potential viewers' chance to experience that ending. But you can explain where the story takes place, who the main characters are, their situation, some of the challenges they face as they attempt to improve their situation or solve a problem, and the message you think the writer or director is attempting to communicate. You can venture your opinion as to whether or not the movie is successful and the rationale for your conclusions. The idea is to review your subject in order to help your readers decide whether or not they want to read the book, see the movie, investigate the social phenomenon—or to give readers enough guidance so they will have some perspective if they do explore further.

For you as the writer, reviews offer additional benefits that can enhance your critical perspectives. Obviously, writing reviews can inspire you to learn about a subject that is new to you as well as to your readers. You are afforded the opportunity to consider points of view different from your own, thereby expanding your intellectual horizons. The review may provide you the opportunity to trace the evolution of an artist or author through changes in style, theme, or developmental phase. Further, writing reviews offers you an occasion for integrating and using your knowledge from other sources, such as other classes or outside interests. All in all, writing reviews can be a refreshing change of pace from the other types of essays that you are learning to write in *Survival*.

With all the opportunities inherent in writing reviews, you do need to be careful not to confuse critical review with literary analysis. When you write a literary analysis essay in Chapter Five, your main task will be to provide your readers with insights into a work of literature–a short story, novel, play, or poem. Literary analysis is the subject of Chapter Five. While the literary analysis is usually a more difficult undertaking than the critical review, both types of essays are frequently assigned in school and college courses. By understanding the essential differences between the critical review and the literary analysis, you will be prepared to write either type.

LESSON ONE—*Planning to Write a Critical Review*

Most critical reviews discuss books, movies, plays, television programs, concerts, recordings, or art exhibits. When the critical essay is written as a review, the writer is usually referred to as a critic. You must be careful, however, that you do not begin to share the popular misconception of the critic as primarily preoccupied with only the negative. The critic's obligation is to be as free as possible from bias in his or her writing, for the task is to "*re*"- *view*, to look again, to evaluate.

A critical review must accomplish the following tasks: first, report what the work (book, movie, play, etc.) does; second, judge how well it does it; third, cite evidence from the work that supports or illustrates your conclusions; finally, be fair.

A critical review that fails to accomplish all of these four objectives is incomplete. If your review fails to "report what the work does," for example, readers who are unfamiliar with the subject will not be able to follow you to your conclusions. If the review reports only what a work does and not "how well it does it," then the essay is merely a summary, not a critical review at all. Most important, if your essay contains no supporting evidence from the work itself, readers will be unable to appreciate your conclusions. Finally, you can never assume that your unsupported opinion will be accepted; in fact, unsupported opinion is as unfair to your subject as is allowing your prejudice to influence your judgments.

Since a critical review is typically a **description** and **evaluation** of something that is new to your readers, it is especially appropriate for many school subjects and courses in which your instructor assigns you to assess a fresh topic; you can write about the topic, expressing the opinions that you formed from firsthand observation; therefore, the critical review is often in first person. Furthermore, the critical review essay is not especially difficult to write because the essential points contained in reviews have become fairly standardized.

The Steps For Writing A Critical Review

1. Read or view the work to be reviewed.
2. Consider the work.
   a. Identify it.
   b. Classify it.
   c. Describe what it does.
3. Evaluate the work's worth.
   a. Is it a success?
   b. Is it a failure?
   c. Is it somewhere in between?
4. Develop a thesis or a point that you wish to illuminate.
5. Cite the evidence to support your judgment.
6. Make an outline.
7. Write the review.

For practice in critical reading, study the following professional written review. Use a dictionary whenever necessary. As you read the review, study the questions on the left-hand side. These are types of comments and questions that you should be asking yourself. Write short answers to the questions. When you write your own critical review essay, you will be answering similar questions in your essay. The following is a professional review of the movie *The Silence of the Lambs*, by Sheila Benson, published in *The Los Angeles Times* on February 13, 1991:

1. Who is the director of the film? What novel does this film come from? What type of film is this?

1. The Jonathan Demme of *Something Wild* or *Melvin and Howard* or *Stop Making Sense* might not be the first director one would think of for suspense or bloody terror; his touch has always seemed lighter, his interests more quirky and off the mainstream. So much for pigeonholing. Demme's vision of *The Silence of the Lambs*, Thomas Harris' truly terrifying novel, is stunning. It is also unusual—as the FBI races to save a kidnapped young woman from a serial killer, Demme concentrates on the hypnotic duel between his two strong central characters, an FBI trainee and a brilliant sociopath, rather than on easy effects calculated to make an audience jump.

2. Who plays the male lead? What is his character's name?

2. They may jump anyway, since *The Silence of the Lambs* (Thursday at selected theaters) is marked by the second appearance of Dr. Hannibal Lector—Hannibal the Cannibal—and Anthony Hopkins' insinuating performance puts him right up there with the screen's great bogymen.

3. What other films/novels is this movie associated with? Which actress plays the female lead?

3. We have seen Dr. Lector's pure evil before: the imprisoned insane psychiatrist/murderer was played mesmerizingly by Brian Cox in *Manhunter*, Michael Mann's adaptation of Harris' earlier novel *Red Dragon*. Later, perhaps realizing the pull of the monster he created, Harris moved Lector to the forefront of *Lambs*, and here in Ted Tally's screenplay he very nearly owns the film. Only nearly—he would have to be superhuman to wrest this film away from Jodie Foster, and Lecter is only super-deviant.

4. What is the female character's name? Who does she work for? What is one of the subplots of the film?

4. Foster's Clarice Starling is a promising FBI trainee in her last year, brought in by Jack Crawford (Scott Glenn), chief of the Bureau's Behavioral Science Section, to do a psychological profile of Lecter. Although Starling isn't let in on the bureau's full agenda, Crawford's hope is that Lecter can be lured into shedding light on one of his own kind, a seemingly random serial killer nicknamed Buffalo Bill who flays the bodies of his women victims for his own, unfathomable purposes.

5. What other work is this film compared to?

5. The build-up to Starling's first meeting with Lecter is as dramatic as the unmasking of the Phantom of the Opera. Warned not to tell him anything personal—"You don't want Lecter inside your head"—the list of things Starling may not do, touch or say is capped by a photograph of Lecter's last victim, a nurse within the asylum whose grisly fate is graphically told and shown to Starling.

6. What is the film rated? Why does it have this rating?

6. Mercifully, Demme doesn't share this sight with us, although there will be a gruesomely clinical tour of one of Buffalo Bill's victims in a later scene. This film is MPAA-rated R for explicit shots of the murder victims, for terror, for scenes of gore and violence and for language.

7. How well does Jodie Foster act in this film?

7. The film swings between Starling and Lecter as though it were moving between sunlight and the chill of fluorescence. Even within the straitjacket of FBI-approved behavior, Foster radiates intelligence, sturdiness, unspoken empathy with the poor dead victims and the most profound human concern.

8. How well does Anthony Hopkins act in this film?

8. Hopkins, sometimes literally straitjacketed, excludes cunning, a laser-keen intellect, patent contempt for most of the world, concentration that could seemingly bend spoons and terrifying physical power. Lecter's persuasiveness becomes particularly threatening when he agrees to trade insights on Buffalo Bill for details of Starling's past, and from these he forges an unsettling bond with her.

9. Who designed the sets? Who is the cinematographer?

9. Our fears about Lecter are heightened by Kristie Zea's production design for his isolation cell: its bars are far apart, separated by super-thick glass, but the visual effect deliberately suggests that the glass isn't there at all, that Lecter could simply reach through the bars to Starling . . . or to us. Demme punches up this immediately as Hopkins and Foster work directly into cinematographer Tak Fujimoto's camera in some of these early, intense scenes, a device that propels Lecter's cajoling, deprecating tirades directly at us.

10. What is the main plot of the film?

10. After Buffalo Bill kidnaps a U. S. senator's feisty, resourceful daughter (Brooke Smith), Crawford pulls Starling into the hunt as his assistant, liking her insights and her deductions.

11. What is the reviewer's criticism of the director?

11. Although Demme's touch with the interplay between Crawford and Starling is deft—Crawford's terseness belying his concern for her—when Starling takes off on her own to follow a Lecter clue to a long-abandoned storage garage, Demme muffs one of the book's prime scenes of terror. He seems unwilling to give this scene its full measure of anxiety, letting it unroll without charge or crescendo. More to his liking are the film's deadpan vignettes of a woman in a male-dominated world, whether it is an FBI Academy elevator or a police examination room in the deep south.

12. Who is the screenwriter?

12. Demme and screenwriter Tally have also done lovely things with the brief flashbacks illuminating Starling's childhood as the adoring daughter of a small town marshall. Foster's subtle, intelligent performance takes it from there, filling in the whole woman; Clarice, coloring under Lecter's cruel mimicry of her almost-buried "rube" accent, flinching at his brutally accurate x-ray of her ambition and her attempt to better herself through the academy.

12.-14. Whose acting is effective? Whose acting isn't so effective?

13. Hopkins' performance may be the film's bravura showpiece, but Foster's goes the whole distance, steadfast, controlled, heartbreakingly insightful, a fine addition to her gallery of characterizations.

14. Who are the supporting actors/actresses and what characters do they play?

14. Although Crawford's search for Buffalo Bill and the Starling/Lecter duel dominate the action, the film is dotted with real, peripheral characters who give it a sense of authenticity: Kasi Lemmons as Starling's supportive roommate Ardilia; Paul Lazar as the sweetly friendly Smithsonian entomologist; Anthony Heald as Lecter's prideful jailer, the smarmy Dr. Chilton, and Ted Levine's terrifying Buffalo Bill, a.k.a. Jame Gumb.

15. Overall, is this a positive of or a negative review?

EXERCISE 4.1

Now that you have read the professional critical review of *The Silence of the Lambs* and answered the questions, you need to practice these skills yourself. Read the following student written critical review. Once you've read through the essay once, go back over each paragraph and indicate what questions were answered in each of the paragraphs. Have your answers checked by your instructor or a tutor.

Stephanie Lensky

Professor Eisenhower

English 1A

1 December 2002

Are the Lambs Finally Silent?

With the release of the film <u>Red Dragon</u> (2002), a remake of the film <u>Manhunter</u> and the first of the Hannibal Lecter trilogy, it's time to revisit the second movie of this series: <u>The Silence of the Lambs</u> (1991). <u>The Silence of the Lambs</u> is one of the best thriller, suspense drama videos, starring Jodie Foster as Clarice Starling and Anthony Hopkins as Doctor Lecter. This film horrifically portrays how evil man can be. This film is made in great detail, and every time it is seen, the viewer picks up another detail not seen before. This quality led the film to win three Academy Awards, including best picture, best male actor, and best female actress. <u>The Silence of the Lambs</u>, a movie that shows how inhuman people can be, has an unusual intricate plot, is suspenseful, well acted, and realistic.

The <u>Silence of the Lambs</u> is an outstanding film because of its unusually complicated plot. Unlike most other films, it has three plots that are so interwoven that they can not survive on their own and combine at the end to create a successful film. At first, the audience thinks that the main plot is going to be the FBI trying to catch the serial killer, Buffalo Bill; in fact, the other main plots to the movie include the escape of Doctor Lecter and Doctor Lecter helping Clarice "silence her lambs." The movie starts by showing Clarice Starling, an FBI student who is picked to investigate the Buffalo Bill murders, conversing with Doctor Lecter, a serial killer. Through many conversations and good police work, Clarice gets closer and closer to the Buffalo Bill killer. The director leaves the movie open so that it may go in several different directions, such as what is going to happen to Doctor Lecter? The question is, will Clarice's lambs stop screaming?

Furthermore, <u>The Silence of the Lambs</u> keeps the audience on the edge of their seats, hearts pounding, stomachs caught in their throats. The director uses many techniques to make this movie so suspenseful. One technique used is the eerie music. Whenever a scary scene is approaching, eerie music in the background makes the viewer anticipate the scary scene that is about to happen. Another technique the director uses is to set up scenes to try to trick the viewer. In one specific scene the audience sees an FBI agent ringing a doorbell. The doorbell seems to be ringing in the serial murderer's house to make the audience believe the FBI is going to catch him, but whose doorbell are they ringing? In addition, to these techniques the director also uses a scary atmosphere to help enhance the suspense. He sets up a showdown between Clarice Starling and the serial killer, Buffalo Bill. He places the two in a pitch black room, and only Buffalo Bill can see because he is wearing night goggles. As Buffalo Bill is staring and reaching for her, she cannot see him, and all she can do is feel her way around the room with her gun drawn, as she shakes tremendously. These few examples leave the audience gasping and nerve wracked.

In addition, the great acting by Anthony Hopkins leads to the development of Clarice Starling's character. The director does an excellent job casting Anthony Hopkins as the lead actor, Doctor Lecter. The antics that he uses to make the audience believe that he is a psychotic serial killer are incredibly believable. The way that he stares at Clarice without blinking when she looks at him gives viewers the creeps. Also, the way he licks his lips when talking to people makes the audience afraid of him. Hopkins' acting helps develop Clarice's character. The director uses flashbacks in order to give the audience the reason for her becoming an FBI agent, but Hopkins' ability to open up her character gives the audience the real meaning of her life. The conversations that Lecter has with Clarice are chilling. When she walks into the room, he knows what lotion or perfume she is wearing. Through conversations they have towards the end of the movie, the audience finds out that Clarice has been raised on a sheep ranch, and can constantly hear the agonizing screams of the lambs in her dreams as they are slaughtered; her entire life has been a flight from these screams, which is why she wants to "silence the lambs" and why she became an FBI agent. Hopkins' acting enables her character to handle what she needs to silence the lambs. Without the great acting that Hopkins provides, Clarice's character would not have been the strong, heroic woman that she turns out to be.

Lastly, this movie portrays a realistic view of how demented people really can be. Some viewers doubt whether or not people really are this insane. Yes, this behavior is unusual, but not unheard of. Unfortunately, this behavior is becoming even more frequent in society today. Remember the Jeffrey Dalmers and the Ted Bundys of the world; they each killed multiple victims in their day and would kill again if back on the streets. Their crimes show that even though this behavior by the serial killers is odd, it is not that unusual. Lecter is a psychologist who killed some of his patients and ate people's livers with fava beans and Chianti. He bites off a police officer's face and kills several other people to free himself. While killing his victims, he never feels remorse; his blood pressure never rises above 80. Lecter has no remorse after killing or after eating people's body parts for dinner. This behavior does not even faze him; it is just part of his daily routine; just as some people tie their shoes, he kills. These are the same characteristics that several real serial killers possess.

This film is very good and quite unusual. The Silence of the Lambs is a very realistic and believable film showing how sick people can really be. This film has many qualities that makes it excellent and has the audience on the edge of their seats, waiting for the outcome. This movie keeps the audience's full attention and is well worth seeing. If you're ready to ride an emotional rollercoaster, then go to your nearest video store and rent it.

You should have a better idea what you will need to include in your own critical review, and you should be thinking about your own topic. You might want to encourage someone to try a new restaurant or see a film that's just come out or to experience an event. It is also possible for you to encourage your reader to revisit a film or restaurant, as the reviewer suggested in the student critical review you have just read. The following exercises should help you to discover an exciting topic for your critical review essay and help you to discover what information needs to be included in your writing.

EXERCISE 4.2

Select a movie review from a newspaper or magazine. Photocopy the critical review. Write in the margins or type on a separate sheet of paper the questions that the reviewer answered. At the end of the review, indicate any questions that you would still like to have answered. Have your exercise checked by your instructor or a tutor. Once your work is checked, include it in your Project Folder.

EXERCISE 4.3

Select a restaurant review from a newspaper or magazine. Photocopy the critical review. Write in the margins or type on a separate sheet of paper the questions that the reviewer answered. At the end of the review, indicate any questions that you would still like to have answered. Have your exercise checked by your instructor or a tutor. Once your work is checked, include it in your Project Folder.

EXERCISE 4.4

Select a TV show, play or concert review from a newspaper or magazine. Photocopy the critical review. Write in the margins or type on a separate sheet of paper the questions that the reviewer answered. At the end of the review, indicate any questions that you would still like to have answered. Have your exercise checked by your instructor or a tutor. Once your work is checked, include it in your Project Folder.

LESSON TWO—Planning the First Draft

Before writing a critical review essay, you must thoroughly read or closely view your chosen and approved work. Then you must **identify** the subject so that your readers may, after reading your essay, find it and experience it themselves (unless, of course, it is a one-time occurrence, such as a concert). This means that for a book, a short story, or a poem, you will need to cite the title, the author, the publisher, and the date of publication. For movies and plays, you need to cite the title, the author, the producer and director, leading members of the cast, and the theater where it is playing. For concerts and other events, you will need to cite the time and place, the performers, and the sponsoring organization. The information needed for identification is usually stated in a sentence or two near the beginning of the essay, although publications that regularly print reviews frequently set aside a place at the beginning for this information where it is presented in a standardized format. You should integrate your identification for any review you write; the standardized heading is optional.

While the **classification** of your subject can frequently be written in a phrase or two, it is an important part of any critical review; by classifying a movie, for example, as a musical, a comedy, a western, a drama, science fiction, a documentary, or some combination of classifications, you will give readers an immediate understanding of what your subject is; furthermore, the classification will give them a reference for comparison by suggesting a category into which it might best fit. Other facts for classification, while seemingly incidental, may help readers to form a frame of reference by relating your subject to other, similar subjects. You should, then, work into your text such classifying details as the "writer's second novel," "the director's first western," "the poet's third collection of poems," "Leanne Rimes' tenth appearance of her current tour," or "first in a new series of Public Television Specials."

The longest part of a critical review will probably be your **description**, which contains specific details about the subject. These details may be presented either in a single block of description or throughout the essay as evidence for your observations. All that is required of you in gathering this descriptive material is **attentive observation** while reading the book, story, or poem; while viewing the movie or play; or while hearing and viewing the concert or other event. A worthwhile essay can result from your careful attention to details. While a description summarizes for readers the content, the writer of a critical review must be careful not to spoil the reader's experience of the story by revealing the outcome. Professional reviewers are usually quite good at summarizing the story without giving too much away. Frequently, they summarize only sample incidents that are representative of what the reviewer considers either successful or unsuccessful. You must always be careful, however, not to write description that is without purpose; all of your description must support your thesis. A real temptation, especially with books and movies, is to write only a plot summary; however, your fundamental task in the critical review is to describe for the purpose of judgment.

Evaluation and Evidence

The most important part of your critical review is the **evaluation:** your opinion. Your evaluation may not be the longest portion of your essay, and it may vary from a rather informal discussion of your reaction to the subject to a structured argumentative judgment based upon considerable reflection and experience. Nonetheless, the evaluation is the most important portion of your essay, the part your reader will be most interested in reading. To support your opinion, you must **give your reasons** and then **cite evidence** that makes your evaluation persuasive and believable. Avoid the temptation to hide your opinion behind general, sweeping pronouncements and such unsupported phrases as "It is the best . . . ," "It is the worst . . .," or "This reviewer likes it." An easy way to avoid this problem is to cite particular aspects of your subject that you feel are especially successful or especially weak.

Using Comparisons

One technique that is popular with reviewers is to compare or contrast a more familiar subject with one that is unfamiliar to your intended readers. This technique is particularly worthwhile in comparing (or contrasting) subjects that are similar. Comparison and contrast offer the opportunity for considerable insight. For example, you might choose to compare (or contrast) books by the same writer, poems with similar form, or movies with similar themes. Some specific examples of subjects that might be reviewed in this fashion are as follows:

1. A critical review of a film—compare or contrast the special effects in *The Matrix* (1999) and *The Matrix: Reloaded* (2003).

2. A critical review of an emerging celebrity—compare or contrast the fighting techniques of Vin Diesel (XXX) with Bruce Willis (*Die Hard*).

3. A critical review of computer games—compare or contrast X-Box (Microsoft) and Play-station 2 (Sony).

4. A critical review of an event—compare or contrast the new art show (boat show, auto show, concert, street festival) opening with a previous similar event.

As you can see from these suggestions, this technique can offer the writer opportunities to *identify, classify,* and *describe* by using *comparison* or *contrast.* Once these steps are complete, the evaluation follows naturally. Does it stand up well against the comparison? Is the work better than the more familiar work or not? Is it worth the expense and time required to experience it? Whether you like or dislike something you are reviewing, you need a good strong thesis that indicates your position; do not leave your readers wondering about your position.

EXERCISE 4.5

Select a topic suitable for a critical review essay and take it through the review steps.

Your choice (be specific):

_____

_____

_____

_____

Have your choice approved.

I. Consider the work.
   A. Identify it.

_____

_____

_____

_____

_____

   B. Classify it.

_____

_____

_____

_____

_____

C. Describe it.

_____

_____

_____

_____

_____

_____

_____

II. Evaluate the work. Is it a success, failure, or somewhere in between? Why?

_____

_____

_____

_____

_____

_____

Have your work checked. Be sure to include it in your Project Folder.

Your Thesis and Outline

Carefully read the following thesis-topic sentence outline for an assigned review. (The student chose a special event, the televised production of an opera).

Devoured by Myths

Thesis: Viewing and hearing the work so well presented on television rather than in a theater better allows the audience to evaluate it as a drama, a tragedy comparable to the Greek original by Sophocles.

1. As was evident in the production, *Elektra* is brief as an opera can be in its one act, yet is bristling with the musical challenges it poses for its large cast, chorus, and orchestra.

2. The Strauss-Hofmannsthal collaboration is strikingly divergent from Sophocles' *Electra* in some ways, and indicates just how different two versions of the same myth can be.

3. In an ordinary reshaping of ancient tragedy, the result of so much omission would impair the opera's truthfulness and force, but the fact is that both *Electra* (Sophocles) and *Elektra* (Hofmannsthal) convey the desired message: revenge is ultimately futile, however noble the cause, however satisfying for the moment.

4. As portrayed by Wagnerian soprano Hildegard Behrens, Strauss's *Elektra* invoked pity and terror, and the camera equally accentuated her peculiar strengths, most of them theatrical.

5. Most of the time, Behrens's voice was equal to the heavy demands placed upon it.

6. From the announcement of Orestes' death through the end of the opera, Strauss's music is perfectly suited to the arousal and subsequent cleansing of one's murderous instincts.

7. The quality of the performance leaves one free to concentrate on the mythic meaning deep within *Elektra*.

EXERCISE 4.6

Take the topic you chose in 4.5 and create the thesis, or main idea, that you wish to pursue for your essay.

_____

_____

_____

_____

_____

EXERCISE 4.7

Cite the main points of evidence that demonstrate the truth of your thesis.

1. _____

_____

_____

_____

_____

2. _____

_____

_____

_____

3. _____

_____

_____

_____

EXERCISE 4.8

Using the main points of evidence that you identified in Exercise 4.7, compose a topic sentence for each.

1. _____

_____

_____

_____

_____

2. _____

_____

_____

_____

_____

3. _____

_____

_____

_____

_____

Have Exercises 4.7 and 4.8 checked before you proceed further. Be sure to include them in your Project Folder.

LESSON THREE—*Writing the Critical Review Essay*

One of the conventions of usage in writing critical review essays that some students find troubling at first is the use of the **present tense**. Most of the essays that you have written in the past (and most of the essays that you have written or will write for this book) are written in past tense. That is not the case, however, for most of the critical reviews (whether they are reviews for this chapter or literary analysis in Chapter Five). This convention rests upon the fact that a story, whether read or viewed, is considered a living entity that may be read or seen time and again. While it is true that you personally may have read something in the past, you may still read it again, and others may read it in the future. In any case, it is still happening, the story is still unfolding, and the plot is still developing, offering suspense and enjoyment at each reading. For example, Captain Ahab is in mortal conflict with the great white whale in *Moby Dick*, and the children are desperately fleeing the rampaging Velociraptors in *Jurassic Park* in the presence of whoever is reading or viewing these works. To see how this works, examine the sample reviews in this chapter.

> AVOID—   Past Tense: In the opening scene of the movie, an accident **claimed** the life of one of the gamekeepers.
>
> CORRECT—Present Tense: In the opening scene of the movie, an accident **claims** the life of one of the gamekeepers.

You have now arrived at the point where you must make some decisions about how to organize your review. Remember, you need to integrate the four essentials—**identification, classification, description**, and **evaluation**—into a review that will have an introduction, a body, and a conclusion. How, for example, can you write the introduction without including some description in addition to the identification and classification? Will you include your description as a block in the body and your evaluation in another block in the conclusion, or will you integrate your evaluation and description? Ideally, these decisions should be made as you organize your review and before you begin your first draft. There is not a single right way to integrate each of a review's elements; a successful essay should result as long as each of the elements is included.

EXERCISE 4.9

Using the material you have assembled in the preceding exercises, write a first draft of your 750-1,000 word critical review. Be sure to show it to your instructor or a tutor. Include it in your Project Folder.

EXERCISE 4.10

After receiving feedback on your first draft, prepare the final copy of your critical review essay. Organize your Project Folder, making sure that your final draft document is on top.

5

The Literary Analysis Essay

Objectives

When you have completed this chapter, you will have

1. selected, had approved, and read a literary work approved by your instructor.

2. practiced critically reading a short story.

3. compared two literary analysis essays.

4. selected and narrowed a topic for a literary analysis essay.

5. developed a thesis sentence.

6. conducted research if necessary.

7. developed an outline.

8. written a 1,000–1,500 word literary analysis essay.

9. compiled a Project Folder.

The Literary Analysis Essay 5

In this chapter you will write a **literary analysis essay**, an essay that explains and interprets a work of literature. A typical assignment might ask you to write 1,000–1,500 words analyzing a short story, novel, play, poem, or film.

Writing a literary analysis essay requires a kind of thinking that most of us do not normally employ when reading a book or watching a film for entertainment. Our brains normally operate on a superficial level as we try to follow the plot of a novel or enjoy the special effects in an action film. To write a literary analysis essay, we have to think about the work analytically.

Analyzing a work of literature involves separating it into its parts and then subjecting them to detailed examination. For example, you might write about one or more of the literary elements of a short story: plot, characters, theme, setting, point of view, tone, style, imagery, and symbols. In literary analysis, the structural elements, meaning, and significance of a work of art are explained to create an understanding of the work as a whole, often by concentrating on a particular aspect of that work. For instance, in her introduction to her literary analysis essay about the short story "The Bride Comes to Yellow Sky," Sandra Ewers indicates in her thesis that she will be analyzing the characters and symbols:

> Steven Crane's short story "The Bride Comes to Yellow Sky" is an illustrative tale of history's inevitable course. On the surface, Crane relates the journey of Marshal Potter and his bride to the small Texas town of Yellow Sky. In a larger sense, however, Crane contrasts a story of the passage of the old West with its simple values and way of life to the arrival of the more complex life and ideas of the civilization from the East, a story of greater historical significance. The characters are not extensively developed; instead, they are simply presented, even understated. Crane's intent is not to draw vivid characterizations but to present objects and characters as symbols with larger meanings.

LESSON ONE—*What Is a Literary Analysis Essay?*

To begin with, a literary analysis essay, like many essays, is expository; that is, it explains. More than anything, it interprets the work for your readers. It creates an understanding of the literary work that your readers probably would not have before reading your essay. In a sense, you are teaching your readers something about the literary work, making them think about it on a deeper analytical level, and by doing so creating a greater appreciation of it.

Second, a literary analysis is focused, or limited, in its topic. For example, rather than writing a comprehensive analysis of the nearly 500 pages in Herman Melville's novel *Moby Dick*, which could not be done in a five to six-page essay, you might focus on one of the following topics:

1. The whaling industry in the mid-19th century as a setting for *Moby Dick*
2. Melville's use of Biblical allusions to illuminate his theme
3. Melville's techniques for increasing suspense
4. Melville's use of symbols for good and evil to illustrate his theme
5. The progression of Captain Ahab's abnormal behavior

Any one of these topics could be the subject of a literary analysis of *Moby Dick*, but you could not write an essay on anything without first focusing on a small aspect, unless you were planning an essay of unlimited length.

To say a literary analysis essay is expository also means that your essay will interpret rather than retell. The literary analysis essay goes a step beyond the traditional book report. The typical book report consists of a plot summary with a few critical comments added at the end. Remember that a literary analysis essay does not merely summarize a story, a novel, a play, or a poem.

Some students confuse literary review and literary analysis. As a result, they try to evaluate the work being discussed. While critical review essays evaluate a work, literary analysis essays strive to illuminate. A review is an attempt to demonstrate that a work is worth reading or reviewing. A review, for example, of a new novel or film, is aimed at readers who are unfamiliar with the work. Furthermore, reviews are often loosely structured, commenting on everything related to the appearance of the work in public; they are often written with an informal, conversational style (see Chapter Four). The literary analysis, by contrast, is an in-depth look at a work aimed at readers who have read or viewed the work. In other words, they are familiar with the subject and are not reading for evaluation but rather for deeper understanding.

A literary analysis essay is written in Standard American English and follows a tightly controlled structure. It includes a clearly stated thesis and topic sentences. Before writing literary analysis essays, most students prepare a thesis-topic sentence outline, and as they write, they follow the outline carefully. The following outline was taken from an essay written by a student. The assignment was to write a 1,000–1,500 word essay analyzing some aspect of the novel *Moby Dick*. After considering several topics, the student-author chose to write about a technique Melville uses to create suspense.

The Gams in Moby Dick: The Creation of Suspense

Thesis: In *Moby Dick*, Herman Melville uses gams, the meeting of two ships at sea, to demonstrate Captain Ahab's obsession, intensify his malignant excitement, and develop suspense for the novel's readers.

1. The first few gams establish the white whale's purported destructiveness and the power the legend of the white whale has upon the crew.

2. The early gams suggest that Moby Dick directs his vengeance at only the one who is directly responsible for inflicting injury upon him.

3. The middle gams are both satirical and function as foils for Captain Ahab and the Pequod.

4. The last two gams clearly foreshadow the imminent and catastrophic conclusion of the tale.

Notice that you can tell exactly what the student's points are, even without being able to read the entire essay. Any well-written analysis should have this obvious structure.

The purpose of the literary analysis essay is to interpret, in depth, one of the following:

1. The author's meaning as it unfolds
2. The author's theme (the central dominating idea of the work)
3. The parts of a literary work and their organization
4. The literary techniques used to develop those elements
5. The significance of the work compared or contrasted with other works
6. The results of applying a particular critical viewpoint, such as historical, formal, analytical, psychological, mythic, feminist, post-colonial, or de-construction.

If you choose the second purpose, your essay will explain the author's point. The theme is very much like the thesis of an essay, except that a theme is not neatly stated at the end of the introduction. Examine the thesis in the outline on page 230 for an example.

Regardless of what aspect of a work you choose to write about, the all-important consideration is that you clearly support whatever position you take in your thesis. Body paragraphs must clearly explain some part of what your thesis states. Use key words or concepts to make the relationship between the thesis and the topic sentences evident. The student author of the *Moby Dick* outline, for example, uses the key word *gam* in each sentence to establish an obvious relationship between the thesis and the topic sentences.

The literary analysis essay explains one possible interpretation of the topic on which you are writing, not the only one. That is, you must understand that one-and-only explanations do not exist. Not even the person who wrote the work can say exactly what it means; everyone's opinion is merely an educated speculation based on a close reading of the work. If you have read the work carefully and honestly considered the possibilities, your opinion is as good as anyone else's.

The key to analysis is to support your observations with specific details and examples from the work in question. Your analysis must seem plausible in terms of the detailed explanation you have composed. Although the main purpose of a literary analysis is not to persuade, you do have the responsibility of organizing a discussion that convinces readers that your analysis is astute.

EXERCISE 5.1

Select a literary work—a short story, a novel, a poem, or a play—that you will read in preparation for writing a literary analysis essay.

Title of Work:_____

Author:_____

Have your selection approved.

LESSON TWO—How to Read a Literary Work for Analysis

Before you can plan a literary analysis essay, you must understand the work about which you wish to write. Far too many students think that simply reading a poem, play, novel, or short story once thoroughly is enough, but once through will develop only a superficial understanding. Follow these steps as you plan your literary analysis paper:

1. Examine the title carefully. The title is often a clue to what is considered important in the work.

2. Consult a dictionary or other source for every word or reference you do not understand. Sometimes a single word, often a unique word, will give a clue to the meaning of the story. The following quote from a short story contains a word that is pivotal to the meaning of the story in which it appears.

   > A sawmill was nearby. Its pyramidal sawdust pile smouldered. It is a year before one completely burns. Meanwhile, the smoke curls up and hangs in odd wraiths about the trees, curls up, and spreads itself out over the valley [. . .]. (Jean Toomer, "Karintha," *Cane)*

   The student who reads this short story and fails to look up the word *wraith* will invariably misinterpret an important clue about the author's meaning. In fact, a "wraith" is a ghost or visible spirit. In this case, the wraith refers to the ghost of a baby who is buried and burning in the sawdust pile.

3. After you have read through the first time, ask yourself about the obvious structure of the work. For instance, is there a geographical, historical, or social aspect to the work? If so, what is it, and how do the characters fit into this setting? Who tells the story? How does that influence the work? Is there a central character, and if so, what conflicts does he or she encounter? How are the different characters related, and what motivates them to do what they do?

4. Think about how the work is organized. Does it have a beginning, a middle, and an end? Are there parts or sections? How is it plotted? Can you trace the development and resolution of the conflict? Is the conclusion the logical outcome of the events and actions of the characters? If you are reading a play, how does what happens in each act relate to the whole play? If you are reading a poem, how does the meaning unfold stanza by stanza?

5. As you read the work the second time, search for deeper meanings. Your understanding of words and images will help you perceive a deeper meaning. You should make notes in the margin or on separate paper during this reading as you speculate about the work. For example, what is the author's purpose in writing this work? Is it to present a slice of life, to make social commentary, or to reveal the complexities of human character? Is the author attempting a combination of purposes? After all is considered, what is the main underlying message of this work? Can you summarize the author's meaning in a paragraph? Can you state the major theme of the work in a single sentence? If you are contemplating symbolism in the work, what are the symbols and what do they mean? What other aspects of the work interest you? Is it possible that the work means different things on different levels, for instance, in terms of pure action and outcome, in terms of social or historical commentary, and on a deeper symbolic level?

6. Ask yourself the significance of all repeated numbers, colors, or images. For example, when an author of one short story uses the number three five times in two pages, the reader should begin to look for a significant relationship among the items described.

You may want to discuss the work with someone else. Just talking about the work will help, but asking questions will promote even more understanding. Always keep asking yourself, What is the author trying to say? What is the point?

If you are unable to decide what the author is saying, you may be wise to do some research either on the Internet or in the library. Even though not expected by instructors who assign literary analysis essays, research will sometimes suggest possible meanings of a work. For instance, if you are reading a short story by the British writer Saki (H. H. Munro), it would probably help you to know that he frequently makes fun of boring adults in his writing. The fact that he was raised by aunts who pretended to care for him (but really did not) might also help you decide what he was thinking as he wrote the story.

If a writer has written about the same type of people or problems in earlier works, you may be able to use them to decide what is important. You might also find it helpful to read about the events that took place at the time the work was written. If you were doing an analysis of John Steinbeck's *Grapes of Wrath*, it might help you to interpret the work if you knew what life was actually like for the farmers who were forced from their lands during the Depression. Often material from other courses, such as anthropology, history, or sociology, may establish a context for a given work. It should take little research to discover such additional information. Ask your librarian for assistance in finding what has been written about the literary work or about the context of the literary work you are studying.

Documenting Your Sources

Any researched information that you include in a literary analysis essay must be documented. Use lead-ins and parenthetical references to integrate researched material, just as you did in your library research essay. Any time you use researched information (secondary sources), be sure to include a Works Cited page at the end of the essay (see Chapter Three and Appendix B). Always collect your research materials in your Project Folder.

EXERCISE 5.2

For practice in critical reading, study the following short story carefully. Use a dictionary whenever necessary. As you read the story, look also at the questions on the left. These are questions and comments you should be asking yourself as you read. Write short answers to the questions in the left-hand margins. Normally, when you are reading a literary work for analysis, you should be writing out questions and comments like these.

Paragraph
Number

THE BRIDE COMES TO YELLOW SKY
By Stephen Crane

1. The author describes the railroad car as a great Pullman with a "dignity of motion." Could this be a symbol? Note that the plains are compared to a river pouring eastward toward a waterfall.

1. The great Pullman was whirling onward with such dignity of motion that a glance from the window seemed simply to prove that the plains of Texas were pouring eastward. Vast flats of green grass, dull-hued spaces of mesquite and cactus, little groups of frame houses, woods of light and tender trees, all were sweeping into the east, sweeping over the horizon, a precipice.

2. The man's face and hands reflect a man of the outdoors; this contrasts sharply with his "new black clothes." He appears out of place. Is this why his glances at other passengers are furtive and shy?

2. A newly married pair had boarded this coach at San Antonio. The man's face was reddened from many days in the wind and sun, and a direct result of his new black clothes was that his brick-coloured hands were constantly performing in a most conscious fashion. From time to time he looked down respectfully at his attire. He sat with a hand on each knee, like a man waiting in a barber's shop. The glances he devoted to other passengers were furtive and shy.

3. Why is the bride embarrassed by her clothes? Is she, too, out of place in the Pullman car? Other passengers have noticed something odd and have stared. Is she an average working woman dressed as a lady? Why else is she embarrassed?

3. The bride was not pretty, nor was she very young. She wore a dress of blue cashmere, with small reservations of velvet here and there, and with steel buttons abounding. She continually twisted her head to regard her puff sleeves, very stiff, straight, and high. They embarrassed her. It was quite apparent that she had cooked, and that she expected to cook, dutifully. The blushes caused by the careless scrutiny of some passengers as she had entered the car were strange to see upon this plain, under-class countenance, which was drawn in placid, almost emotionless lines.

4. The groom does not seem to know much about his bride.

4. They were evidently very happy. "Ever been in a parlour-car before?" she asked, smiling with delight.

5-8. The bride has never been on a train before. What does she mean by the word *fine*? What is Jack's attitude toward the expense of eating in the diner?

9. The groom, Jack, has apparently been on trains before. What does the comment "He had the pride of an owner" mean? Is he showing off for his new bride?

10. Why does Jack's happiness make him appear ridiculous to the porter? Why does the porter bully the newly married pair? And why are other travelers laughing at them? Are the bride and groom such obvious "country cousins"?

5.   "No," she answered; "I never was. It's fine, ain't it?"

6.   "Great! And then after a while we'll go forward to the diner, and get a big layout. Finest meal in the world. Charge a dollar."

7.   "Oh, do they?" cried the bride. "Charge a dollar? Why that's too much for us ain't it, Jack?"

8.   "Not this trip, anyhow," he answered bravely. "We're going to go the whole thing."

9.   Later he explained to her about the trains. "You see, it's a thousand miles from one end of Texas to the other; and this train runs right across it, and never stops but four times." He had the pride of an owner. He pointed out to her the dazzling fittings of the coach; and in truth her eyes opened wider as she contemplated the sea-green figured velvet, the shining brass, silver, and glass, the wood that gleamed as darkly brilliant as the surface of a pool of oil. At one end a bronze figure sturdily held a support for a separated chamber, and at convenient places on the ceiling were frescos in olive and silver.

10.   To the minds of the pair, their surroundings reflected the glory of their marriage that morning in San Antonio; this was the environment of their new estate; and the man's face in particular beamed with an elation that made him appear ridiculous to the Negro porter. This individual at times surveyed them from afar with an amused and superior grin. On other occasions he bullied them with skill in ways that did not make it exactly plain to them that they were being bullied. He subtly used all the manners of the most unconquerable kind of snobbery. He oppressed them; but of this oppression they had small knowledge, and they speedily forgot that infrequently a number of travelers covered them with stares of derisive enjoyment. Historically there was supposed to be something infinitely humorous in their situation.

11-14. Time is the subject in these paragraphs. Both have watches—could they be symbols? Since it is the arrival time in Yellow Sky that seems crucial, this is an interlude before whatever will happen when they arrive. With more than three hours before their arrival, Jack seems happy.

15. Their waiter in the dining car, although friendly and kind, "patronizes" the couple, but they do not even notice. Or do they choose to ignore the waiter's behavior to avoid looking foolish?

16. Jack becomes increasingly nervous as the train draws nearer his home town of Yellow Sky. Why?

11.   "We are due in Yellow Sky at 3:42," he said, looking tenderly into her eyes.

12.   "Oh, are we?" she said, as if she had not been aware of it. To evince surprise at her husband's statement was part of her wifely amiability. She took from a pocket a little silver watch; and as she held it before her, and stared at it with a frown of attention, the new husband's face shone.

13.   "I bought it in San Anton' from a friend of mine," he told her gleefully.

14.   "It's seventeen minutes past twelve," she said, looking up at him with a kind of shy and clumsy coquetry. A passenger, noting this play, grew excessively sardonic, and winked at himself in one of the numerous mirrors.

15.   At last they went to the dining-car. Two rows of Negro waiters, in glowing white suits, surveyed their entrance with the interest, and also the equanimity, of men who had been forewarned. The pair fell to the lot of a waiter who happened to feel pleasure in steering them through their meal. He viewed them with the manner of a fatherly pilot, his countenance radiant with benevolence. The patronage, entwined with the ordinary deference, was not plain to them. And yet, as they returned to their coach, they showed in their faces a sense of escape.

16.   To the left, miles down a long purple slope, was a little ribbon of mist where moved the keening Rio Grande. The train was approaching it at an angle, and the apex was Yellow Sky. Presently it was apparent that, as the distance from Yellow Sky grew shorter, the husband became commensurately restless. His brick-red hands were more insistent in their prominence. Occasionally he was even rather absent-minded and far-away when the bride leaned forward and addressed him.

17. Jack Potter feels guilt about marrying without talking it over with the citizens of Yellow Sky. Why should a town marshal who is a well-respected member of the community ask permission?

17.   As a matter of truth, Jack Potter was beginning to find the shadow of a deed weigh upon him like a leaden slab. He, the town marshal of Yellow Sky, a man known, liked, and feared in his corner, a prominent person, had gone to San Antonio to meet a girl he believed he loved, and there, after the usual prayers, had actually induced her to marry him, without consulting Yellow Sky for any part of the transaction. He was now bringing his bride before an innocent and unsuspecting community.

18. Apparently, Jack's guilt is due to his own sense of duty. Why is his marriage an "extraordinary crime"? What do the lines "At San Antonio he was like a man . . . in that remote city" mean?

18.   Of course people in Yellow Sky married as it pleased them, in accordance with a general custom; but such was Potter's thought of his duty to his friends, or of their idea of his duty, or of an unspoken form which does not control men in these matters, that he felt he was heinous. He had committed an extraordinary crime. Face to face with this girl in San Antonio, and spurred by his sharp impulse, he had gone headlong over all the social hedges. At San Antonio he was like a man hidden in the dark. A knife to sever any friendly duty, any form, was easy to his hand in that remote city. But the hour of Yellow Sky—the hour of daylight—was approaching.

19. How could his marriage be so important to the town? What kind of reception does he expect? What kind of reception do married couples usually receive?

19.   He knew full well that his marriage was an important thing to his town. It could only be exceeded by the burning of the new hotel. His friends could not forgive him. Frequently he had reflected on the advisability of telling them by telegraph, but a new cowardice had been upon him. He feared to do it. And now the train was hurrying him toward a scene of amazement, glee, and reproach. He glanced out of the window at the line of haze swinging slowly in toward the train.

20-22. He is going to sneak from the station to his house to avoid friends and the brass band. In paragraph 19, Jack thinks his friends will not forgive him; yet here he thinks that the citizens will be happy about his marriage and offer congratulations—explain the apparent contradiction.

20.   Yellow Sky had a kind of brass band, which played painfully, to the delight of the populace. He laughed without heart as he thought of it. If the citizens could dream of his prospective arrival with his bride, they would parade the band at the station and escort them, amid cheers and laughing congratulations, to his adobe home.

23-25. Both feel guilty about the marriage. Do they seem to understand one another without discussion?

26. The word *traitor* drives home the idea that Jack is not loyal to the townspeople. Pause here to note the point of view from which the story is told. The narrator tells the story and seems to know everything about what will happen and what the people are thinking and feeling. How would the story be different if it were told from the limited point of view of one of the characters?

27-28. Why does the porter treat the couple differently now?

21.   He resolved that he would use all the devices of speed and plainscraft in making the journey from the station to his house. Once within that safe citadel, he could issue some sort of vocal bulletin, and then not go among the citizens until they had time to wear off a little of their enthusiasm.

22.   The bride looked anxiously at him. "What's worrying you, Jack?"

23.   He laughed again. "I'm not worrying, girl; I'm only thinking of Yellow Sky."

24.   She flushed in comprehension.

25.   A sense of mutual guilt invaded their minds and developed a finer tenderness. They looked at each other with eyes softly aglow. But Potter often laughed the same nervous laugh; the flush upon the bride's face seemed quite permanent.

26.   The traitor to the feelings of Yellow Sky narrowly watched the speeding landscape. "We're nearly there," he said.

27.   Presently the porter came and announced the proximity of Potter's home. He held a brush in his hand, and, with all his airy superiority gone, he brushed Potter's new clothes as the latter slowly turned this way and that way. Potter fumbled out a coin and gave it to the porter, as he had seen others do. It was a heavy and muscle-bound business, as that of a man shoeing his first horse.

28.   The porter took their bag, and as the train began to slow they moved forward to the hooded platform of the car. Presently the two engines and their long string of coaches rushed into the station of Yellow Sky.

29. Potter is like a man going to his death. Is that what is about to happen?

29. "They have to take water here," said Potter, from a constricted throat and in mournful cadence, as one announcing death. Before the train stopped his eye had swept the length of the platform, and he was glad and astonished to see there was none upon it but the station agent, who, with a slightly hurried and anxious air, was walking toward the water-tanks. When the train had halted, the porter alighted first, and placed in position a little temporary step.

30. The station-agent sees the couple leaving. Does he react as Jack feared he would?

30. "Come on, girl," said Potter, hoarsely. As he helped her down they each laughed on a false note. He took the bag from the Negro, and bade his wife cling to his arm. As they slunk rapidly away, his hang-dog glance perceived that they were unloading the two trunks, and also that the station-agent, far ahead near the baggage car, had turned and was running toward him, making gestures. He laughed, and groaned as he laughed, when he noted the first effect of his marital bliss upon Yellow Sky. He gripped his wife's arm firmly to his side, and they fled. Behind them the porter stood, chuckling fatuously.

II

31-33. The scene shifts abruptly to the Weary Gentleman Saloon "twenty-one minutes" before the train arrives. Who all is there? What is a "drummer"? Could this be the "lull before the storm"? This abrupt shift in time and in scene tells you something about how the story is organized. What does it tell?

31.   The California Express on the Southern Railway was due at Yellow Sky in twenty-one minutes. There were six men at the bar of the Weary Gentleman saloon. One was a drummer who talked a great deal and rapidly; three were Texans who did not care to talk at that time; and two were Mexican sheep-herders, who did not talk as a general practice in the Weary Gentleman saloon. The barkeeper's dog lay on the board walk that crossed in front of the door. His head was on his paws, and he glanced drowsily here and there with the constant vigilance of a dog that is kicked on occasion. Across the sandy street were some vivid green grass plots, so wonderful in appearance, amid the sands that burned near them in a blazing sun, that they caused a doubt in the mind. They exactly resembled the grass mats used to represent lawns on the stage. At the cooler end of the railway station, a man without a coat sat in a tilted chair and smoked his pipe. The fresh-cut bank of the Rio Grande circled near the town, and there could be seen beyond it a great plum-coloured plain of mesquite.

32.   Save for the busy drummer and his companions in the saloon, Yellow Sky was dozing. The new-comer leaned gracefully upon the bar, and recited many tales with the confidence of a bard who has come upon a new field.

33.   "—and at the moment that the old man fell downstairs with the bureau in his arms, the old woman was coming up with two scuttles of coal, and of course—"

34-37. Scratchy Wilson is apparently a much-feared person. Although the drummer is oblivious, how do the others react?

34.   The drummer's tale was interrupted by a young man who suddenly appeared in the open door. He cried: "Scratchy Wilson's drunk, and has turned loose with both hands." The two Mexicans at once set down their glasses and faded out of the rear entrance of the saloon.

35.   The drummer, innocent and jocular, answered: "All right, old man. S'pose he has? Come in and have a drink anyhow."

38. The barkeeper's actions leave no doubt that all take the danger from Wilson as a very real threat. Why is the bar compared to a chapel?

39-50. The author uses the drummer to relate essential background information to the reader. What can Scratchy Wilson be expected to do?

36.   But the information had made such an obvious cleft in every skull in the room that the drummer was obliged to see its importance. All had become instantly solemn. "Say," said he, mystified, "what is this?" His three companions made the introductory gesture of eloquent speech; but the young man at the door forestalled them.

37.   "It means, my friend," he answered, as he came into the saloon, "that for the next two hours this town won't be a health resort."

38.   The barkeeper went to the door, and locked and barred it; reaching out of the window, he pulled in heavy wooden shutters, and barred them. Immediately a solemn, chapel-like gloom was upon the place. The drummer was looking from one to another.

39.   "But say," he cried, "what is this, anyhow? You don't mean there is going to be a gunfight?"

40.   "Don't know whether there'll be a fight or not, answered one man, grimly; but there'll be some shootin'—some good shootin'."

41.   The young man who had warned them waved his hand. "Oh, there'll be a fight fast enough, if any one wants it. Anybody can get a fight out there in the street. There's a fight just waiting."

42   The drummer seemed to be swayed between the interest of a foreigner and a perception of personal danger.

43   "What did you say his name was?" he asked.

44.   "Scratchy Wilson," they answered in chorus.

45.   "And will he kill anybody? What are you going to do? Does this happen often? Does he rampage around like this once a week or so? Can he break in that door?"

46.   "No; he can't break down that door,"
replied the barkeeper. "He's tried it three
times. But when he comes you'd better lay
down on the floor, stranger. He's dead sure
to shoot at it, and a bullet may come
through."

47.   Thereafter the drummer kept a strict
eye upon the door. The time had not yet
been called for him to hug the floor, but,
as a minor precaution, he sidled near to
the wall. "Will he kill anybody?" he said
again.

48.   The men laughed low and scornfully
at the question.

49.   "He's out to shoot, and he's out for
trouble. Don't see any good in experimen-
tin' with him."

50.   "But what do you do in a case like
this? What do you do?"

51. Jack Potter is connected to the action in
town. Obviously, the townspeople think
Potter is the only one who can stand up to
Wilson. At this point, who do you think
Potter's antagonist is, the townspeople or
Wilson?

51.   A man responded: "Why, he and Jack
Potter—"

52-59. The marshal role Jack has taken on
earns respect but obvious danger, too. Do
the townspeople seem to take it for
granted that Potter should fight Scratchy
on a regular basis?

52.   "But," in chorus the other men interrupted, "Jack Potter's in San Anton'."

53.   "Well, who is he? What's he got to do
with it?"

54.   "Oh, he's the town marshal. He goes
out and fights Scratchy when he gets on
one of these tears."

55.   "Wow!" said the drummer, mopping
his brow. "Nice job he's got."

56.   The voices had toned away to mere whisperings. The drummer wished to ask further questions, which were born of an increasing anxiety and bewilderment; but when he attempted them, the men merely looked at him in irritation and motioned him to remain silent. A tense waiting hush was upon them. In the deep shadows of the room their eyes shone as they listened for sounds from the street. One man made three gestures at the barkeeper; and the latter, moving like a ghost, handed him a glass and a bottle. The man poured a full glass of whisky, and set down the bottle noiselessly. He gulped the whisky in a swallow, and turned again toward the door in immovable silence. The drummer saw the barkeeper, without a sound, had taken a Winchester from beneath the bar. Later he saw this individual beckoning to him, so he tiptoed across the room.

57.   "You better come with me back of the bar."

58.   "No, thanks," said the drummer, perspiring; "I'd rather be where I can make a break for the back door."

59.   Whereupon the man of bottles made a kindly but peremptory gesture. The drummer obeyed it, and, finding himself seated on a box with his head below the level of the bar, balm was laid upon his soul at sight of various zinc and copper fittings that bore a resemblance to armour-plate. The barkeeper took a seat comfortably upon an adjacent box.

60. Scratchy Wilson is "a wonder with a gun—a perfect wonder." What evidence is there that he is a character left from an older, wilder West?

60.   "You see," he whispered, "this here Scratchy Wilson is a wonder with a gun—a perfect wonder; and when he goes on the war trail, we hunt our holes—naturally. He's about the last one of the old gang that used to hang out along the river here. He's a terror when he's drunk. When he's sober he's all right kind of simple—wouldn't hurt a fly—nicest fellow in town. But when he's drunk—whoo!"

61. As the trouble starts, the men in the bar wish Potter was back. How do you know Potter is a skillful gunfighter and that there have been previous fights?

61.   There were periods of stillness. "I wish Jack Potter was back from San Anton'," said the barkeeper. "He shot Wilson up once—in the leg—and he would sail in and pull out the kinks in this thing."

62. What effect does Scratchy's rampage have on the men in the bar?

62.   Presently they heard from a distance the sound of a shot, followed by three wild yowls. It instantly removed a bond from the men in the darkened saloon. There was a shuffling of feet. They looked at each other. "Here he comes," they said.

III

63-65. Which articles of Scratchy's clothing seem incongruous? Why does the author go out of his way to make Wilson appear a misfit? Note that Section Three of the story begins here.

63.   A man in a maroon-coloured flannel shirt, which had been purchased for purpose of decoration, and made principally by some Jewish women on the East Side of New York, rounded a corner and walked into the middle of the main street of Yellow Sky. In either hand the man held a long, heavy, blue-black revolver. Often he yelled, and these cries rang through a semblance of a deserted village, shrilly flying over the roofs in a volume that seemed to have no relation to the ordinary vocal strength of a man. It was as if the surrounding stillness formed the arch of a tomb over him. These cries of ferocious challenge rang against walls of silence. And his boots had red tops with gilded imprints, of the kind beloved in winter by little sledding boys on the hillsides of New England.

64.   The man's face flamed in a rage begot of whisky. His eyes, rolling, and yet keen for ambush, hunted the still doorways and windows. He walked with the creeping movement of the midnight cat. As it occurred to him, he roared menacing information. The long revolvers in his hands were as easy as straws; they were moved with an electric swiftness. The little fingers of each hand played sometimes in a musician's way. Plain from the low collar of the shirt, the cords of his neck straightened and sank, straightened and sank, as passion moved him. The only sounds were his terrible invitations. The calm adobes preserved their demeanour at the passing of this small thing in the middle of the street.

65.   There was no offer of fight—no offer of fight. The man called to the sky. There were no attractions. He bellowed and fumed and swayed his revolvers here and everywhere.

66. Wilson is unable to find any human to shoot, so he picks on the dog. Note the foreshadowing in paragraph 31.

66.   The dog of the barkeeper of the Weary Gentleman Saloon had not appreciated the advance of events. He yet lay dozing in front of his master's door. At sight of the dog, the man paused and raised his revolver humourously. At sight of the man, the dog sprang up and walked diagonally away, with a sullen head, and growling. The man yelled and the dog broke into a gallop. As it was about to enter an alley, there was a loud noise, a whistling, and something spat the ground directly before it. The dog screamed, and, wheeling in terror, galloped headlong in a new direction. Again there was a noise, a whistling, and sand was kicked viciously before it. Fear-stricken, the dog turned and flurried like an animal in a pen. The man stood laughing, his weapons at his hips.

67-68. He cannot enter to buy another drink, and no one will even yell back to him. Are you surprised that he leaves the saloon so quickly?

67.   Ultimately the man was attracted by the closed door of the Weary Gentleman saloon. He went to it and, hammering with a revolver, demanded drink.

68.   The door remaining imperturbable, he picked a bit of paper from the walk, and nailed it to the framework with a knife. He then turned his back contemptuously upon this popular resort and, walking to the opposite side of the street and spinning there on his heel quickly and lithely, fired at the bit of paper. He missed it by a half-inch. He swore at himself, and went away. Later he comfortably fusilladed the windows of his most intimate friend. The man was playing with this town; it was a toy for him.

69. Jack Potter is called Wilson's "ancient antagonist." Is this referring to the marshal's age and ability? Or is it focusing the reader's attention on the fact that only Potter is capable of stopping Wilson? How does his chanting reveal again that he is a character from the vanishing old West?

69.   But still there was no offer of fight. The name of Jack Potter, his ancient antagonist, entered his mind, and he concluded that it would be a glad thing if he should go to Potter's house, and by bombardment induce him to come out and fight. He moved in the direction of his desire, chanting Apache scalp music.

70. Although Scratchy is working himself into a rage, his confrontation with the house seems part of a ritual. Explain (remember the chanting).

70.   When he arrived at it, Potter's house presented the same still front as had the other adobes. Taking up a strategic position, the man howled a challenge. But this house regarded him as might a great stone god. It gave no sign. After a decent wait, the man howled further challenges, mingling with them wonderful epithets.

71. How much time has probably elapsed since paragraph 31? How has the author skillfully and dramatically set the scene for a climax?

71.   Presently there came the spectacle of a man churning himself into deepest rage over the immobility of a house. He fumed at it as the winter wind attacks a prairie cabin in the North. To the distance there should have gone the sound of a tumult like the fighting of two hundred Mexicans. As necessity bade him, he paused for breath or to reload his revolvers.

IV

72-73. Where do you expect Scratchy Wilson to be?

72.   Potter and his bride walked sheepishly and with speed. Sometimes they laughed together shamefacedly and low.

73.   "Next corner, dear," he said finally.

74. Wilson could shoot Potter easily. Why does he wait?

74.   They put forth the efforts of a pair walking bowed against a strong wind. Potter was about to raise a finger to point the first appearance of the new home when, as they circled the corner, they came face to face with a man in a maroon-coloured shirt, who was feverishly pushing cartridges into a large revolver. Upon the instant the man dropped his revolver to the ground and, like lightning, whipped another from its holster. The second weapon was aimed at the bridegroom's chest.

75-77. The story has been building to this point since the beginning. Do you expect violence and death?

75.   There was a silence. Potter's mouth seemed to be merely a grave for his tongue. He exhibited an instinct to at once loosen his arm from the woman's grip, and he dropped the bag to the sand. As for the bride, her face had gone as yellow as old cloth. She was a slave to hideous rites, gazing at the apparitional snake.

76.   The two men faced each other at a distance of three paces. He of the revolver smiled with a new and quiet ferocity.

77.   "Tried to sneak up on me," he said. "Tried to sneak up on me!" His eyes grew more baleful. As Potter made a slight movement, the man thrust his revolver venomously forward. "No; don't you do it, Jack Potter. Don't you move a finger toward a gun just yet. Don't you move an eyelash. The time has come for me to settle with you, and I'm goin' to do it my own way, and loaf along with no interferin'. So if you don't want a gun bent on you, just mind what I tell you."

78. Did you expect Potter to be armed? Is a gun a symbol here of more than one idea?

78.   Potter looked at his enemy. "I ain't got a gun on me Scratchy," he said. "Honest, I ain't." He was stiffening and steadying, but yet somewhere at the back of his mind a vision of the Pullman floated: the sea-green figured velvet, the shining brass, silver, and glass, the wood that gleamed as darkly brilliant as the surface of a pool of oil all the glory of the marriage, the environment of the new estate. "You know I fight when it comes to fighting, Scratchy Wilson; but I ain't got a gun on me. You'll have to do all the shootin' yourself."

79-80. Why does Wilson's face go "livid" when he finds Potter is unarmed? Is he playing a game with the marshal or does he believe Potter is lying?

79.   His enemy's face went livid. He stepped forward, and lashed his weapon to and fro before Potter's chest. "Don't you tell me you ain't got no gun on you, you whelp! Don't tell me no lie like that. There ain't a man in Texas ever seen you without no gun. Don't take me for no kid." His eyes blazed with light, and his throat worked like a pump.

80.   "I ain't takin' you for no kid, answered Potter. His heels had not moved an inch backward. "I'm takin' you for a damn fool. I tell you I ain't got a gun, and I ain't. If you're goin' to shoot me up, you better begin now; you'll never get a chance like this again."

81. Wilson tries to humiliate the marshal. Why?

81.   So much enforced reasoning had told on Wilson's rage; he was calmer. "If you ain't got a gun, why ain't you got a gun?" he sneered. "Been to Sunday-school?"

82-87. Why is Wilson overwhelmed by news that Potter is married? Why is he "like a creature allowed a glimpse of another world?"

82.   "I ain't got a gun because I've just come from San Anton' with my wife. I'm married," said Potter. "And if I'd thought there was going to be any galoots like you prowling around when I brought my wife home, I'd had a gun and don't you forget it."

83.   "Married!" said Scratchy, not at all comprehending.

84.   "Yes, married. I'm married," said Potter, distinctly.

85.   "Married?" said Scratchy. Seemingly for the first time, he saw the drooping, drowning woman at the other man's side. "No!" he said. He was like a creature allowed a glimpse of another world. He moved a pace backward, and his arm, with the revolver, dropped to his side. "Is this the lady?" he asked.

86.   "Yes; this is the lady," Potter answered.

87.   There was another period of silence.

88-89. What does Wilson mean when he says, "I s'pose it's all off now?" What is all off?

88.   "Well," said Wilson at last, slowly, "I s'pose it's all off now."

89.   "It's all off if you say so, Scratchy. You know I didn't make the trouble." Potter lifted his valise.

90. Why is marriage a "foreign condition" to Scratchy?

90.   "Well, I'low it's off," Jack, said Wilson. He was looking at the ground. "Married!" He was not a student of chivalry; it was merely that in the presence of this foreign condition he was a simple child of the earlier plains. He picked up his starboard revolver, and, placing both weapons in their holsters, he went away. His feet made funnel-shaped tracks in the heavy sand.

After the first reading of "The Bride Comes to Yellow Sky," you may have more questions than answers. If so, it is time to reread and think carefully about the story. When you finally have answers to all your questions, you are ready to study an essay about the story.

LESSON THREE—The Structure of a Literary Analysis Essay

At this point you may be asking yourself what the essay you are expected to write should look like. Examine the student-written literary analysis essay on the following pages. As you read the essay on the right-hand pages, consider the accompanying explanations on the left-hand pages.

The essay on "The Bride Comes to Yellow Sky" is limited by a carefully written thesis because the assignment was to write a 1,000-word essay. Had the student been writing a longer essay, she would have composed a much broader thesis. Notice, also, that she does not use a divided thesis, demonstrating that a divided thesis is an option, not a requirement. Both are equally correct; either one can result in a successful literary analysis.

Heading

The heading is standard. It should look just like the one on your argumentative essay. On the upper left corner of the first page, place the following:

1. Your name
2. Instructor's name
3. Course title
4. Date paper is to be submitted

Title of Essay

The title of the essay is centered at the top.

Page Numbers and Headers

Begin numbering your essay on the first page with your last name and the number 1 in the upper right corner. Subsequent page numbers follow your last name: e.g., Bronson 2. (If you are required to have a title page, do not number it; if you include an outline page, it should be Roman-numbered following your name: e.g., Bronson i.)

Present Tense

Analysis essays on literary works are written in present tense because if you were to re-read the work, the characters would still be doing the same things. The present tense is the way readers think about what is happening; consequently, that is the tense you should use in writing about those actions. Thus, you would say:

"Jack Potter **is** the marshal in the story."

                NOT

"Jack Potter **was** the marshal in the story."

Title Page

If your instructor requires a traditional title page instead of a heading on the first page of the essay, it should look just like the sample title page for the research essay (see page 135 for detailed directions).

Outline Page

If your instructor requires an outline page, see pages 137-139 for instructions and a sample outline.

Purpose of Essay

The purpose of any literary analysis essay is to explain the work's meaning or the author's technique. In this essay the student does both: She explains the theme of changes and she interprets the symbols that Crane uses to elaborate on his theme.

Sandra L. Ewers

Professor Mehaffy

English 1A

21 April 1995

A Historic Day in Yellow Sky

Stephen Crane's short story "The Bride Comes to Yellow Sky" is an illustrative tale of history's inevitable course. On the surface, Crane relates the journey of Marshal Potter and his bride to the small Texas town of Yellow Sky. In a larger sense, however, Crane contrasts a story of the passage of the old West with its simple values and way of life to the arrival of the more complex life and ideas of the civilization from the East, a story of greater historical significance. The characters are not extensively developed; instead, they are simply presented, even understated. Crane's intent is not to draw vivid characterizations but to present objects and characters as symbols with larger meanings.

The Pullman car is the first symbol of the East presented in the story. With its elaborate interior, the parlor-car expresses the greater sophistication of Eastern culture, for the velvet, brass, and finely-polished wood furnishings found in the coach would not be useful or practical in an adobe house or a Texas saloon. Rather, the harshness of the frontier demands sturdy, functional furniture and equipment requiring little care. The superior attitude of the porter and the scornful conduct of the other passengers, all Easterners, toward the weather-worn marshal implies the culture of the West is primitive and unrefined. The westward movement of the train, a powerful machine of steel run by steam, signifies that the advancement of Eastern culture into the Western frontier is an accelerating force which cannot be checked. It is almost as though the West rushes to meet the East. As the train moves westward, "the plains of Texas were pouring eastward . . . all were sweeping into the east, sweeping over the horizon, a precipice."

Transitions

The relationship between the thesis and the topic sentences must be clearly established. Here the writer uses repetition of a key word to remind the reader of the relationship. (The key word is symbol.)

The paragraphs are joined by transitions to make sure the essay flows smoothly. The first body paragraph is read immediately after the thesis, so a smooth transition is achieved by the words *first symbol*.

To relate the second paragraph to the previous paragraph, the author begins the second paragraph, "In addition to objects, characters are used as symbols." The words *in addition to objects* and *symbols* create the transition.

To connect the third paragraph with the second paragraph, Ewers begins the third paragraph, "While Scratchy Wilson and his bride represent the opposing forces of old and new, [. . .]. This transition connects with the discussion of Scratch Wilson in paragraph two. The key transitional words are *Scratchy Wilson*.

In addition to objects, characters are used as symbols. The marshal's bride, for instance, is a sexual metaphor for the ideals and principles of Eastern society. First, women traditionally represent complexity over men in literature because women are viewed as biologically more complex. Beyond this simple representation, women are not only bearers of the children of the next generation, but they also protect the customs valued by the culture for posterity. Second, the arrival of the bride in Yellow Sky portends feminine values supplanting the current masculine values of the town. Women, for instance, culturally value peace over conflict. As a result, Yellow Sky can no longer permit Scratchy Wilson his binges of drunken shooting. Furthermore, the bride's new status as the marshal's wife will change the caliber of the entire town, since the marriage anticipates a more complex life approaching all the town's residents. The appearance of other women, children, churches, schools, and libraries in the town will closely follow the bride's, permanently changing the lives of all the men in Yellow Sky.

Described by the town bartender as "kind of simple," Scratchy Wilson represents what remains in the town of the life and values of the old frontier. Requiring sturdy men and offering only simple food, simple clothing and simple shelter, the life of the early West was severe and arduous. Scratchy's clothes symbolically convey that the encroachment of the East upon the West has been gradual. Unsuitable in the wilderness, the flannel shirt he now wears was sewn in a New York ghetto. Furthermore, Scratchy sports a pair of red-topped boots with gilded imprints that would have made him the object of contemptuous humor in previous times. However modern Scratchy may dress, he is not truly able to fit into the transitional progress of town life. Rather, he is tolerated because among the men the old skills remain respected, and Scratchy is "a wonder with a gun."

While Scratchy and the bride represent the opposing forces of old and new, the marshal and the other town residents exemplify the groups intermediate to the vanishing frontier and the approaching civilization. These are the

Sentence Variety

Paragraphs should contain different sentence types. Too many of any particular type of sentence will create boring writing. However, do not worry about writing a variety of different sentence types when you write the first draft. Those are inserted during the revision process.

Conclusion

The concluding paragraph summarizes the observations made in the essay.

ordinary, hard-working men who brought the law and established order to the wildlands subdued by men like Scratchy. Specifically, the marshal symbolizes change. Because the marshal did not consult the town about his intent to marry, town residents are neither aware nor prepared for the changes in the marshal and, therefore, for the town that lie ahead. In this manner, Crane suggests that the course of history is neither determined nor prevented by any one person or group.

The simple frontier life giving way to a more advanced and complex civilization is symbolized by Scratchy's acquiescence to the marshal's bride. To Scratchy, Jack Potter seems less masculine with the bride. Even though, according to the code of the West, Scratchy can challenge and fight the marshal, man to man, gun to gun, Scratchy is defenseless against the power of progress. Even Scratchy's primitive code will not permit gunning down an unarmed man in front of his bride. Guns cannot prevent the inexorable course of history. With the arrival of the bride, Yellow Sky, the West, is maturing, and Scratchy, still a child, has no role to play. As Scratchy turns and dejectedly trudges away from the newlyweds, his boot heels leave deep imprints in the sand, illustrating that the old West will soon become only memories. Before long, gusts of wind blowing in from the hot prairie will shift the grains of sand; the frontiersmen, along with their ideals, their values, and their code will have vanished.

EXERCISE 5.3

Read the following literary analysis essay "From Inside the Cage" by Stefanie Oudiz, and compare it with "A Historic Day in Yellow Sky" by Sandra Ewers. Whereas Ewers relies on her own close reading of the story along with previously acquired knowledge about the history of the Western frontier, Oudiz combines her close reading and literary research about Maya Angelou and the historical context of *I Know Why the Caged Bird Sings* to gather evidence to support her thesis and supporting points. Whereas Ewers combines an analytic and historical critical approach, Oudiz relies more on a combination of biographical, historical, and feminist critical perspectives.

Stefanie Oudiz

Professor Sessano

Eng 1B

26 November 2002

From Inside the Cage

"I'm a Woman, Phenomenally. Phenomenal Woman, that's me." —Maya Angelou

In the year 1970, the cultural framework constructed during the 200 years since the inception of the United States of America was crumbling in a vortex of social unrest and protest. Two of the strongest forces for change in this time were the Civil Rights Movement and the Women's Rights or Feminist movement. Although neither of these movements has truly ended or achieved all of its goals, both did gain enough momentum to change the way African Americans and women were viewed, represented, and treated, and each group was thereafter allotted more opportunities in society. However, despite that these movements were occurring at relatively the same time, they generally did not collaborate. Illustrating this gap is the criticism that the Civil Rights Movement received for being mostly led by men and often exclusive of black women; meanwhile, the Feminist movement was also criticized because many perceived it to have only addressed the concerns of middle-class white women. Consequently, many black women of the time went unheard in the midst of the battlefield that the country had become.

It is therefore expected that when Maya Angelou published the first volume of her autobiography, <u>I Know Why the Caged Bird Sings</u>, in that year, it was interpreted by many as a unifying cry of black women across the country. Comparable to Richard Wright's <u>Black Boy</u>, it became, and still is, used as a voice for the idea of a common black female experience. Whether Angelou intended <u>Caged Bird</u> to be a universal or personal statement, the book clearly presents how being both black and female did uniquely shape her experience as a child.

Angelou introduces her life to the reader with a depiction of her concept of beauty as applied to herself as a black girl living in the South. It is the evolution of this opinion on her appearance that reflects Marguerite Johnson's (Angelou's childhood name) growing perception of what it means to be a black woman. In the 1930s South, and traditionally in all Western culture, beauty was considered to be the essence of true womanhood. Therefore, critic Sidonie Smith points out, being African American in Stamps, Arkansas, means being automatically born without the capacity for full womanhood because being beautiful and being white are inseparable. Marguerite's fantasy of being white is a haunting portrayal of this fact: "I was going to look like one of the sweet little white girls who were everybody's dream of what was right with the world [. . .]. Wouldn't they be surprised when one day I woke out of my black ugly dream, and my real hair, which was long and blond, would take the place of the kinky mass that Momma wouldn't let me straighten? My light-blue eyes would hypnotize them" (Angelou 1-2). Despite that Marguerite endures taunts from other black children about her looks, her self-image is rooted in the notion that the ideal is white and, consequently, nothing that resembles herself. Marguerite's perception of beauty is indicated to have evolved years later when she watches a Kay Francis film and thinks to herself that the white actress not only resembles her mother, but is not as beautiful as her mother. Because Marguerite realizes this she is also able to withstand the cruel jokes that the white audience members make about the black chauffeur of the movie; Marguerite thus finds for herself the definition of beauty regardless of any racial barriers.

Surrounding Marguerite and having perhaps the most influence on her are the other black women in her life, beginning with her grandmother Annie Henderson, or "Momma." Critic Sondra O'Neale emphasizes Annie's defiance of the stereotyped powerless Black woman confined to the kitchen of a white woman as a so-called "Mammy" by being a strong member of her community that both blacks and whites depend upon (28). Her ability to maintain such a solid position across the race barriers of her segregated Southern town of Stamps, Arkansas, would not be the result of just her financial success without the distinct aura of dignity that emanates from her. Marguerite observes the powerful force behind this quality of her grandmother when Momma firmly resists retaliation to the insults of an impudent group of "powhitetrash" girls. "How long could Momma hold out? What new indignity would they subject her to? [. . .] Momma never turned her head or unfolded her arms, but she stopped singing and said, ''Bye, Miz Helen, 'bye, Miz Ruth, 'bye, Miz Eloise [. . .].' Whatever the contest had been out front, I knew Momma had won" (Angelou 26-27). After the grime-covered powhitetrash girls leave without acknowledging Annie in return with a respectful "Mrs.," Annie orders Marguerite to go wash her face in order to, according to critic Pierre Walker, maintain "personal dignity through the symbolic importance of cleanliness and politeness." Correspondingly, an episode of chastising Marguerite's blasphemous use of the phrase "by the way" proves Annie's conviction to righteousness in action. "When Bailey tried to interpret the words with: 'Whitefolks use "by the way" to mean while we're on the subject.' Momma reminded us that 'Whitefolks' mouths were most in general loose and their words were an abomination before Christ" (Angelou 86-87). Walker compares this scene with the powhitetrash scene in how Annie demonstrates a superior attention to proper detail that is firm in the face of any assumptions of black inferiority.

Representing different yet equally important aspects of the black female experience is Marguerite's mother, Vivian Baxter. Whereas Critic Sheri Metzger proclaims Vivian to have "had little impact on her daughter's life," the profound lessons in being a black woman that are taught to Maya by her mother prove this statement wrong. In Angelou's description of Vivian, she uses a popular saying of the time that she heard often from her mother: "Sympathy is next to 'shit' in the dictionary, and I can't even read" (Angelou 175).

Although Vivian is kind, she is steadfast in the ideal of self-reliance and

makes it clear to Marguerite that every person has full responsibility for

his or her own life. This means that although she herself may be an illiterate

black woman, she is capable of standing on her own without accepting handouts

or standing in soup kitchen lines despite the stereotypes, points out O'Neale

(25-27). While Maya is living with her mother in St. Louis, she observes that

although her mother is a trained nurse, she does not rely on that profession

because it does not fit her lifestyle and is capable of making a living instead

by cutting poker games. No matter what, "Mother was competent in providing

for us" (Angelou 58). Vivian's character is thus the representative of the

blues/street culture of the time that required a sense of what O'Neale calls

"urban survival" (27). Marguerite's mother forcefully contradicts the

traditional roles of black women, as Angelou explains, "She wouldn't bust suds

for anybody nor be anyone's kitchen bitch. The good lord gave her a mind and

she intended to use it" (Angelou 175). As a black woman, she also demonstrates

her ability to hold power and control in her relationships with men, critic

George Kent observes. Vivian's boyfriend Mr. Freeman demonstrates this point

with a personality that revolved around Vivian's mere presence. Vivian's

essence as that of a non-compliant woman is what O'Neale attributes to being

the "unsung spirit" in the progress of blacks in the United States (O'Neale

31).

The strength in black womanhood that Marguerite has learned from her

grandmother and mother faces its greatest challenge when she is raped by Mr.

Freeman. "The act of rape on an eight-year-old body is a matter of the needle

giving because the camel can't. The child gives, because the body can, and

the mind of the violator cannot" (Angelou 65). It is the ensuing silence that

Marguerite operates under throughout the next five years that reveals her

conflict in healing as a black girl. Silence in her case speaks loudly because it is a principal element in the common cultural reactions to the abuse of women and to racism. When the Civil Rights Movement and Feminists spoke out against these atrocities of society, they named silence as a perpetuating force in the problems. In Marguerite's case, guilt for what has happened propels her into such a state of fear that her words are poisonous to all those around her. Yet Metzger explains that this silence did not begin with the rape but rather with Maya's upbringing; Annie had taught her to avoid speaking with white people because it was a risk to her life as a girl of color. This custom is secured in Marguerite's demeanor by Mr. Freeman when he threatens her life and the life of her brother should she tell anyone of his sexual abuse. The tradition of silence in her life has fastened Maya in the idea that silence is a means of survival. It provides the same false sense of protection that Civil Rights and women's activists meant to reveal as being ultimately detrimental. Essentially, silence is a means for any victim to preserve what little they are left with after the attack rather than risk greater assault when they try to retrieve what has been taken by their perpetrators. Maya's feelings of guilt give her silence a second role as punishment. She accepts Mr. Freeman's lawyer's insistence that she incited the rape and is bombarded with the fear that everyone around her can see the figurative stains she bears. Because Marguerite's only experience with sex is as a loveless act of one person's will over another, she then projects this mode onto her later sexual experiences, as many rape victims do. She views her first consensual intercourse as a means of proving her heterosexuality and thereupon uses a boy solely for his body just as Mr. Freeman had used her. Likewise, Angelou later becomes a prostitute in the second volume of her autobiography, Gather Together in My Name. The effects of rape on Angelou's life are like the branches of mold permeating through a loaf of bread and spoiling it. Moreover, her resistance to its damage is the same effort that she is constantly making against the dangerous blade of racism and sexism.

Corresponding to Marguerite's experiences with other African Americans are her encounters with whites that are just as consequential to her developing sense of race. Angelou explains in her prologue, "If growing up is painful for the Southern black girl, being aware of her displacement is the rust on the razor that threatens the throat. It is an unnecessary insult" (Angelou 3). When a white ex-sheriff arrives at Marguerite's home in Stamps to warn of a possible Klan raid, Angelou describes her hatred at the time as directed at the sheriff, not the terrorizing Klan members. "His confidence that my uncle and every other black man who heard of the Klan's coming ride would scurry under their houses to hide in chicken droppings was too humiliating to hear" (14). What frustrates and angers Marguerite is that this white man rides up gallantly on his horse to distribute a charitable warning as if her uncle and the other members of their community were helpless victims devoid of dignity and trembling under white supremacy. Marguerite is fully aware of her subhuman consideration by whites and eventually acts out against it while working in the kitchen of a white woman named Mrs. Cullinan. Because Mrs. Cullinan decides to take the liberty of addressing Marguerite by "Mary" to accommodate her own convenience, Marguerite defiantly breaks a dish of Mrs. Cullinan's heirloom china, provoking Mrs. Cullinan to shout her name as "Margaret." According to critic Edward Eller, this would be called an act of the "courage to be human." Critic Sidonie Smith interprets that the act "is assuming the consciousness of rebellion as the stance necessary for preserving her individuality and affirming her self-worth." Angelou's outlook on racial oppression evolves over the course of the novel from anger to action as she becomes capable of expressing her right to be treated as a human being.

Nearly every scene in Maya Angelou's childhood as depicted in I Know Why the Caged Bird Sings is somehow affected by her membership to black womanhood, which many believe has given her a strong voice for overcoming the obstacles that it brings. Sidonie Smith resolved in her essay "The Song of a Caged Bird: Maya Angelou's Quest after Self-Acceptance" that the black American girl of Angelou's book "has succeeded in freeing herself from the natural and social bars imprisoning her." But when asked in an interview how she escaped this "cage," Angelou replied, "How the hell do you know I did escape" (McMurray)? According to Carol Franks in <u>Masterpieces of Women's Literature</u>, Angelou asserts that her work is about survival (282). Just because Angelou has survived does not mean that the rusted razor is not still held to her neck and the necks of all other black women. Throughout all of the alleged universal and personal experiences that Angelou has described, she does not exalt her ability to break free of the chains of oppression; she offers her account of the feat of merely living, and surviving, inside the cage.

Works Cited

Angelous, Maya. <u>I Know Why the Caged Bird Sings</u>. New York: Bantam Books, 1971.

Eller, Edward E. "Critical Essay on <u>I know Why the Caged Bird Sings</u>." <u>Nonfiction Classics for Students</u> Vol 2. <u>Literature Resource Center</u>. Gale Group Databases. American River College Lib., Sacramento, CA. 1 Nov. 2002 <http://www.infotrac.galegroup.com>.

Franks, Carol. "I Know Why the Caged Bird Sings." <u>Masterpieces of Women's Literature</u>. Ed. Frank N. Magill. New York: Harper, 1996. 282-284.

Kent, George E. "Maya Angelou's <u>I know Why the Caged Bird Sings</u> and Black Autobiographical Tradition." <u>Kansas Quarterly</u> 3 (Summer 1975): 72-78. <u>Literature Resource Center</u>. Gale Group Databases. American River College Lib., Sacramento, CA. 31 October, 2002 <http://www.infotrac.galegroup.com>.

McMurry, Myra K. "Role Playing as art in Maya Angelou's <u>Caged Bird</u>." <u>South Atlantic Bulletin</u> 2, (May 1976): 106-111. <u>Literature Resource Center</u>. Gale Group Databases. American River College Lib., Sacramento, CA. 1 Nov. 2002 <http://www.infotrac.galegroup.com>.

Metzger, Sheri E. "Critical Essay on <u>I Know Why the Caged Bird Sings</u>." <u>Nonfiction Classics for Students</u> Vol II. Gale Group Databases. American River College Lib., Sacramento, CA. 1 Nov. 2002 <http://www.infotrac.galegroup.com>.

O'Neale, Sondra. "Reconstruction of the Composite Self: New Images of Black Women in Maya Angelou's Continuing Autobiography." <u>Black Women Writers 1950-1980</u>. Ed. Mari Evans. New York: Anchor Books, 1984. 25-35.

Smith, Sidonie Ann. "The Song of a Caged Bird: Maya Angelou's Quest after Self-Acceptance." <u>The Southern Humanities Review</u> (Fall 1973): 365-375. <u>Literature Resource Center</u>. Gale Group Databases. American River College Lib., Sacramento, CA. 31 Oct. 2002 <http://www.infotrac.galegroup.com>.

Walker, Pierre A. "Racial Protest, Identity, Words, and Form in Maya Angelou's
I Know Why the Caged Bird Sings." _College Literature_ Vol. 22 No. 3 (1995):
91-105. _Literature Resource Center_. Gale Group Databases. American River
College Lib., Sacramento, CA. 31 Oct., 2002 <http://
www.infotrac.galegroup.com>.

EXERCISE 5.4

Read the literary work approved in Exercise 5.1.

Work Selected:_____

LESSON FOUR: *Writing the Literary Analysis Essay*

After studying the samples, you should now be ready to write your own literary analysis essay. As with all other essays you write, following a deliberate step-by-step procedure will produce a well-written paper with a minimum of frustration. The following approach is suggested:

After selecting and reading a literary work:
1. Identify some aspect of the work you want to examine. (This is your topic.)
2. Develop a thesis sentence.
3. List the points you want to present as evidence.
4. Gather your evidence, conducting research if necessary.
5. Plan how you will arrange your evidence.
6. Develop an outline.
7. Write your essay, documenting any research included.
8. Revise, revise, and revise until your essay represents your best effort.
9. Collect all of your work in a Project Folder.

Identify a Topic for Examination

The first step in developing any essay, of course, is to identify the topic about which you plan to write. As always, be certain your topic is one that you can develop into an essay that is worthy of your effort. Whatever you do, do not choose a topic merely because it sounds easy or because you think your instructor is interested in it. The following are topics you might consider if you were preparing to write an essay on "The Bride Comes to Yellow Sky."

Sample topics:
1. Jack Potter's extraordinary crime
2. Why Potter and his bride appear ridiculous to others on the train
3. Crane's use of color in the story
4. How Crane uses Scratchy Wilson to make a point
5. Crane's use of minor characters to develop Potter's character
6. The role of time in the story
7. The significance of setting in the story
8. Crane's use of characters and objects as symbols (This topic is the one used by the author of the essay, "A Historic Day in Yellow Sky.")

EXERCISE 5.5

Select a topic from the literary work approved in Exercise 5.1.

Topic Chosen:_____

Develop a Thesis

As with every essay you write, developing a thesis sentence is crucial in a literary analysis essay. (If you need to review thesis development, turn back to Chapter One.) Although a literary analysis is not an argument, the thesis statement is similar to one in an argument because in your thesis you must present your readers with a claim about the literary work, or interpretation of it, that they may not understand initially or one with which they may disagree. Then in the body of your literary analysis essay you must present evidence to support your thesis idea.

For this essay, simply convert the topic that you chose in Exercise 5.5 into a working thesis sentence. At the time you develop the outline for your essay, you will write a refined thesis sentence. The best way to do this is to begin by asking a "thesis question." Although we can only speculate about how the authors of the two sample essays in this chapter developed their thesis sentences, we can use them as examples for you to follow.

Examples

Topic:	Crane's use of characters and objects as symbols
Question:	What is Crane's point in using characters and objects as symbols?
Working thesis:	Crane presents characters and objects as symbols.

Topic:	The influence of being black and female on Angelou's childhood.
Question:	How did being black and female influence Angelou's childhood?
Working thesis:	*I Know How the Caged Bird Sings* shows the influence of being black and female on Angelou's childhood.

EXERCISE 5.6

Develop the topic you wrote for Exercise 5.5 into a working thesis, and copy it below:

_____

_____

_____

Have your thesis sentence checked.

List the Points That You Want to Present as Evidence

After writing your thesis sentence, you will need to make a list of the points that you want to present as evidence in order to persuade your readers that your essay is sound. These points can then be developed into topic sentences for the body paragraphs.

Examples

Crane's use of objects and people as symbols:

1. The train represents the East.
2. The marshal represents forces of change.
3. The bride represents civilization.
4. The townspeople represent an intermediate society.
5. Scratchy represents the frontier.
6. The showdown represents the frontier giving way to civilized life.

Childhood influences on Angelou as the result of being black and female:

1. Her concept of beauty
2. Influential black women in her life–her grandmother
3. The influence of her mother
4. How Angelou's strength was challenged when she was raped
5. The influence of whites on Angelou

Arranging Your Evidence

Before your write your outline, give some consideration to the order in which you will arrange your evidence. What you should strive for is a chain of evidence that unfolds in some logical order. You may use **chronological order** that begins with the event that occurs earliest in the work being analyzed and progresses event by event to the last. You may use **comparison or contrast order**, for example, if you are comparing two works or different characters in a story. Or you may use **order of importance**, beginning with the least important point and progressing to the most important. **General to specific order** is another way to arrange your evidence, progressing from broad concepts, historical or biographical background, for instance, to more specific points closely linked to specific passages in the work. In considering how to arrange your evidence, review your thesis and imagine how you might organize the body of your essay and then choose an organizational pattern that seems appropriate.

EXERCISE 5.7

In what order will you arrange your evidence?_____

Gather Your Evidence–Supporting Your Points

The best evidence with which to support your points is specific references to or quotations from the text of the story, novel, play, or poem you are analyzing. Each point presented as evidence will need to be developed through explanation and examples. Specific details can be **summarized** as evidence. Notice the three-step pattern followed in the example that follows. 1) The point is made in the topic sentence. 2) The point is explained further. 3) Specific details summarized from the story are used as an example.

Example

1) Described by the town bartender as "kind of simple," Scratchy Wilson represents what remains in the town of the life and values of the old frontier. 2) Requiring sturdy men and offering only simple food, simple clothing and simple shelter, the life of the early West was severe and arduous. 3) Scratchy's clothes symbolically convey that the encroachment of the East upon the West has been gradual. Entirely unsuitable in the wilderness, the flannel shirt he now wears was sewn in a New York ghetto. Furthermore, Scratchy sports a pair of red-topped boots with gilded imprints that would have made him the object of contemptuous humor in previous times.

Lines, phrases, and passages **quoted** from the work are often used as supporting examples in literary analysis essays. One way to collect useful quotations is to review the work rapidly, looking for passages that relate to the various points you plan to make and then copying them on note cards, on paper, or on your computer. (Be sure to note the exact page of each citation in parentheses at the end of each citation as soon as you write it down because it may be difficult to relocate it later.)

In the *MLA* style, which you should use for this essay, up to four typed lines from a story or novel can be included in a paragraph without indenting the quotation. These short quotations must be set off with quotation marks, and the page number must be placed at the end with a period immediately after the parentheses.

Example

> Margurite's mother forcefully contradicts the traditional roles of black women, as Angelou explains, "She wouldn't bust suds for anybody nor be anyone's kitchen bitch. The good lord gave her a mind and she intended to use it." (Angelou 175).

When quoting five or more typed lines, you must "block" the quote, indenting each line one inch. Quotation marks are not used in block quotes. (Review page 152 in Chapter Three for details about the block style.) One to three lines of poetry can be included without indenting them, setting them off with quotation marks, and using slash marks (/) to separate the lines of poetry. When quoting four or more lines of poetry, indent them in the block style. Dialogue from a play is quoted in the block style.

Conduct Research—Optional

The literary analysis essay is not a research paper; therefore, you do not need to use secondary sources. (Note: Your instructor may not allow you to use any research information for this essay, believing that your interpretation should be entirely your own.) If, however, you are unsure of yourself and do not understand the work well enough to write a literary analysis even though you have read the work several times and discussed it with others, you may decide to do some research, either in the library or online.

ONLINE RESEARCH

If you look online for information that will help you gain a deeper understanding of your work, you must be careful to locate information that is reputable. If you are not careful, you may encounter suspect interpretations of the work by people not trained to read literature. If, for example, you conduct a *Google.com* search for sources about J. D. Salinger's novel *The Catcher in the Rye*, you will encounter the top ten web sites out of 84,800 possible sites. If you search for William Shakespeare's play *Hamlet*, you will find 83,400 sites. With so many web sites available, you must choose your sources carefully, and you must also avoid the temptation to "lift" one of the essays about your work that you might find posted online. That would be plagiarism. You can study someone else's essay and refer to it, giving proper credit to your source, but ultimately you must write your own original literary analysis essay no matter how much research you do.

To avoid encountering so many sources, you can narrow your search, using your topic as a guide. For instance, you could search for "symbols and *Catcher in the Rye*" or "setting and John Steinbeck's *Grapes of Wrath*."

ONLINE ASSISTANCE

Valuable assistance, both about the elements of literature, and how to write essays about literature can be obtained from many web sites. Other online sources are available only through your library.

Examples

Writing About Literature:
http://owl.english.purdue.edu/handouts/general/gl_lit.html

Writing Papers of Literary Analysis:
http://unix.cc.wmich.edu/~cooneys/tchg/lit/adv/lit.papers.html

Writing About Prose:
http://uwc.tamu.edu/handouts/writing/prose.html

Writing Essays About Literature:
http://www.citadel.edu/citadel/otherserv/wctr/writinglit.html

Literary Analysis Guide:
http://www.goshen.edu/english/litanalysis.html

Writing About Fiction:
http://owl.english.purdue.edu/handouts/general/gl~fiction.html

The Academy of American Poets:
http://www.poets.org/index.cfm

Favorite Poem Project:
http://www.favoritepoem.org/

Writing About Poetry (Hamilton College):
http://www.hamilton.edu/academic/Resource/WC/WwritingaboutPoetry.htm

Questions to Ask of Any Poem:
http://www.gmu.edu/departments/writingcenter/handouts/poetry.html

Reading Poetry (U Wisconsin-Madison):
http://www.wisc.edu/writing/Handbook/ReadingPoetry.html

Elements of Drama:
http://www.csustan.edu/english/reuben/pal/append/axh.html

Writing About Film (George Mason U):
http://www.gmu.edu/departmentgs/writingcenter/handouts/film.html

LIBRARY RESEARCH

In the library you can begin your research by using the online public access catalog. If you are researching a major literary work or classic, you can look up the author's name in the online catalog or look up the title of the work to see if any books about the work are available. If, however, you are researching a less known work or a short story or poem, you will need to consult one or more of the specialized literary books and indexes which are often located in the Reference Department. Your library may have some of the following:

General Literary Sources

Beacham's Encyclopedia of Popular Fiction
Chicano Literature: a Reference Guide
Literature and Its Times: Profiles of 300 Notable Literary Works and the Historical Events

That Influenced Them

Masterplots: 2010 Plot Stories & Essays from the World's Fine Literature

Masterplots II (American Fiction Series)

Masterplots II (Short Story Series)

Oxford Companion to African American Literature

World Literature and Its Times: Profiles of Notable Literary Works and the Historical Events That Influenced Them

Biographical Sources

African American Writers
American Women Writers: From Colonial Times to the Present
American Writers
British Writers
Contemporary Authors
European Writers
Latin American Writers
Something About the Author

Literary Criticism Sources

Contemporary Literary Criticism
Drama Criticism
Magill's Critical Survey of Drama (English)
Magill's Critical Survey of Poetry (English)
Poetry Criticism
Shakespearean Criticism
Short Story Criticism
Twentieth Century Literary Criticism

Literary Criticism Indexes

Novel:

American Novel
Contemporary Novel
Continental Novel
English Novel Explication

Short Story:

American Short Fiction Criticism and Scholarship, 1959–1977
Short Fiction Criticism
Twentieth Century Short Story Explication

Poetry:

American and British Poetry
English Poetry: 1900–1950
Index to Criticisms of British and American Poetry

Drama:

American Drama Criticism
Drama Criticism
Modern Drama

If you find helpful sources which you use in your essay, either in direct quotations or ideas that you summarize, you must be certain to give credit to your sources by documenting them so that you are not plagiarizing. Use the *MLA* style with lead ins., internal documentation, and a Works Cited page. Collect all of your notes, photocopies, and Internet downloads, and place them in the Project Folder for this assignment.

EXERCISE 5.8

Conduct any online or library research necessary to help you understand the work you are analyzing or how to write a literary analysis essay. Collect all of the research in your Project Folder.

Developing an Outline

After developing the thesis and gathering your evidence, write an outline for your essay. An outline should become as normal a part of your writing procedure as choosing a topic and writing a thesis. A basic thesis-topic sentence outline may be adequate for you, but you can also use an elaborate outline format such as the one used by the author of the essay on "Yellow Sky" (see below). The advantage of the more elaborate outline is that it makes it easier to develop the outline into an essay.

1. Repeat the title of your essay at the top of the page.
2. Double-space and write your thesis. Precede your thesis sentence with the word "Thesis," followed by a colon.
3. Skip three spaces after the thesis and write your topic sentence outline: a consecutively numbered list of all the topic sentences that appear in the body of your essay. (Double-space.)

OR

You may use a more elaborate outline that shows the major ideas used in each paragraph to support the topic sentence. Many students find that the more complete outline, such as the one below, makes the essay easier to write. (Double-space before each new topic sentence.)

A Historic Day in Yellow Sky

Thesis: Crane's intent is not to draw vivid characterizations but to present objects and characters as symbols with larger meanings.

I. The train is the first symbol of the East presented in the story.
   A. The elaborate interior of the parlor car expresses the greater complexity of the advancing culture.
   B. The superior attitude of the porter and other passengers implies the simplicity of Western ways.
   C. The westward movement of the train symbolizes the accelerating force of the advancing culture.

II. The bride is a sexual metaphor for the ideals and principles of Eastern society.
   A. Women are viewed as more complex.
   B. Feminine values will replace masculine values.
      1. Women value peace.
      2. Women do not value conflict.
   C. The marriage depicts the complex future of the town.
      1. Children will soon appear.

     2. Schools, churches, and libraries will follow.

    D. The lives of all the men will change.

III. Scratchy Wilson represents the simple life and values of the frontier life.

    A. The frontier is severe; the men are tough.

    B. Scratchy's clothes say the encroachment of the East upon the West has been gradual.

        1. The flannel shirt would have been impractical in the wilderness.

        2. The red-topped boots would have been ridiculed.

    C. Scratchy does not fit into the transitional progress of town life.

        1. He is tolerated because old ways are still valued.

        2. His skill with a gun is respected.

IV. The marshal represents the groups intermediate to the frontier and the approaching Eastern societies.

    A. These men tamed the land conquered by men like Scratchy.

    B. The marshal is the symbol of change to Yellow Sky.

    C. The marshal does not advise the town of his intent to marry; therefore, they are unaware of and cannot be prepared for the changes.

    D. The course of life and the sweep of history is fate.

V. Simple frontier life giving way to a more advanced culture is symbolized by Scratchy acquiescing to the bride.

    A. Scratchy cannot fight against the power of progress.

    B. Yellow Sky is becoming a grown-up town.

    C. The boot tracks in the sand symbolize the fading away of the old West.

EXERCISE 5.9

Write an outline for the thesis you wrote in Exercise 5.6.

_____

_____

_____

_____

_____

_____

_____

_____

_____

_____

_____

_____

_____

_____

_____

_____

_____

_____

_____

_____

_____

_____

Have your worked approved, and place your outline in your Project Folder.

Writing the Essay

Once you have completed the other steps, writing the literary analysis essay is not difficult. In fact, at this point little more than an expansion of your outline is required. One final note of caution should be sounded, however; do not expect to go from outline to final draft in one swift step. Begin by writing a preliminary draft. Writing the first draft gives you an opportunity to revise extensively. Also, if you have used information from other sources, you must insert documentation in the first draft, using lead-ins and parenthetical references, and compile your Works Cited. Then, when your preliminary draft is written, corrected, and revised, you are ready to write the final document.

Reminders:

1. While the occasional use of first person is acceptable, the use of third person is preferable.
2. With literary subjects, you should use the present tense.

Use the sample student essays from this chapter for models of what your completed essay should look like.

EXERCISE 5.10

Write the first draft of your literary analysis essay. After receiving feedback about its strengths and weaknesses, make revisions, and place it in your Project Folder.

EXERCISE 5.11

After you write the final draft of your literary analysis, proofread it one more time to discover and correct any errors. Place your final document in your Project Folder.

Project Folder

Include the following work in your Project Folder (in the order listed):

1. Final document (on top)
2. Outline
3. First draft
4. Copy of poem or short story (if required)
5. Research materials (on bottom)

6

The Investigative Essay

Objectives

When you have completed this chapter, you will have

1. selected a problem to investigate.
2. conducted secondary research.
3. engaged in primary research, including interviews.
2. conducted secondary research.
4. written a thesis sentence and outline.
5. drafted a 1,250-1,500 word investigative essay.
6. received feedback and revised the essay.
7. produced the final document in the required format.
8. compiled a Project Folder.

The Investigative Essay 6

An investigative essay explores a problem in depth and provides plausible solutions. At first glance the investigative essay may appear similar to the library research essay because it requires research and includes documentation and a Works Cited page. But the two essays are dissimilar in some important ways. As you proceed through this chapter, these differences will become quite apparent.

One of the advantages of writing this popular kind of essay is the open-ended nature of the investigative assignment. It gives you the freedom to do something different that may include a personal involvement in a subject that matters to you. In addition to developing your own topic, the investigative essay assignment provides you with the opportunity to gather information without spending nearly as much time on the Internet and in the library as you would with a research essay. You will substitute primary research for some of the secondary research you would do for a research essay. The depth of your investigative research probe will determine the success of your essay. And this means **primary research**. Primary research is the kind you do personally: for example, experiments you perform in science and psychology laboratories, surveys, on-the-scene reporting, or reading original documents, such as letters and memos. **Secondary research**, by contrast, refers to Internet and library investigation; reading reports, books, periodicals, newspapers, and pamphlets; and viewing documentary films. Both primary and secondary sources are valid; however, for essays on local, current topics, primary sources are more powerful persuaders than secondary sources. Therefore, as a general rule, if both primary and secondary sources are available, you should include both in the preparation of your investigative essay.

The culminating step after researching a problem is to write an essay. For example, in your sociology class you might be assigned to write a term paper discussing the problems of single parenting. At work you might be assigned to a team that will write a report recommending a solution to a product quality problem. In either situation you should be able to write a report that defines a particular problem, presents several solutions, discusses and evaluates them, promotes the best one, and makes recommendations for implementing them. Furthermore, you should be able to write by yourself, with a co-writer, or on a writing team.

LESSON ONE—*Identify a Problem*

Choosing a good topic for the investigative essay is a challenge; however, it is easier than you might first imagine. For example, your regional newspaper is full of local problems begging for solutions. The Internet is another good source of problems to be researched. You might try one of the online indexes such as *Google Web Directory*. You might, for instance, try the "Society—Terrorism" category just to see how many potential topics are available.

Examples

Biological and Chemical Terrorism
Cyber Terrorism
Environmental Terrorism
Nuclear Terrorism
Suicide Terrorism
Terrorist Organizations
US Domestic Terrorism

With the Internet your problem isn't finding problems to research, it's actually choosing just one from the many that are available.

You may discover a problem that is sufficiently narrowed right from the beginning. More likely, though, you will first decide upon a general subject area and then discover within it the topic for your investigation. To work your way from a problem area to the specific problem you will investigate, use one of the techniques you have learned for narrowing subjects:

Brainstorming
Freewriting
Clustering
Analytical Questioning
Focused Questioning

Begin by locating a problem area that interests you, for example, intellectual property. Then divide that problem area into more specific topics.

Example

Brainstorming List

copyrights
plagiarism
DVD encryption
music freedom
Napster and MP3 sharing
open sources–computers
piracy
patents
free access
boycotts
royalties
file servers

Next, carefully consider whether the problem is sufficiently narrowed to be suitable for a 1,250-1,500 word paper. Again, employ one of the prewriting discovery techniques.

Example

Focused Questions

Subject: Terrorism

Narrowed topic: How to prevent nuclear terrorism

Are nuclear reactors sufficiently protected?

Can terrorists build nuclear weapons?

Are nuclear weapons and materials adequately protected from theft?

How dangerous are "dirty bombs?"

What can we do?

Considerations When You Are Identifying a Problem

1. Select a problem that really interests you.
2. Choose a problem that will also be of interest to whoever will be reading your essay.
3. Select a controversial topic or one with several possible solutions.
4. As an alternative, think about the possibility of investigating a problem in your workplace.
5. Identify a problem that will allow you to conduct both primary and secondary research.
6. Make certain that it is feasible to conduct whatever primary research will be needed.
7. Select a problem that can be investigated within the time frame available.
8. If you will be working with a co-writer or on a project team, make certain that you are all in agreement on the choice of topics.

EXERCISE 6.1

Using the prewriting techniques that work for you, identify a problem area that interests you, and within it identify the topic that you will investigate for your essay. (Your instructor may want to see your prewriting exercises.) Write your final topic in the space below.

Final topic:_____

_____

Have your topic approved.

LESSON TWO—Secondary Research

After identifying a problem, the next step in the planning phase is to conduct secondary research. To gather background information during your secondary research, you should use your library just as you would for any research project. Begin by searching a variety of sources: magazines, newspapers, books, professional journals, reference books, pamphlet file materials, recordings and video cassettes, CD-ROMs, electronic information services and databases. If your library has electronic indexes, begin with those before exploring other sources such as the pamphlet file and reference books. If the technology for electronic searching is available, instruct the computer to search for and print a list of references on your narrowed topic. Then highlight the references listed that look worthwhile or fill out a working bibliography card for each reference that you intend to locate and read. The reference librarians can be of enormous assistance at this stage of your investigation.

You might prefer to start your secondary research on the Internet. While searching for a topic on the Internet, you may have already discovered some promising web sites. Conduct the same kind of systematic search you did while gathering material for your library research essay, seeking out differing viewpoints and evaluating your sources carefully. As with all your other essays, collect all of your printouts in a Project Folder.

When you have located at least fifteen references and written a working bibliography listing for each, begin reading your sources and taking notes. Unlike a research essay, you do not need to take notes on a large number of sources. In fact, you may need only half as many. At this point, you should be certain that you have a sufficient number of sources; that is, do you have enough sources to be assured of a well-documented essay? The investigative essay, like the research essay, should contain a minimum of **ten** sources of information. However, the investigative essay may need only five secondary sources. The other five sources may come from your primary research.

EXERCISE 6.2

Prepare at least fifteen working bibliography listings for the most promising secondary sources for your investigative essay. (Have your working bibliography listings approved.)

EXERCISE 6.3

Using your working bibliography, find and read enough sources to develop an understanding of the topic. Take notes on the problem and the possible solutions you discover in your reading. Have your notes approved, and place them in your Project Folder.

LESSON THREE—*Primary Research Planning*

When you have finished taking notes on your secondary sources, you should understand the subject thoroughly enough to become involved personally. You should have a general understanding of the problem and any solutions that have been proposed by others. If you are working on a local problem, your secondary research should have enabled you to put the problem into perspective.

Primary research, the investigation of an issue firsthand, can be conducted in a number of ways. You may choose to conduct and interview, distribute a survey, organize a focus group, examine original documents, view picture evidence, conduct a site visit, or record an event on video or digital camera.

Interviews

The most commonly used method of conducting primary research is to talk to people individually, interviewing them about the problem you have identified. To be an effective interviewer, you will need to plan ahead, discovering whom you might interview, setting up appointments, and deciding what to ask them. This will require you to select carefully those who can give you the most information about your topic.

Choosing People to Interview

Deciding whom to interview is your first step. Who might be willing to talk to you, who can help you better understand the nature of the problem, its possible consequences, and ways of solving the problem? Your first feeling, understandably, might be that you don't know anyone who can help you. The best thing to do is to start asking people you know if they know anyone who could speak knowledgeably about the problem you are investigating. Ask your instructors, relatives, classmates, friends, relatives, and co-workers. Study local news articles on your topic carefully, looking for the names of people you might interview, including the reporter who wrote the article. Often, too, someone you interview will refer you to someone else, even giving that person a call to help set up an appointment. As one lead follows another, you will find more and more potential sources. Look for those people who would be most likely to be involved with the problem you are investigating. Use good judgment, looking for people to interview who can speak with authority on the topic either because of the work they do or because of relevant personal experience. Suppose you were investigating teenage marriage as a problem. The following mix of people would provide you with information from different viewpoints:

1. a school counselor
2. a psychology instructor
3. an employee at a local family planning center
4. a parent of a married teenager
5. married teenagers
6. an author on the subject
7. a member of the clergy
8. an anthropologist
9. a social historian

EXERCISE 6.4

List five or six people you would like to interview as primary sources for your essay. (Add names to your list as new leads develop.)

	Name	Role/Position	Telephone Number
1.			
2.			
3.			
4.			
5.			
6.			

Have your list reviewed.

Writing the Questions

After deciding who can give you the information you need, you are ready to begin developing your questions. You need to investigate the seriousness of the problem locally and determine what is being done—or what could be done—to resolve it. Before you interview anyone, you should have six to ten carefully developed questions.

Your questions must elicit thoughtful responses. That is, make certain the person you interview cannot answer your questions with a "yes" or "no," or your interview will be over very quickly. If you were preparing an essay on the problems of teenage marriage and you asked someone the following questions, you would find that the first version of each is inadequate.

Examples

(weak) Are many teenagers marrying?

(revised) Why are so many teenagers choosing to marry?

(weak) Is enough being done to counsel teenagers who wish to marry?

(revised) What do you think should be done to discourage teenage marriage?

The basic problem with the two "weak" questions above is that they fail to require the interviewee to express any more than a one-word opinion. Remember, the person you interview is a valuable source with information you want; treat the person accordingly. Many interviewers ask the people they speak with to explain how they would do things differently if they had the authority.

Besides reducing your nervousness during an interview, possibly the most significant advantage of writing out your questions in advance is that you are forced to think about your topic in depth. Until you have thought seriously about the topic and its possible solutions, you will never truly understand the topic. Putting the questions on paper will require this thoughtfulness.

EXERCISE 6.5

Write six to ten questions to ask the people you identified in Exercise 6.4.

1. _____

_____

2. _____

_____

3. _____

_____

4. _____

_____

5. _____

_____

6. _____

_____

7. _____

_____

8. _____

_____

9. _____

_____

10. _____

_____

Have your questions approved, and place a copy in your Project Folder.

Scheduling Your Interviews

Now you are ready to begin contacting people to schedule interviews. Persuading people to agree to an interview is remarkably easy, provided you approach them with respect and confidence. When you call for an interview appointment, you should identify yourself and explain the topic you are investigating. Explain exactly why you want the interview. Do not attempt to flatter your way into an appointment; just explain why you think the person's experience or connections would be helpful to you. One final point to emphasize as you request an interview is that you will keep the interview as brief as possible. This approach should reward you with an interview, but if not, simply move on to the next person on your list. No successful investigative essay depends on a single source.

Conducting the Interview

If you are prepared, your interview will be productive. Before your interview appointment, review the notes of your secondary research. If others have suggested solutions to the problem you are investigating, be certain to be familiar with them. Mentioning proposed solutions in your interview will clearly establish your interest in and knowledge of the topic. If your interviewees discover you are informed, they will be more willing to assist you.

Part of being prepared for your interview is being certain that you take sufficient paper and several pens. It is also a good practice to take a typed list of your questions with you to the interview. Have the list out and ready before you start the interview. It would be very distracting to forget your questions or to search through pages of loose notes looking for them.

Be on time for your interview. Arrive early enough to catch your breath and organize your interview materials. If an emergency arises so that you are unable to keep your appointment, telephone as soon as possible, suggesting that the interview be rescheduled.

Further hints for conducting successful interviews:

- Maintain eye contact as much as possible.
- Request permission to use a tape recorder if you wish to use one.
- Take notes (even if you are taping the machine might not clearly record everything you need).

- Transcribe your tape or rewrite your notes immediately after the interview (while all the information is fresh in your mind).

> **NOTE!** Telephone interviews are sometimes acceptable; they can involve less time for both you and the person interviewed. However, you must be no less prepared with intelligent questions than if you interview in person. Also, the answers to your questions may not be as complete during telephone interviews as during personal interviews.

EXERCISE 6.6

Conduct the interviews you have scheduled. Prepare for each one carefully following the advice given in this lesson. Follow through immediately after each interview, rewriting your notes or listening to your tape and making notes. Send a thank-you letter to each person interviewed. (Have your interview work approved and file your interview notes in your Project Folder.)

Focus Group Option

Originally used for marketing research in business, focus groups are frequently used by researchers investigating a problem. With a little planning you can conduct a focus group right at school. Simply assemble a cross section of students in a place where they can talk, for example, at a table in the cafeteria. Then ask them a short series of open-ended questions that solicit their opinions or feelings about a particular problem, for instance, cheating on campus. Then listen carefully, taking notes on the conversation. If possible, have a classmate or friend take notes or tape-record the discussion. Then later, review your notes, analyzing the comments of the focus group participants.

Other Kinds of Primary Research

If you are conducting other kinds of primary research, organize your task carefully, keeping in mind the time frame within which you must operate. One student, for example, made a trip to the Farallon Islands, twenty-five miles from San Francisco by boat, to investigate, first hand, environmental problems on the islands. To arrange the trip, the student had to write to two government agencies for permission to visit the islands (a wilderness area and bird refuge). Twice, storms forced postponement of the trip to the rugged islands. All of these preparations were made in addition to interviews with environmentalists, government officials, and instructors at a local university.

EXERCISE 6.7

Conduct other research that you have planned. (Have your record of that research approved, for example, journal, survey tallies, video record of site visit and place it in your Project Folder.)

LESSON FOUR—Organizing the Essay and Writing the Working Thesis

When your primary research has been completed and the notes have been written, you should have all the information needed to write the essay. But be cautious, for it is here that you may feel a tremendous temptation to simply begin writing. Nevertheless, one important step remains: the deliberate, concentrated plan for organizing your essay. A well thought-out plan not only results in a better essay but makes the essay much easier to write. Rather than false starts at writing, you should begin by creating an outline. The organization of your notes and thoughts into an outline should begin with your working thesis.

Tailor Your Thesis to Your Organization

Before writing your working thesis, think about the body of your essay. Review the information you have gathered and organized, and decide whether you plan to concentrate on a discussion of the problem in the body paragraphs or whether you will devote most of them to one or more solutions to the problem. Are you more interested in educating your readers about the problem or ways of solving the problem? Your working thesis should reflect whatever emphasis you decide upon.

If you decide that your sole purpose is to convince your readers that a serious problem exists, you can devote all of the body paragraphs to different aspects of the problem. In that case your working thesis should be straightforward, simply stating the problem (see the **Type I** diagram on page 246.)

Thesis Examples—Type I (Problem Only)

Nuclear reactors are highly vulnerable to terrorist attacks.

Nuclear reactors are highly vulnerable to terrorist attacks due to inadequate protective measures.

Because protective measures are inadequate, nuclear reactors are highly vulnerable to terrorist attacks.

You may decide, however, that although more body paragraphs should be about the problem, one or more body paragraphs should be about the solution (see **Type IIA** diagram on page 247). Your working thesis should be written to emphasize the problem but include something about the solution.

Example—Type IIA (Emphasis on Problem)

Nuclear reactors are highly vulnerable to terrorist attacks until adequate protective measures are implemented.

Nuclear reactors are highly vulnerable to terrorist attacks; therefore, more adequate protective measures should be implemented.

A third option is to write fewer body paragraphs about the problem and more paragraphs about solutions see **Type IIB** diagram on page 248). This is the organization to use if you plan

tional plan if you want to devote the majority of your discussion to the merits of a particular solution, hoping to persuade your readers that that solution should be implemented. Your working thesis should reflect this emphasis.

Examples–Type IIB (Emphasis on Solution)

More adequate protective measures should be implemented to protect nuclear reactors from terrorist attacks.

Because nuclear reactors are highly vulnerable to terrorist attacks, more adequate protective measures should be implemented.

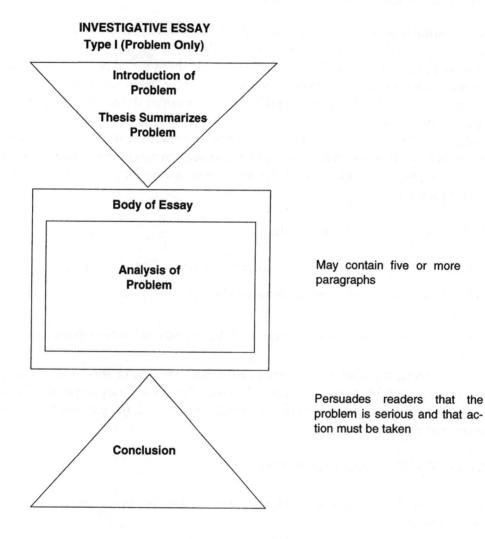

INVESTIGATIVE ESSAY
Type I (Problem Only)

Introduction of Problem

Thesis Summarizes Problem

Body of Essay

Analysis of Problem

May contain five or more paragraphs

Conclusion

Persuades readers that the problem is serious and that action must be taken

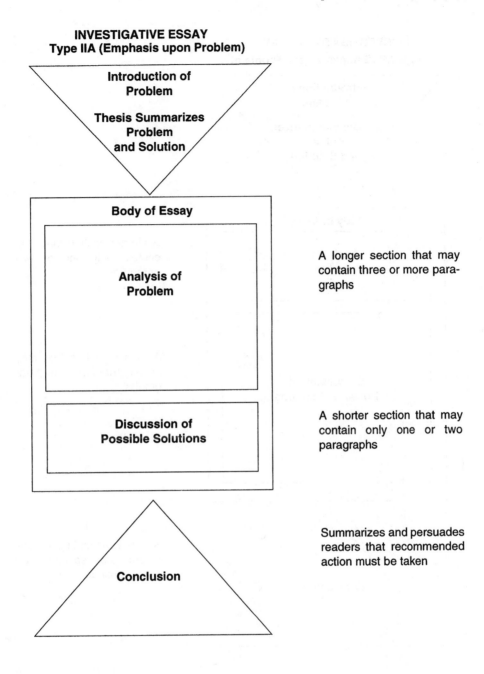

INVESTIGATIVE ESSAY
Type IIA (Emphasis upon Problem)

Introduction of Problem

Thesis Summarizes Problem and Solution

Body of Essay

Analysis of Problem

A longer section that may contain three or more paragraphs

Discussion of Possible Solutions

A shorter section that may contain only one or two paragraphs

Conclusion

Summarizes and persuades readers that recommended action must be taken

INVESTIGATIVE ESSAY
Type IIB (Emphasis upon Problem)

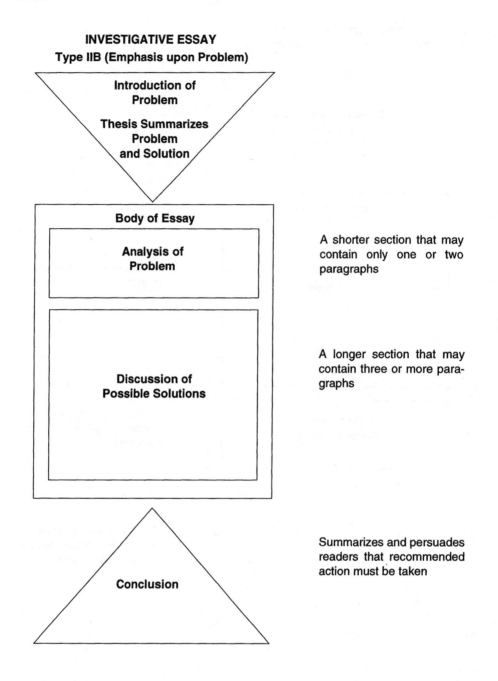

Introduction of
Problem

Thesis Summarizes
Problem
and Solution

Body of Essay

Analysis of
Problem

A shorter section that may contain only one or two paragraphs

Discussion of
Possible Solutions

A longer section that may contain three or more paragraphs

Conclusion

Summarizes and persuades readers that recommended action must be taken

Read the first sample student essay, "Organ Shortages." It follows the Type 1 organization. Ka Yan Chan's thesis is stated at the end of the second paragraph: "Because the organ transplants are so successful, the number of people wanting them far exceeds the number of organs available, creating serious controversies that limit the potential of the donation system." The problem of there not being enough donated organs available for all of the patients who need them is analyzed, but the real problem being discussed is the many controversies associated with organ transplant policies and procedures and the need to settle those controversies. Only then can enough organs be made available. The author does discuss the steps needed to solve the problem, but only briefly in the concluding paragraph of her essay. This brief discussion was intended as a closing device, not an in-depth discussion of the solutions.

Ka Yan Chan

Professor Kitching

ENGWR 300

4 April 2003

Organ Shortages

Angela Rushford was a 4-year old girl in need of a kidney transplant. She was suffering from a life-threatening kidney disease. Her family members were unable to help because they were medically incompatible, so her parents put her on the wait list for a kidney transplant. But the odds did not look good, considering that there are 53,000 others on the list. Months passed, and Angel's health was steadily deteriorating. After nearly a year and still no kidney, Angela's parents, scared and frustrated, decided to try their luck and posted an ad in the local newspaper. David Herper, a 38-year old welder, happened to see their ad and decided to call. It so happened that the testing showed that his blood type was a close match to Angela's, so he decided to donate a kidney to her. The operation took place on January 3, 2003. Through his selfless and courageous act, David Herper gave Angela a second chance in life (Hansen).

Angela was very fortunate to have received her transplant in time. Many Americans are not so lucky. Like many medically advanced countries, the United States is currently facing organ shortages. The following statistics are cited in a CQ Researcher article: "More then 80,700 Americans are waiting for kidneys, hearts, livers and other organs, and the number grows by 115 every day. But only about 66 patients a day receive transplants." Moreover, the article reports, an average of 17 people die each day because of the lack of organ donations. According to the article, the increase in demand for organ transplants is due to the effectiveness of the procedure. "'The transplant community is a victim of its own success,' says Mark Fox, a physician at the University of Oklahoma College of Medicine. 'If transplantation didn't work, we wouldn't have so many people on the waiting list.'" (Hansen). Because the organ transplants are so successful, the number of people wanting them far exceeds the number of organs available, creating serious controversies that limit the potential of the donation system.

The biggest controversy about the shortage of organs is the debate about why the shortage of donated organs even exists in the first place. According to a CQ Researcher article, "Experts cite several reasons why the U.S. donation rate for cadaveric organs is only 50 percent." Perhaps the biggest reason is that many of those who sign the donor cards fail to inform their family of their decision before they die. Even though donor cards are legally binding, doctors do not want to go against the family's wishes in fear of lawsuits and bad publicity. Some families are unwilling to agree with the donation due to the stress of the situation, for instance, if a family member has just died in a traffic accident, shooting, or some other sudden tragedy. Other reasons for refusing to allow the donation of organs, according to the article, are religious beliefs, fear that the body will be disfigured, and distrust of the health-care system by minorities (Hansen). A USA Today article states, "The primary reason for the shortage of donated organs harkens back to 1984, when Congress passed the National Organ Transplant Act, which outlawed the buying and selling of organs." Another reason given in the article is that allocation regulations which have led to "a system whereby patients can receive a transplant only after their health status deteriorates to a point that their chances for long-term survival, even with a transplant, are greatly diminished" (Carlstrom).

Currently minorities have the lowest number of donors, especially African Americans, because they have a hard time trusting the healthcare system. Minorities believe that the system for distributing organ donations favors wealthy white transplant applicants. They also fear that doctors would let the donor die once they received the permission to obtain their organs (Hansen). Due to the low number of donations, the shortage of organs is particularly significant. An article on the Coalition on Donation web site reports that "35 percent of all patients waiting for kidney transplants are African Americans" and that "African Americans and other minorities are three times more likely to suffer from end-stage renal disease than Whites." However, "Transplant success rates increase when organs are matched between members of the same ethnic and racial group." Thus, a shortage of organs can greatly affect the minority population, resulting in minority patients having to wait longer to receive transplants and suffering more deaths ("Critical Shortage").

Another major controversy, due to the extreme shortage in the supply of organs, is the question of who should be able to receive an organ transplant. The USA Today articles states, "Current rules established by United Network for Organ Sharing (UNOS), a private organization that allocates organ harvested by cadavers, called cadaveric organs, specify that donated organs must go to the sickest patient first and stay within a particular region" (Carlstrom). According to a CQ Researcher article, UNOS has certain rules they follow for each organ. For every organ that becomes available, they use a sophisticated program to rank all the potential recipients on the waiting list. Several factors that determine the ranking, including the potential recipient's blood and tissue type, the status of his or her immune-system, and how long they have been on the waiting list. They also take into account the medical urgency. By doing so, the organ is given to the sickest person on the waiting lists (Hansen). However, this sickest-first policy is not universally supported. The USA Today article takes the viewpoint that this policy "is myopic." "For instance, the two-year organ-graft survival rate for patients who are in intensive care before their liver transplants is approximately 50%, compared to 75% for transplantees who are still relatively healthy. Given these differences, it makes sense to perform transplants on patients before they become critically ill." (Carlstrom).

In addition, surgeons oftentimes struggle with the decision of who to give the organ to. Christopher Rudge, a London surgeon, gives an example of the kind of "nightmare" decision he faces: "'You can have a kidney which will fit either a man in his forties with a job and three children, or a retired single woman in her sixties without dependents'" (Palmer 68). The problem of patient selection is compounded by subtle subjectivities among physicians. Dr. Rudge cites changing distribution guidelines: "It used to be the case, for instance, that younger patients automatically had priority over older ones. That has changed over the last ten years? Why? 'The surgeons themselves have got older,' suggested Dr. Rudge. 'It may make us not quite so keen on the inflexible age cut-off'" (Palmer 68). Another problem with this system is that some believe that organs should not be given to alcoholics, smokers and those who are sick due to their own unhealthy behaviors. Alvin H. Moss, a director of the Center for Health Care Ethics and Law at the University of West Virginia, for example, believes that those who destroy their livers due to drinking should not compete equally with other candidates for liver transplants (Hansen).

Along with the controversies over why there is a lack of donor organs and who should receive them, an equally intense debate continues about whether donors should be paid for their organs. Some experts believe that if financial incentives were used, a significant increase in organ donations would occur. According to David L. Kaserman, a professor of economics at Auburn University in Alabama, "We're losing some 6,000 people per year to the organ shortage—more then twice the number killed in September 11 terrorist attacks. It's completely unethical to let so many people die every year simply because some people think it's wrong to pay donors" (Hansen). Andy Barnett and David Kaserman estimate that $1000 to $3000 should be paid to each donor. Paying donors would eliminate organ shortages and help reduce health care costs, such as kidney dialysis which costs $44,000 per year (Williams). Supporters of paying donors argue that people should have the right to sell their organs if they please. "If we agree that people have property of themselves, i.e., own themselves, they have the right to dispose of themselves anyway they please so long as they do not violate the property rights of others" (Williams).

Opponents of paying donors, however, consider financial incentives to be morally and ethically wrong. They believe that by doing so would exploit the poor and promote a black market for organ sales. Some even think that the idea would lead to children being raised for "spare parts" (Hansen). Many critics argue that financial incentives would force the poor to agree to donate their organs even if it violates their religious and moral beliefs. Pediatrician Michelle Peterson, president of the Nebraska Medical Association, fears that incentives would pressure poor families to "pull the plug" too soon on their loved ones (Hansen). Examples of incentives exploiting the poor can be seen in India. According to the article, "Selling Organs for Transplants is Unethical," an Indian woman was forced by her husband to sell one of her kidneys for money. As soon as he received the money for the donation, he left his wife to go gambling (Palmer 63). Others fear that by providing financial incentives, some might try to make money by murdering and selling body parts in the black market.

Other suggested solutions to the organ shortage problem are also highly controversial. One idea is that women would be paid or volunteer to conceive specifically for transplantation purposes. Proponent John Robertson claims, "In terms of fetal welfare, no greater harm occurs to the fetus conceived expressly to be aborted, as long as the abortion occurs at a stage at which the fetus is insignificantly developed to experience harm, such as during the first trimester" (61). But inasmuch as abortion, in general, is already a highly emotional moral and ethical issue, this idea if put into practice surely would be strenuously opposed by anti-abortionists. Incensed by even the suggestion of planned abortions for organ harvesting, they argue that to do such an inhumane act would be incredibly wrong. Other ideas include the idea of using fetuses that are already aborted by abortions, which is equally controversial. Yet another idea, proposed as a treatment possibility by scientists, is using transplanted tissues developed from stem cells to replace damaged or diseased cells or repair damaged organs. However, the ability to actually apply the results of current stem-cell research may lie many years in the future. Furthermore, like abortion, the subject of stem-cell research is also highly controversial because it involves the use of embryonic stem cells ("Stem Cell Research").

Another controversial solution is xenotransplantation, the transplanting of animal organs to humans. As reported in the CQ Researcher article, baboon or other primate organs transplanted into humans were rejected within a short time. But recent studies have shown that there might be hope in transplanting pig organs instead. Raising pigs for organs is cheaper and faster than raising baboons. In addition, fewer ethical objections are raised regarding the harvesting of pig organs for transplants (Hansen). According to an ABC News article, "Pig organs are closer in size to actual human organs than those of monkeys and pig farms are already ubiquitous while monkey and ape populations are threatened all over the world" (Brewster).

Nevertheless, scientists worry that viruses might be transmitted from animals to humans through xenotransplantation. Although not transmitted through xenotransplantation, the flu virus that killed 20-40 million people in 1918 was transmitted from pigs, and the current AIDS pandemic apparently was transferred from chimpanzees (Hansen). Scientists critical of xenotransplantation fear porcine endogenous retrovirus (PERV), a virus embedded in every pig's chromosomes. In 1997 xenotransplantation experiments involving pig cells and pig livers were halted when scientists discovered that PERV could infect human cells. Although no patients have contracted PERV thus far, experts remain skeptical because PERV, like AIDS, can be undetected for years. Two companies currently have been breeding pigs from parents that have the problem gene taken out of their DNA (Hansen). The whole idea of breeding animals for spare parts, however, is controversial from the moral and ethical standpoints. Some find it morally and ethically wrong to use animals in such ways while others believe that animals should be used to save lives (Hansen).

Through all the controversy and fierce debate, organ shortage is a very serious problem. In order to solve this problem, the system must change, but the controversies regarding the proposed solutions make changes difficult and prolong the shortage. Strong leadership and consensus building among physicians and researchers is needed to solve the shortage. First, consensus needs to be reached on a fair allocation system that favors no economic, ethnic, or age group. The current UNOS rules, although well intentioned, need to be reconsidered, particularly the policy of giving highest priority to the patients who are the sickest. Also, more effort should be spent promoting public awareness about organ donation in order to reduce the reluctance of people to consider organ donation, especially among minority groups traditionally suspicious of the organ donor system. Next, guidelines for providing financial incentives for organ donations need to be developed that won't allow the poor to be exploited or a global black market to develop. Third, medical research related to organ transplants should continue. Xenotransplantation research should be encouraged, although experiments with humans should be strictly limited until potential medical problems and moral/ethical objections can be resolved. Although burdened with its own scientific and moral controversies, stem cell research related to organ replacement is another solution that deserves more support. Until these steps are taken, far too many people will die unecessarily.

Works Cited

Brewster, Bill. "Are Pigs the Solution to Organ Shortages?" <u>ABC News</u>. 3 Nov.

    2002. 26 March 2003 <http://abcnews.go.com/sections/living/Daily News/

    pigorgans 991103.html>.

Carlstrom, Charles T. "Organ Transplant Shortages: Matter of Life and Death."

    <u>Find Articles</u>. Nov. 1999. <u>USA Today</u>. 26 March 2003 <http://

    www.findarticles.com/cf_0/ml272/2654_128/57564082/print.jhtml>.

Hansen, Brian. "Organ Shortages." <u>CQ Researcher</u>. 21 Feb. 2003.13.7 (2003) CQ

    Press. American River Library. Sacramento, CA. 20 March 2003. <http://

    0-library.cqpress.com.lasiii.losrios.edu/cqresearcher/

    documnet.php?id=cqresrre2003...>.

Mahoney, Julia D. "Should We Adopt A Market Strategy to Organ Donation?"

    <u>The Ethics of Organ Transplantation: Advances in Bioethics</u>. 7.

    Netherlands: Elsevier Science Ltd, 2001. 67.

Palmer, Alasdair. "Selling Organs for Transplants Is Unethical." <u>Biomedical

    Ethics Opposing View Points</u>. USA: Greenhaven Press, 1998. 63-68.

Robertson, John A. "Rights, Symbolism, and Public Policy in Fetal Tissue

    Transplants." <u>The Ethics of Organ Transplants: The Current Debate</u>. USA:

    Prometheus Books, 1998. 61-64.

"The Critical Shortage Facing the African Community." 2003 United Network for

    Organ Sharing. 5 April 2003 <http:www.shareyourlife.org/africanamerican/>

"Stem Cell Research: Medical Progress with Responsibility; a Report from the

    Chief Medical Officer's Expert Group Reviewing the Potential of

    Developments in Stem Cell Research and Cell Nuclear Replacement to Benefit

    Human Health." Department of Health, 16 August 2000 <http://

    www.doh.gov.uk/cegc/ stemcellreport.htm>.

Williams, Walter E. "My Organs Are for Sale." <u>Ideas on Liberty</u>. Oct. 2002. 20

    March 2003 <http://www.gmu.edu/departments/economics/wew/articles/ fee/

    organs.html>.

Now read the second sample student essay., "Daycare" by Kimberly Brokaw. Its organization is Type IIA, although the solution section is almost as long as the problem section. Four paragraphs are devoted to the problem and three to the solution. The essay is interesting because it compares daycare in the United States with that in other industrialized countries and because it includes personal anecdotes of the author who had previously been a professional daycare operator. The essay also includes primary research in the form of private interviews. The writer focuses on government solutions to the problems of inadequate training of daycare personnel and the high cost of daycare. The essay's basic premise is that daycare is not just the working mother's problem—it's a family and social issue.

Kimberly Brokaw

Professor Mehaffy

English 1-A

19 April 1995

Daycare

Every day millions of parents must rely on strangers to care for their children. The issues of daycare, including who provides it and how much it should cost, are a major source of problems for working parents. Oftentimes this care is inadequate. Of the Western industrialized nations, only the United States, Britain, and Canada do not have family daycare policies (Foreman, "How East" F4). While many countries have very successful programs, the United States has an outdated view on daycare. According to one author, there are three main reasons why America has such a poor childcare system: an ambivalence towards working mothers, a lack of a coordinated system, and a resistance toward government involvement in childcare (Foreman, "Working Parents" n.pag). Although our current daycare system is not effective for working parents, solutions exist for the many problems these parents face.

Daycare, according to parents, is expensive. However, when people ask daycare providers if they think daycare is too expensive, they get a different reply. According to the pamphlet Women, Work and Childcare, childcare is the fourth largest expense of working parents. The cost of childcare ranges from $2,400 to $9,000 annually per child, with low-income households spending approximately 25 percent of their incomes on childcare alone (National Commission n.pag). Because many families cannot afford this kind of expenditure, they are forced to leave their children alone or in a childcare situation that may be cheaper but not safe. While parents complain of the rising costs of daycare, those who provide childcare complain of long hours and low wages. Lily Monem, a family daycare provider, works from 7:30 a.m. until 6:30 p.m. She charges $20 to $25 a day. Her hourly wage is much less than most people make today in the working force. The discrepancy between parents and providers is a major problem with our current daycare system. Parents are turning away from typical daycare situations because they simply cannot afford the cost, especially if they have more than one child.

One concern parents have with daycare is the fear that the provider could intentionally or unintentionally hurt a child. Every parent's worst nightmare is that someone will hurt his or her child. A student who is the mother of a young child said, "I feel like he comes home with more cuts and bruises than when I am with him" (Heverly). In the media in recent years, we have seen cases of daycare providers who have become so frustrated with children in their care that they have actually shaken the children to death. Stories like these only promote the feelings of anxiety that parents experience every day when they leave their children in the care of someone else. Most daycare providers don't intentionally hurt the children in their care, but often they have too many children in their care to give them adequate supervision and to prevent all of the minor spills and tumbles that are bound to occur. As a retired daycare operator, I know from first-hand experience that with five or six children in my care, youngsters were sometimes falling or hitting each other, and I just didn't have enough hands or eyes to stop them all before there were minor cuts or bumps.

Availability is another big issue for working parents. While our society has shifted from working 9-to-5 shifts Monday through Friday to working around the clock, daycare providers have not adjusted to this demand for longer hours. Parents today are working day and/or night and need childcare at all hours of the day/night. Oftentimes parents who work late (or early) shifts cannot find adequate care for their children. As one working father put it, "My shifts vary sometimes from week to week. It is very hard to keep daycare providers because they get frustrated with my changing hours, and a lot of times I work nights, and they [daycare providers] don't want to watch kids late at night" (Ginocchio). Situations like this are a great source of frustration for many working parents.

Currently, daycare providers receive little scrutiny or training. The licensing process is simple. All prospective providers must do is go to a meeting and sign some papers, and as long as they don't have a felony on their records, they can become daycare providers. Ten to fifteen years ago, these guidelines were not even enforced, according to a retired daycare provider. She says the system was extremely lax in past years (Perrine). It is almost more difficult to obtain a driver's license than it is to get a daycare license. Parents entrust the care of their children to the licensed professionals for 8 to 10 hours a day. It is frightening to think that daycare providers are required to have little training or knowledge about children and how to handle them. Having once owned a daycare myself, I know that I was required to have only a C.P.R. certification and an additional eight hours of training per year; anything else I did was by my own choice. The lack of good training programs for daycare providers causes many parents to fear for the safety of their children.

The first step in reforming or building a daycare system is for parents to demand better training for daycare providers. Parents are most often the best advocates for their own children (Goffin and Lombardi 32). A set training program should be implemented with requirements that all daycare providers must meet in order to be licensed. As a former daycare owner, I know the importance of learning how to deal with different children who have conflicting attitudes, needs, wants, and ways of expressing themselves in order to be prepared to handle potentially frustrating situations. A good screening process needs to be developed. One type of screening that should be implemented is personal interviews for all prospective daycare owners. A working mother said, "How do I know the person caring for my son has the patience to deal with six kids and still treat my son with love and respect" (Vasquez). Requiring potential caregivers to undergo personal interviews and screening would help weed out the people who cannot handle the pressure.

A second step that we need to take is to implement subsidized daycare programs. It doesn't matter how well prepared caregivers are if working parents can't afford to pay for childcare. An example of a daycare system that wasn't expensive was the former East Germany's. The state paid all daycare fees ($8 a day). The infant and toddler centers were run by the state, and almost 100 percent of their 3- to 6-year-olds were in a kindergarten-type program (Foreman, "How East" F4). In the United States, on the average, parents pay more for daycare than anywhere else (Williams B6). Companies must become more aware of employee needs and offer childcare programs, such as providing flexible benefits and voucher programs (both of which are programs that help working parents pay for daycare). Some government programs are available to parents, such as federal income tax credits (for working parents) and subsidized childcare (for low-income parents). Parents need to be informed about these programs so they may take advantage of them (Miller and Weissman 27). Making daycare affordable is not easy, but it is possible. Some programs exist already that parents just need to know about.

Another solution to the daycare dilemma working parents face is for them to use alternatives to typical paid childcare. Some parents already are choosing these options. Oftentimes parents overlook the best person or people to care for their child--a family member. In a growing trend, more parents are leaving their children with spouses or even the children's grandparents. A 1984 survey revealed that approximately 29 percent of parents were leaving their children with a relative (Rubin 24). If relatives aren't available, another popular idea is to trade babysitting with someone. There are many options out there; sometimes it just takes a little creativity. Parents need to ask around and find other people in similar situations. Many of the alternatives to regular daycare cost much less money than the typical family daycare situation.

Daycare is a topic of major concern for millions of people. Every day it affects families all over the country. Unfortunately, it has been a neglected subject by the government because it has been viewed as a problem of working parents, not the government. For leadership in making daycare policies, the government should look to the former East Germany, a small country that led the world in childcare policy. The national policy in the former East Germany was that the task of raising children is not one which parents should or would want to bear alone (Foreman, "How East" F4). We live in a very advanced society, and we need to bring daycare out of the Stone Ages and into the here and now. Daycare would greatly benefit from better training programs and assistance from the federal government. Parents also need to be more informed of programs that already exist and to become more creative in finding daycare for their children.

Works Cited

Foreman, Judy. "How East Germany Provides Total Childcare." <u>Sacramento Bee</u> 25

    Dec. 1980: F4.

- - - "Working Parents Around the World." <u>Boston Globe</u> n.d.: n.pag.

Ginocchio, Guy. Private Interview. 4 Apr.1995.

Goffin, Stacie, and Joan Lombardi. Speaking Out: <u>Early Childhood</u>

    <u>Advocacy</u>. Washington, D.C.: NAEYC, 1988-89.

Heverly, Melissa. Private Interview. 4 Apr. 1995.

Miller, JoAnn, and Susan Weissman. <u>The Parents' Guide to Daycare</u>. New York:

    Bantam Books, 1986.

Monem, Lily. Private Interview. 2 Apr. 1995.

National Commission on Working Women of Wider Opportunities for

    Women. <u>Women, Work and Childcare</u>. 1988: n.pag.

Perrine, Vickie. Private Interview. 3 Apr. 1995.

Rubin, Sylvia. "The Best Place." <u>San Francisco Chronicle</u>. 4 May 1984: 24.

Select Committee on Children, Youth, and Families. <u>U.S. Children and Their</u>

    <u>Families: Current Conditions and Recent Trends</u>, 1989. Washington, D.C.:

    U.S. Government Printing Office, 1989.

Vasquez, Stacie. Private Interview. 1 Apr. 1995.

Williams, Norman. "Sacramentans May Pay More for Childcare." <u>Sacramento Bee</u>

    16 Sept. 1992: B6.

EXERCISE 6.8

Circle the type of organization plan to use (Type I, Type IIA, or Type IIB). In the space below write a working thesis sentence appropriate for the organizational plan you will use.

_____

_____

_____

EXERCISE 6.9

Write a thesis topic sentence outline for your essay. Have your outline approved and place it in your Project Folder.

LESSON FIVE—Writing and Editing the Essay

Now you are ready for the culminating phases of your investigation: writing and editing an essay that will effectively communicate the results of your investigation. Concentrate on developing your outline and integrating the mass of information you have accumulated. The actual writing techniques are the same as with the library research essay, so if you need to review, refer again to Chapter Three.

If possible, have someone who can provide constructive feedback read the first draft of your essay—a peer editing group, your instructor, a classmate, tutor, friend, co-worker, or relative. If time permits, let your first draft "cool" a day or two. Then when you read it again, you will probably see improvements that can be made that would not have occurred to you otherwise. Furthermore, the cooling-off period may allow you to accept some of the revision suggestions that your readers made that seemed unacceptable when they were first made. All experienced writers will tell you that every writer needs an editor, with no exceptions. Learning to keep an open mind when receiving feedback about your writing is an important part of becoming a competent writer.

EXERCISE 6.10

Write the first draft of your investigative essay.

EXERCISE 6.11

Have at least one person read your first draft and make suggestions for improving its content, organization, and sentence structure. (Your instructor may make this a peer-editing exercise in class.) Place your first draft, along with any feedback and revisions, in your Project Folder.

EXERCISE 6.12

After you write your first draft and receive feedback on it, revise the essay and prepare the final document. Use the required format and proofread it carefully, correcting any errors you find. Place the final document in your Project Folder.

7

Essay Exams

Objectives

When you have completed this chapter, you will have written or studied each of the following:

1. writing processes for essay exams
2. short essay answers
3. longer in-class essays
4. open-book exams
5. take-home exams
6. proficiency exams

Essay Exams 7

To complete your development from an inexperienced writer to an accomplished one, you must learn to write different kinds of essay examinations. This task has been left for last to make certain you have the writing experience necessary to perform well under the pressures of essay testing. By adapting the organizational strategies covered in the previous chapters of this book, you can confidently answer almost any kind of essay question assigned. Confidence is a big factor in writing successful exams, and knowing beforehand how to organize different types of essay examinations will help tremendously in building the self-confidence you need. In this chapter you will learn strategies for writing short essay answers, longer in-class essays, open-book exams, take-home exams, and proficiency exams.

LESSON ONE—Short Essay Answers

When assigned short essay questions, write answers that are condensed paragraphs. Each answer should contain a topic sentence and several supporting sentences. Begin each answer with a topic sentence that clearly states the essential generalization. Suppose, for example, the following question were asked:

> What was the significance of Brown v. Board of Education to the African-American community?

Your topic sentence might read:

> In Brown v. Board of Education the Supreme Court declared unconstitutional the separate but equal doctrine that was used by whites to force African-Americans to use separate public schools.

This **topic sentence** directly answers the question:

In Brown v. Board of Education. . .	Repeats name of case to let reader know that the answer is written on required subject (introductory phrase)
. . . the Supreme Court declared unconstitutional the separate but equal doctrine . . .	States the crucial generalization that must be made about the case (main clause of sentence)

... that was used by whites to force African-Americans to use separate public schools.

Completes topic sentence by relating answer to the portion of the question, "What was the significance . . . to the African-American community?" (dependent clause following the main clause)

Follow the topic sentence with two or three sentences, each of which serves as a combined primary and secondary support sentence. Making each support sentence perform double duty allows you to condense your paragraph without sacrificing the details necessary to convince your instructor that you really know the material. The strategy is to write support sentences that obviously support the topic sentence with key generalizations and to intersperse these generalizations with facts. To accomplish this task, you will have to use complex sentences, devoting independent clauses to your primary generalizations and dependent clauses and phrases to your secondary supporting details. Study the following support sentences for the previous sample topic sentence:

Support Sentence #1

Questioning the validity of racial segregation in public schools, Chief Justice Warren delivered the unanimous opinion of the court that segregation of children in public schools solely on the basis of race, even though the schools may be equally well equipped and staffed, denies minority children equal educational opportunities.

Support Sentence #2

Citing results of psychological experiments, Warren stated that to separate children from others of the same age and educational qualifications solely because of their race creates a feeling of inferiority as to their community "status that may affect their hearts and minds in a way unlikely to ever be undone."

Notice the tremendous concentration of generalization and fact achieved in these support sentences. If the second sentence were converted to conventional primary and secondary support sentences, they might look like this:

Chief Justice Warren cited the results of scientific experiments by psychologists to support the court's opinion. He stated that researchers had found that separating children from others of the same age and educational qualifications solely because of their race creates a feeling of inferiority. The children feel that their status in the community is lower. This feeling "may affect their hearts and minds in a way unlikely to ever be undone."

Comparing the two versions of support sentence #2, you will see that the recommended version is a single complex sentence whereas the longer version is made up of four complete sentences. Study the following breakdown:

Condensed Version	Expanded Version
1) Citing results of psychological experiments, . . .	1) Chief Justice Warren cited the results of scientific experiments by psychologists.
2) . . . Warren stated that to separate children from others of the same age and educational qualifications solely because of their race creates a feeling of inferiority . . .	2) He stated that researchers had found that separating children from others of the same age and educational qualifications solely because of their race creates a feeling of inferiority.

Condensed Version	Expanded Version
3) . . . as to their community status . . .	3) The children feel that their status in the community is lower.
4) . . . that "may affect their hearts and minds in a way unlikely to ever be undone."	4) This feeling "may affect their hearts and minds in a way unlikely to ever be undone."
1 sentence—50 words	4 sentences—71 words

EXERCISE 7.1

Write a short essay answer no more than three sentences answering one of the following questions:

1. How does the structure of an introductory paragraph differ from the structure of a body paragraph?
2. What are the best ways to find a job?

_____

_____

_____

_____

_____

_____

_____

_____

_____

_____

_____

_____

_____

_____

_____

_____

_____

_____

_____

_____

_____

_____

_____

_____

_____

Have your writing checked for accuracy and completeness.

EXERCISE 7.2

For practice, answer this three-part short essay question:

What is a thesis, where is it located, and how should it be written?

Use the following paragraphs as a source of information. Write a topic sentence, and support it with two sentences that combine primary and secondary support. Compress as much information as possible in your support sentences.

Logically, most writers write the introductory paragraph of their essays first. This is as it should be. It does not follow, however, that you should begin by writing the first sentence of it; indeed, it would be more accurate to say you should write the last sentence of your introductory paragraph first. This statement may sound absurd, but it makes far more sense than it would first appear. Since the thesis sentence is the most important sentence of the entire essay, it should be given your complete attention before you begin writing the first line. Frequently, the thesis is called the central idea because it is the idea around which your entire essay is built. If the introduction of your essay has no central idea to hold it together, the essay will fail. Without the thesis statement, the essay may wander aimlessly and be ineffective.

The introductory section of every essay must have a thesis sentence for two distinct reasons. First, a thesis sentence will present the main idea you intend to stress in the rest of the essay. In a single sentence the thesis will preview the explanation or argument to follow in the body and conclusion of the essay; that is, it will assert an idea to be elaborated upon or an argumentative statement to be supported. Second, the thesis sentence will control your writing. By asserting the specific idea you want to elaborate upon, your thesis will narrow your topic and limit the discussion that follows.

Both the presentation of your main idea and the limitation of the essay's scope are important; however, both must be worked out before you begin writing your essay. If you do not have a thesis sentence written out before you write the essay, you will often forget your main idea long enough to cause problems. Forgetting your point, however briefly, may result in statements being included that are not directly related to the idea you are trying to communicate. Statements of this nature are irrelevant, and every instructor will note such statements as errors because they weaken your essay.

Topic Sentence:_____

_____

_____

_____

_____

Support Sentence #1:_____

_____

_____

_____

_____

Support Sentence #2:_____

_____

_____

_____

_____

Have your sentences checked.

LESSON TWO—Writing Longer Essay Exams in Class

While an objective test determines a student's ability to recognize correct information, the in-class essay exam enables an instructor to ascertain student ability to interpret and use information. Furthermore, the essay exam practically eliminates guessing while it encourages thoughtfulness and organization. As a result of the emphasis on these qualities in evaluation, you should expect to demonstrate your competence by writing many essay exams. They will often be the source of a major portion of course grades.

Preparing To Write Essay Exams

The three-phase writing process can be adapted for use in essay exams. As with all other writing assignments in *Survival*, you must begin with the planning and drafting stages. You will, of course, be under pressure to write essay exams in a limited amount of time; consequently, you will need to shorten the process to have more time to write. But you must not allow yourself to omit the process completely because students who do their planning and drafting consistently earn better grades on their written work. You will find that your essay exam grades will improve if you follow the strategies you have learned and practiced in the first six chapters of *Survival*.

Consider the following abbreviated version of the writing process outline you have been working with throughout the text. By following this procedure, you could develop an organized approach to writing in-class assignments. The suggested time allotments given in parentheses are for a two-hour exam.

Planning

  Reading before coming to class; annotate the reading; mark relevant sentences

Assignment Analysis (10 minutes)

  Analyze the question or assignment carefully; find the keywords

Time Budget

  Planning (15 minutes)
  Writing (60 minutes)
  Editing—final copy (20 minutes)
  Reread (15 minutes)

These suggested time allotments can be varied to suit individual writing styles, but assignment analysis and time budgeting are essential to avoid confusion and running out of time before the writing project is complete.

You usually won't be allowed to bring research notes or books to class when you are to write an in-class essay exam. The ideas you present in your essay will, therefore, have to be based on the information stored in your memory. In such a situation, your information gathering will consist of doing your planning: brainstorming, freewriting, clustering, analytical questioning, and focused questioning. If you don't write out your information before you begin your in-class essay, you will almost certainly forget some of the ideas and facts you had intended to offer as proof of your assertions. This step takes little time; however, you may wish to limit yourself to five or ten minutes for prewriting exercises, definitely to no more than fifteen minutes.

Your instructors will expect you to write a 500-word essay or at least two 250-word essays in a one-hour examination period. Writing 500 words or more in one hour may sound impossible to you now, but you can do it if you are properly prepared and know how to approach such an assignment.

To do well on an in-class exam, know the subject matter thoroughly. But in addition to the knowledge of subject matter, you must have the resourcefulness to apply your knowledge when faced with unexpected questions. Systematically studying the material covered by the text and thoughtfully anticipating the questions that might be asked are the best ways of acquiring the knowledge needed for essay exams. But you already know that. What you may not know is that it is possible to arm yourself with an organizational strategy that will be useful in almost any essay exam situation. Being prepared, you will be much freer to concentrate on the writing assignment than if you have to worry about how to organize the essay. This strategy is an adaptation of the basic three-part organizational plan presented in earlier chapters of this text. To employ this strategy, follow these eight easy steps:

1. **Clarify the Assignment.** Make certain that you analyze the required examination question carefully before you begin to write. Essay-exam topics can be quite complicated, and you should never begin writing until you have read and reread the question several times. Take a calm approach, refraining from writing until you have carefully studied the required topic and surveyed your knowledge. Look for key direction words in the exam question. Overlooking these words may result in your misunderstanding what you are to write. If you are asked to analyze how the space shuttles can be used to benefit American business in the future, do not write an exam about past benefits. You simply would not be writing the essay your

instructor wanted. Many key direction words are commonly used by instructors, but the following fifteen are most frequently encountered. Study this list of words and definitions carefully.

a. **Analyze**—to examine closely, separating the basic parts, steps, or essential features. You may write a critical analysis or chronological analysis.

b. **Attack or defend**—to be for or against, taking a position. Write an argument, pro-con if possible.

c. **Compare**—to explain similarities, parallels. An instructor may actually want you to compare and contrast: to stress likenesses and differences. Before you write, make a list of your points of comparison and contrast.

d. **Contrast**—to stress differences.

e. **Define**—to explain what something means, or what something is. Begin with a basic definition and use examples to make it clear.

f. **Discuss**—to explain, to analyze, to elaborate, possibly to debate. This is a vague term, so carefully ponder what direction to take.

g. **Elaborate**—to explain further, to develop a detailed explanation of something. Take care to use enough primary and secondary support; go into details.

h. **Evaluate**—to judge, or to analyze critically, discussing the strengths and weaknesses but not necessarily taking a position.

i. **Examine**—to analyze.

j. **Explain**—to clarify, to recite, to interpret, to explicate, to summarize. The term "explain" covers all expository writing strategies. Do not write an argument.

k. **Illustrate**—to clarify through the use of an extended example or several short examples. Do not forget to begin with your basic generalization.

l. **List**—to write down a series of points. Use a 1, 2, 3, or first, second, third approach.

m. **Outline**—to discuss briefly, a skeletal discussion, the relationship of major and minor parts.

n. **Summarize**—to review briefly, omitting details. A review of major or main ideas.

o. **Survey**—to briefly review all of the parts of something in order to gain perspective.

2. **Develop a Thesis.** As rapidly as possible, formulate a thesis sentence. You can use an umbrella or a divided thesis, but be careful to avoid writing a thesis that is too broad. Your thesis must control the scope of your essay. You might, for instance, focus your essay by writing, "Congress must take immediate steps to balance the budget." A divided thesis such as "Congress must eliminate all farm subsidies, cut all oil subsidies, eliminate pork barrel projects, and remove welfare fraud to balance the budget" would also focus your essay effectively. The thesis often comes from the prompt question itself.

3. **Write an Outline.** Make a list of four or five points or ideas you hope to have time to cover—a simple outline. If you can, number them in order of importance or interest to your instructor. Because you are writing an essay exam, you should begin with the most important or interesting point and proceed down the list, discussing the least important idea last. You do not need to use full sentences at this point.

4. **Use Short-Cuts Where Possible.** Do not write a full introductory paragraph when you are writing an essay exam unless your instructor specifically requires one. Make your thesis sentence the first sentence of your first paragraph, or isolate it, making it the first paragraph even though it is just one sentence. Time will be limited, and your instructor will be more interested in your knowledge of the facts than a formal beginning. Examine the student-written essay exam on page 276; the writer effectively uses an isolated thesis. Compare it to the essay on page 278 to see how the thesis can be incorporated into the first body paragraph on a short exam.

5. **Explain Ideas Fully.** Write a paragraph for each point discussed. Begin each paragraph with

a clear topic sentence. If possible, add at least four sentences of support for each topic sentence. Use both primary and secondary support sentences. Include plenty of specific details, and above all, use examples whenever they will demonstrate to your instructor that you know the material.

6. **Eliminate Traditional Concluding Paragraph.** Do not write a concluding paragraph that summarizes your essay and asserts the importance of what has been written as you would in a traditional essay. Instead, write a single concluding sentence and place it at the end of the last paragraph; or simply stop writing when you have completed your last point. Your last sentence must not give your reader the idea that you were too rushed to finish—even if you were. Create the impression that you have said everything you wanted to say and that you had ample time to finish.

7. **Make Corrections Quickly as You Write.** Do not plan to recopy your essay; there will usually not be time. Corrections can be made by crossing out words and writing either above or after what is crossed out.

8. **Edit Your Final Copy.** Take at least 15 minutes to proofread your work. Look for lapses in sentences and sentences that do not make sense. Correct misspelled words, and rewrite awkward sentences. Many instructors will allow you to use a dictionary during an essay exam. Finally, in the upper left corner, write your name, the instructor's name, class title, and the date.

Study the sample essay exams that follow. Keep in mind that they were written under the pressure of a two hour-time limit and that the writers were not allowed to refer to text or notes. As you read the sample essay exams, notice these characteristics:

1. Single-sentence or short introductory paragraph: immediately begins answering question.
2. Good paragraph structure: strong topic sentences, plenty of primary and secondary support— each body paragraph at least four or five sentences long
3. Logical order of ideas: usually the most important point is stated in first body paragraph
4. Conclusion summarizes the essay in a single sentence placed at the end of the last body paragraph
5. Essay carefully proofread

SAMPLE ESSAY QUESTIONS

Sample In-Class Essay #1

Topic: Analyze the causes that prompt the characters to act as they do in the short story "The Autopsy."

An analysis of "The Autopsy" reveals that all four living characters in the story are in many ways products of their environment.

The clearest example of this is the old fishmonger. The author describes him in great physical detail, making it clear that his work and hard life have made great demands upon him. His body, his face, and his hands all show the effects of the hard life he has lived. Perhaps even more tragically, the old man's emotions have been conditioned by the environment. It becomes apparent to the reader early in the story that the man is considered by the other characters to be lower class, hardly worth noticing. For instance, when the narrator arrives at the hospital for the business meeting and finds the fish merchant there, his feelings are made perfectly obvious. The narrator, even after recognizing the old man, does not bother to acknowledge him. It is not surprising that with the indifference shown him, the fishman accepts the role of an inferior person in society, expecting the cruel treatment from others that they almost automatically extend to him.

If the fishman represents the inferior role in a racially prejudiced society, the pathologist is surely the antithesis. Obviously accustomed to controlling his environment, the doctor notices no irregularities in his treatment of others. An example of his lack of feeling is given in the beginning of the story. As the doctor enters the hospital, he not only ignores the fishman, but he does not even verbally greet his visitor. It is apparent the doctor was raised in an environment which taught him to consider all members of other races as inferiors. In addition, he obviously believes that the power of his position makes him superior to some or most members of his own race. During the scene in the autopsy room when the old man is viewing his wife's body, the doctor is oblivious to any human quality or suffering. Two things could contribute to his lack of feeling; the first is his profession. Working at a job where he does not deal with living patients could have removed basic feelings of compassion towards others. The second, a more likely factor, could be his environment. A person in his position in a racist society could come to feel he is above common people, especially some old, black fishmonger who accepts the role of an inferior.

Another, more obvious example of the effects of environment can be seen in the lab assistant. The author uses a very graphic incident to illustrate the callousness of the lab assistant. Using the dead woman's thigh as a pin cushion while the husband watches him sew up the woman's mutilated body clearly illustrates the assistant's inability to feel compassion for the grieving man in front of him. This incident clearly suggests that the assistant has been influenced by the unfeeling doctor. While working on the old man's wife, the assistant displays the same feelings of social superiority as the doctor. An assumption that position and race separate humanity is obvious in both the doctor and the assistant.

Finally, the most ambiguous character is the narrator. He is also shown to be a product of a racially segregated society by his actions during the first meeting with the fishman. Unlike the doctor, the narrator does notice the old man; indeed, he acknowledges some human qualities in him. But while he is quick to notice his appearance, this businessman does not feel compelled to greet or console the old black man. Although the reader becomes aware of an uneasiness in the narrator, there is little action from him to indicate true compassion during the post-mortem scene. The reader is almost led to believe the narrator's sense of unease comes from embarrassment and not compassion. In the narrator, as well as the other characters, the reader is aware of a sense of position. Although the narrator may be uncomfortable due to some inner pangs of compassion, it is obvious the fishman, the doctor, and the lab assistant see nothing wrong with the roles they play, suggesting their actions are the result of environmental conditioning.

—*K. C. Boylan*

Sample In-Class Essay #2

The students taking this exam were given the following instructions and were to respond to an essay that first appeared in *Newsweek* magazine. The article, written by Ginny Carrol, reported on a interview with Captain Carol Barkalow of the U.S. Army. The title of the article, "Women Have What It Takes," sums up the point of the article. According to Captain Barkalow, women should have every right to ask for combat duty if they want to fight on the front lines. She pointed out in the interview that women have fought in wars in the past, that the death of a woman warrior should be considered no more tragic than the death of a man warrior, and that the interpersonal relationships between men and women soldiers on the battlefield would be no different than the traditional relationship between men on the battlefield.

In "Women Have What it Takes," Captain Barkalow makes a case for military women being allowed to fight in combat. Write an essay in which you agree or disagree with her position.

Women Have What It Takes

During the past few decades, there has been a growing controversy over the issue of allowing women to serve in the military. Carol Barkalow, a West Point graduate and commander of an air defense platoon and a truck company, spoke to *Newsweek* writer Ginny Carroll concerning the subject shortly after the invasion of Kuwait and resulting Gulf War. In her interview, Ms. Barkalow took the position that women were fully capable of serving in the military and were equal to men in their overall suitability. While such a position may well raise some conservative eyebrows, a review of similar roles women have played in American history will demonstrate the veracity of Ms. Barkalow's belief.

During the American Revolution and the Civil War, a number of women were involved both overtly and covertly in the war efforts. In both wars, soldiers involved in active combat were later discovered to be women disguised as men. In many cases, the women involved were so convincing in their roles that the men they fought alongside and camped with refused to believe they were in fact women. In at least one instance, the United States government paid a pension to the husband of a "soldier" following her death. In addition to this type of direct combat involvement, other women acted as spies and couriers. For instance, during the Civil War, abolitionist Harriet Tubman and Sojourner Truth, both black women, tirelessly worked as spies to promote the success of the Union army and risked certain death if they were caught.

The history of women in the military continued into the present century with the advent of World War II. With fighting taking place in so many arenas, women were not at liberty to take a passive role, even had they been so inclined. While women were unable to serve in active combat, military positions were found for them in organizations such as the WACS and WAVES. In fact, one such woman was employed as General Eisenhower's driver, and other women filled a number of similar positions. Back in the United States, many women played an active role in the war effort by seeking employment and training in naval yards and factories, and the war-time stereotype of Rosie the Riveter was born. Although their jobs were primarily in the private sector rather than in direct, combat-related activities, the job duties of women in war work were hard and physically demanding. Because they were successful and dedicated in carrying out their efforts, women were able to prove to their male counterparts that they could undertake such responsibilities when called on to do so.

Within the last few decades, women have been accepted into military and paramilitary roles traditionally within the purview of men and have found success in those positions. As Carol Barkalow pointed out in her *Newsweek* interview, West Point began admitting female candidates in 1980. By 1990, men in the military had begun to recognize women as their peers because women had shown themselves to be worthy of their regard. Similarly, and at about the same time, civilian police departments began to hire and train female officers as a result of the Affirmative Action requirements mandating the hiring of minorities. While veteran male police officers were skeptical at first, women officers have since proven their competency on the job, on patrol, and not just behind a desk in a station house.

Although the idea of women in combat is still somewhat controversial, it is an idea whose time has come. It is axiomatic that diehard conservative males will continue to oppose the idea of women in the forefront of active combat, but as Carol Barkalow so eloquently pointed out, strong, valid arguments exist to refute each and every point of opposition. During the 200-plus years the United States has been in existence, women have made slow but steady gains in obtaining the recognition of their abilities and equality they deserve, and the battle has frequently been a difficult one. The experience of battling against those people they value and hold closest to them for so many years has made women inherently suitable to battle those who threaten the peace and liberty of us all. In fact, given the opportunity, women just may do a better job!

—Kim Powers

EXERCISE 7.3

Assume you are writing an in-class exam for a health education class, and your instructor has told you to prepare to write on physical fitness. Try to anticipate the essay examination questions that you might be asked. List three potential questions:

1._____

_____

_____

2._____

_____

_____

3._____

_____

_____

NOTE: The following examination (Exercise 7.4) must be completed during a single class period.

EXERCISE 7.4

At the very beginning of the class period in which you plan to write your practice examination, ask your instructor for your question and go to work immediately.

Write in ink; use 8 1/2 x 11-inch paper; write only on one side of the page; and skip every other line. Proofread your work.

Your practice examination will be evaluated and returned to you, or it will be evaluated with you in a conference. The following checklist will be used. Study it so you will know the basis upon which you will be graded.

EVALUATION CHECKLIST

1. Knowledge of subject (Coverage?)
2. Thesis (Short introductory paragraph. Does it address the prompt directly?)
3. Essay structure (Strongest idea first?)
4. Topic sentences (At beginning of each body paragraph?)
5. Primary and secondary support sentences (Details?)
6. Sentence construction
7. Proofreading

Probable Grade _____

LESSON THREE—Open-Book Exams

Occasionally, an instructor will allow you to refer to your texts and notes during an in-class essay examination. Open-book exams, however, are not easy to write; they present special problems. The main problem is time pressure. Since you will be required to write at least 500 words during a typical essay exam—often in a fifty-minute class period—you cannot take much time to plan your answers. To function effectively during an open-book exam, you must formulate your thesis and an outline rapidly, then begin to write your paragraphs, using, whenever possible, information you need from your books and notes. Because of time limitations, however, you have to know exactly what information you want to use and where to find it. Therefore, studying before an open-book exam is just as important as studying before a closed-book exam.

The best organizational strategy for you to use is the one outlined in the previous lesson. Dispense with the introductory paragraph—concentrate on writing a good thesis sentence. Use your best point first, and write just one concluding sentence instead of a full concluding paragraph.

Quoted materials must be enclosed in quotation marks and documented, and any material closely summarized or paraphrased should be documented, too. Use lead-ins also. Use parenthetical documentation.

Study the following essay, written as one part of an open-book examination in an American literature course. Again, notice how the thesis sentence, the first sentence, directly addresses the essay question.

Question: Discuss the use of nature as a symbolic motif in William Faulkner's *The Bear.*

Nature symbolism in *The Bear* by Faulkner is dominated by the bear and Sam Fathers as symbols of the spirit of the wilderness.

"Old Ben is the wilderness, the mystery of man's nature and origins beneath the forms of civilization; and man's proper relationship with the wilderness teaches him liberty, courage, pride, and humility" (Hoffman and Vickery 325). Sam Fathers, the son of a Negro slave and a Chickasaw chief, symbolizes human ability to achieve the proper relationship to nature through contact with the wilderness. Both Sam Fathers and the bear bring Ike to an awareness of the wilderness, which he realizes is slowly vanishing. " 'So it won't be until the last day. When even [the bear] don't want it to last any longer' " (Faulkner, 205). Because of his initiation into the mystique of the wilderness, Ike takes it upon himself to preserve the spirit of the wilderness after the killing of the bear and the death of Sam Fathers by refusing to contribute to its physical destruction. By repudiating his inheritance of the land, Ike hopes "to hold the earth mutual and intact in the communal anonymity of brotherhood" (Faulkner 247), a lesson he has learned from the wilderness. Ultimately, Faulkner juxtaposes the wilderness, a desired element in human well-being, with civilization, a corrupt evil that is a result of people not having a proper relationship to nature. The wilderness emerges as human salvation from civilization, but it is dying as that same civilization threatens to destroy it.

EXERCISE 7.5

If you feel that you need to practice writing an open-book exam (or if your instructor feels you need to practice), have your instructor assign you a topic, and decide on the time limits, sources you may use, and documentation required.

Have your practice exam evaluated.

LESSON FOUR—Take-Home Exams

Instructors frequently assign take-home exams. Students are usually relieved upon hearing they will be able to write their exams outside of class because they want to be free of the tremendous time pressure of the in-class exam and because they need more time to study. Often, however, their relief is short-lived, for take-home exams can be very demanding. It is not unusual for multiple-part exams to be assigned, each part requiring a response of 500 words or more; furthermore, students are usually given less than a week to complete a take-home exam. These requirements are a great hardship on students who have heavy study loads or who work.

When your instructor assigns a take-home exam, be certain you understand exactly what is required and what is allowed. Your best strategy in take-home exams—unless your instructor is adamant that you should not do any more than asked for—is to go above and beyond what is required. Some instructors will mark essays down if students go over the allowable length. Other instructors will mark essays down if students include references to library sources that were not requested. Take the time and effort to construct your answers carefully. Each take-home essay you write must be carefully constructed and carefully edited.

Study the following essay. Students taking this exam were to analyze a specific essay by Russell Baker, entitled "School vs. Education."

The students assigned this take-home essay were given the following instructions and limitations.

Take-Home Essay Assignment

Background: In "School vs. Education," Russell Baker satirizes the American educational system by exaggerating its problems at each stage of a person's life. Can you recognize any part of your education process in his descriptions? Or have your educational experiences been vastly different from what Baker describes? Or have your educational experiences been somewhat the same and somewhat different?

Topic: Write an essay comparing or contrasting your educational experiences with that of Russell Baker.

Guidelines:

1. 750–1,000 words in length
2. address the topic
3. have clear essay structure, with an identifiable thesis statement and topic sentences
4. refer clearly to Baker's essay
5. carefully edit the essay
6. include clear examples supporting your ideas.

The following essay was submitted by a student who took the exam.

Ben Lorton

Professor Sessano

English 1A

5/27/03

                    ABC: Anything But College

Something new is learned every day. That's good because according to

Russell Baker, ascertainment of knowledge does not come from school

instruction. Russell Baker explains this in his essay "School vs. Education"

by dividing the learning process into three stages: before school, during

school and college—formal instruction, and after the completion of college.

Although he exaggerates the failings of the American education at each of

these stages, Russell Baker's essay caused me to ponder my educational

experiences.

In recalling the preschool phase of education, my experiences are vastly

different from what Baker describes. Baker writes, "By the age of six the

average child will have completed the basic American education and be ready

to enter school." This "basic American education," is taught in the first

stage of education—preschool, which is interpreted literally to mean before

taking that giant leap of a first step into a classroom in Baker's essay.

He writes, "From television, the child will have learned how to pick a lock,

commit a fairly elaborate bank holdup, prevent wetness all day long, get

the laundry twice as white, and kill people with a variety of sophisticated

armaments." However, I do not remember learning much of this in my

"preschool" stage because my parents had a firm control over what I observed

on television. As most kids around six years old do when Mom has a headache

and Dad is mowing the lawn, I watched television. I remember "Sesame Street"

as being one of my favorite programs to watch. "Sesame Street" found its

way onto my TV screen, for its day-time programming consists of educational,

yet fun, themes with cast and Muppets displaying exemplary behavior in hopes of convincing children that they are supposed to learn and have fun at the same time. Singing along with friends like Big Bird, Bert and Ernie, and even Oscar the Grouch, I learned my alphabet, how to count, and how to add and subtract. I remember vividly one show's animation for the number nine. Since they have nine lives, I assume that is why cats were used in the representation. I remember the sound of the cats when the Count said, "Repeat after me ... that's one-meow, two-meow, three-meow...nine-meow! That's nine meowing cats. Meow, Meow, Meow!" Other shows, or should I call them cartoons, that I liked to watch were the "Smurfs" and "Scooby Doo." These shows excited my imagination with captivating who-done-it plots. These shows demonstrated teamwork and friendship—the necessary social skills one needs in society that some adults are still searching for. Therefore, although Baker claims lock-picking, bank hold-ups, and other "no-no's" are presented in children's programming, I did not pick up on these mischievous acts when watching television; instead, my attention focused on learning the alphabet, how to count, and how to play and work with others appropriately.

Baker continues, "From watching his parents, the child, in many cases, will already know how to smoke, how much soda to mix with whiskey, what kind of language to use when angry, and how to violate the speed laws without being caught"; in this, I agree. My parents, although both educated, did demonstrate these behaviors in front of me. I remember my father and mother, my mother especially, firing up cancer sticks after meals; however, I do not smoke, and I have not smoked a cigarette to this day—yuck! I also remember my father coming home from work and mixing his Wild Turkey Straight Kentucky Whiskey with 7-Up, a T-7 if you will, which is one of my preferred alcoholic beverages today. I also remember our car rides, especially with my mother, and the braking at the intersections from 50 mph to the posted 30 mph, in order to avoid being spotted by the lurking traffic cop, or on the freeway, she would switch two lanes over if she spotted a cop car in the rearview mirror. This behavior carried over without a doubt. I am always speeding here and there, and keeping an eye out for the boys in blue; maybe it's the video games, maybe it's the movies; maybe it's the fear our system has come to instill in our minds. Whatever the reason, from watching my parents, I learned these behaviors and practice some of them today, which puts me in agreement with Baker for this stage.

Next, according to Baker, "the child is ready for the second stage of education, which occurs in school." At this point in Baker's essay, he refers to teachers walking out on their jobs and the actions of a segregated America in the 1950s and 1960s—people "stoning buses, and cracking skulls" of those whom are pigmented differently. Although this happened close to a half century ago, these events still invade the newspapers of American today. My education, however, still differed from Baker's explanation. I was enrolled in Merryhill Country School (MCS), a private preparatory school, which is a Nobel Learning Communities Institute for Instruction, where the teachers seemed to care, even though they'd put you on time out during recess for no reason valid enough for me, at least. The instruction in this school was heavily focused on pushing the students, and at $400.00 a month tuition, each student achieved successfully. There were no walkouts or bus stonings; there were no fights that I can remember; everyone at the school knew each other and respected each other, even at that young age. During this stage of formal instruction, Baker writes, "the child learns that life is for testing." At this school, I agree. SAT's scores were given the utmost attention, and teachers made sure each student knew how important success is. I would assume I, along with the rest of my classmates at MCS, was one of the smart kids Baker refers to as the one that "the teacher puts intelligent demands upon," for I remember what was expected of us at Merryhill Country School.

After Merryhill, I attended John Kennedy High School, which happened to be a public school. This was my first experience outside of the sheltered private institution. In the public school system, the teachers differed as well as the class sizes. Since there was no tuition to be paid, classes were overfilled, and instruction did not always make its way through the thick layers of my head. The individualized instruction was missing; therefore, my grades dropped, and as Baker put it, "there [was] very little incentive to stop being dumb." After somehow graduating high school, I thought it would be a grand idea to enter college with the horrible study habits I had mastered in high school. This was a bad idea. My attendance pattern, which wasn't the best in high school, showed up my first few semesters of college, and by not coming to class, I earned "Ds," "Fs," and "Ws," and exited college to work at a handful of part—time jobs for minimum wage. Baker doesn't write about this stage of struggle in his essay, yet almost all the college students I know are currently or already have gone through it. It was in this stage of my life that I learned the most. I realized that world was full of ruthlessness and that it had no heart. Nobody cared, and if I needed to get something done, I would have to do it myself. This was the most valuable lesson I could have learned from my three-year absence from college, and I'm glad I learned it when I did. Baker does refer to this when he writes, "The student learns that the race is to the cunning and often, alas to the unprincipled." However, he refers to this after the student has learned that he or she has not been admitted to graduate school. Since my lesson has been learned and I have re-entered college, I feel that I will have a running start when that time comes to prosper "in medicine, at the bar, or in the corporate boardroom."

In summary, I remember moments of my education that were similar and others that were different from Baker's point of view. It is exceptionally arduous to separate what one learns in school from what one learns by simple surveillance in this frenetic world. I believe schools cannot teach everything people need to know in life. Schools prepare students for the working world, and schools train students to think critically so that when they are presented with a real life problem, they can handle it. But life likes to throw curve balls at each of us, and that is what the school cannot teach. That is what parents are for. Even they can not completely prepare their young for what the world will bring, yet our parents have given us a good start, and it is up to us to finish it.

LESSON FIVE—*Proficiency Exams*

Schools commonly require students to write proficiency exams to demonstrate their writing ability prior to awarding some major degree or certificate. Most colleges and universities, for example, require students to pass a proficiency exam before they receive their bachelor's degree. Some schools refer to such exams as the WPE, the Writing Proficiency Examination. In most states, those students who go on to earn their teaching credential must pass another writing proficiency test. There are many other writing proficiency exams students may be required to pass, depending on their majors.

Writing these proficiency exams is in some ways easier than writing short-time in-class exams. When writing proficiency exams, you will typically have two hours or more to complete the writing. When writing such essays, you should write fully developed introductory and concluding paragraphs as well as fully developed body paragraphs. Plan to write an essay that is 500-750 words long, and make sure you edit your work carefully before you submit it.

Proficiency exams are usually graded holistically by a committee made up of experienced instructors. Your exam will be read by at least two readers, both of whom must agree that your essay is either passing or failing. In some schools all exams that receive a failing score are read by a third reader to give the student the benefit of the doubt. The term "graded holistically" refers to the fact that the instructors reading the exams are not allowed to make any marks on your exam; they simply read the exam to gain an overall impression and then compare its qualities to a scoring guide they have in front of them. The following scoring guide is typical.

SCORING GUIDE

4   The 4 essay reflects an exceptional performance of the writing task.
  • thesis is clearly stated, may be compelling or thoughtful
  • organization is exceptionally clear, transitions effective
  • uses appropriate details and analyzes their significance
  • fluent, demonstrating a clear command of language and varied sentence structure
  • virtually free of errors in sentence structure, grammar, and mechanics

3   The 3 essay reflects adequate performance of the writing task.
  • a central idea focuses the essay
  • adequate organization and development
  • may have a few problems in sentence structure, diction, and mechanics
  • demonstrates adequate command of language and some sentence variety

2   The 2 essay approaches adequate performance of the writing task.
  • may have an unfocused or simplistic central idea
  • may be poorly organized, or may lack detail and specificity
  • frequent problems in diction, grammar, mechanics, and sentence structure, which impede meaning

1   The 1 essay is clearly inadequate.
  • may lack a central idea
  • may lack coherence or adequate development although it may address the topic
  • multiple errors in sentence structure, grammar, and mechanics impede understanding

Student essays given 4 or 3 scores by instructors are passing exams; those given 2 or 1 scores are failing exams. However, some schools use a six-point scale where 6, 5, and 4 exams pass and 3, 2, and 1 exams fail. You should examine it carefully so you will know what your readers will expect when they read your exams.

Most proficiency exams will list two topics and ask you to choose one of them. When you receive your exam topics sheet, look quickly at both topics and choose one that looks interesting. After you have chosen one, stay with it: do not change topics, even if you later find that you don't like the one you have chosen. Changing topics after you have started will almost certainly lead to failure because you won't have sufficient time left to develop the second topic.

The topic you are given to write on when you take a proficiency exam will be general rather than specific. That is, you can confidently expect that you will be asked to write about something that everyone should know enough about to write a 500-750 word essay. Consider the typical proficiency exam topic below:

> Many parents are concerned about the negative effect of television on their children. Write an essay in which you explain what some of the physical, social, and psychological effects are that cause parents to worry. Include specific examples to support your ideas.

When writing on a topic such as this one, look carefully at the assignment and you will often see exactly what is desired in the way of a response. Here, the body paragraphs should include at least three, one describing each of the following effects: physical, social, and psychological. You could write more than this but not less.

The following is a typical holistic exam topic that has been given often in proficiency examinations.

EXAM TOPIC:

Aging is an inevitable process about which people hold differing views. Some people are bothered by the physical process of growing older: the changes in appearance, activities, and health. Others, however, believe the mental changes—more knowledge, maturity, ability to understand life—far outweigh the physical inconveniences of growing older. Obviously, there are both positive and negative aspects involved in the process of growing old.

THE TOPIC TO WRITE ON:

Discuss some of the positive and negative aspects of growing older, and explain why you feel aging is ultimately either a positive or a negative experience.

The first step in writing on this, as with any written assignment, is to analyze the question. The topic clearly states that you are to discuss both the "positive and negative aspects" of growing older. The topic also asks you to "explain why you feel aging is ultimately either a positive or a negative experience." You could easily discuss the positive and negative aspects in the introduction and then explain the point of the essay in the thesis. The body of the essay would then give as many examples as possible to support the major idea. The student who wrote the following exam used that approach.

What Do You Mean, Old?

Nobody asks for it, nobody wants it, everyone tries to avoid it, everybody fights it, but, so far, everyone eventually grows old unless he or she dies prematurely. Although growing old is a natural state of affairs, most people would just as soon avoid having to experience the physical problems that come along with old age. Even those who champion the advantages of aging don't look at newborns with their petal-soft skin, sparkling eyes, and flexible joints and wish them dry, wrinkly skin, droopy, dim eyes, and stiff, painful joints. But given the fact that virtually all humans would rather grow old than die before having a chance to enjoy life, most look forward to old age with a mixture of apprehension and anticipation. After all, growing old is not only a time when the body deteriorates; it is also a time when people have time to enjoy free time, family, and friends. Because growing old is a challenging and worthwhile adventure that calls into action all the mental, emotional, and physical resources that people have available, there are realities and myths which need to be addressed.

No one can deny that recognizable attitudinal and mental changes occur as people grow older. Many reach a "generative" state when past fifty. This is a time when many individuals search to put meaning into their lives and their work. Oftentimes these people might change jobs or even careers. They look for fulfillment by leaving something good for posterity. As they grow past that, in the later years, there can be a sense of peace and accomplishment because of a life well spent. In these years people in general use the faculties, experiences, and wisdom they have gathered over the years to guide the next generation. Although it takes them longer to learn new skills, it is a mistaken notion that old people must be forgetful and can't learn new things. A recent article in *Scientific American* discussed how many people continue to learn throughout life and published a picture of a ninety-nine-year-old who had just graduated with a Bachelor of Arts! And many of us can remember hearing that Colonel Sanders started a new business adventure, Kentucky Fried Chicken, after he retired.

While growing older, people can continue to be emotionally balanced. Good emotional habits need to be acquired while young and continued throughout life. By learning good stress-coping techniques and being open to change—change does not mean death—people can carry on normal, happy, fulfilling lives regardless of their age. George Burns is a good example of this. His wife and show business partner died many years ago, yet he not only survived, but with good coping skills, he went on to make many more money-making movies and made countless appearances on television shows and in theaters. Many centenarians, when asked what their longevity secrets are, repeatedly remark, "I didn't worry," "I left it up to the Lord," "I drank a glass of wine every day," and the like. George Burns might suggest that his daily cigar is responsible for his longevity. The similarity between all those who have lived exceptionally long lives is that they had the ability to live their lives "one day at a time." Being emotionally balanced can give older people an edge in dealing with younger ones as they teach them, thus helping to leave a good legacy.

The physical process of growing old is viewed by many as the hardest with which to cope. Obviously, it is true that there are many physiological changes which also affect the emotions and the mind. There is no dichotomy here. Throughout our lives we lose about twenty-five percent of our neurons, and there are other changes in the remaining neurons. This affects the communication between brain and body. Also, muscles tend to shrink in size. Hormones decline. These are very real physiological changes. However, some myths must be expelled from people's minds. One medical doctor, in his book *Growing Old is Not for Sissies*, described his lifestyle and showed pictures of himself—his muscles are far from flat and flabby! Much of the physical deterioration commonly accepted as a normal part of aging is simply from lack of use. It has been consistently proven that exercise does help stiff joints. The synovial fluid needs to be moved so it does not crystallize and make the joints stiff. Ninety-year olds have been put on gentle exercise programs, and their muscles have increased in size. In a study conducted in the United States, several older citizens were able to give up their walkers after a steady program of exercise. Disabilities due to coronary heart disease have been reversed by using a good exercise program. And how much better is prevention? Good regular exercise, a prudent, low-fat, mostly vegetarian diet, good stress coping skills, and quiet "time outs" keep people feeling young and healthy into old age. In the same issue of *Scientific American* mentioned previously, there were pictures of centenarians swimming and engaging in various lively activities.

People should remember that mental changes can be channeled into positive experiences, that the emotions can be tamed and used to benefit posterity, and that physical changes can be monitored to a great extent. It seems that life is just a matter of living each day, each minute, looking forward to the next day with clear cognitive skills, wholesome emotions, and a healthy, toned body. Can it happen? Absolutely! Is it happening to people?" Yes. The questions to ask are, "If you didn't know how old you were, how old would you be?" and "If you had seventy more years to live, how would you plan to spend them?" A woman in France just turned one hundred twenty years old. This is, according to scientists, as long as humans can live under the conditions people are familiar with at this time. People would do well to plan their lives according to the one hundred twenty-year time line. They would have quite an incentive to keep good mental, emotional, and physical habits so as to guarantee themselves a happy, healthy, and long life.

—Lillian Manship

Chapter Seven Test

To prepare for the Chapter Seven Test, you will need to review Chapter One through Chapter Six of *Survival*. Your final essay exam will require you to demonstrate a thorough knowledge of the writing strategies presented in these chapters. (You will not, however, be tested on your knowledge of documentation.) When you have completed all of the work in Chapter Seven and you have reviewed Chapters One through Six, ask your instructor for the Chapter Seven Test. Your instructor may give you one of the following:

1. A closed-book exam (500-750 words)
2. An open-book exam (500-750 words)
3. A take-home exam (750-1,000 words)

If the examination is to be written in class, it must be completed during a single class period. If your first attempt is not acceptable, you may be allowed to revise your examination or to write another one on a different topic. (You may be asked to rewrite or revise your take-home exams, too.) Your instructor will make this decision.

APPENDICES

APPENDIX A
Sentence Structure and Mechanics

Writing is one of the gauges that scholars employ to judge the level of intellectual development achieved by a civilization. Ancient peoples who had not perfected a written language had to rely wholly upon oral communication. The oral tradition of our ancestors is, of course, rich in story and myth. However, speaking to contemporary people across the centuries without writing means that much of what these people's lives were like, what frightened them, what brought them joy, what they thought about, is left to our speculation from hints derived from their technology, their art, and the stories that survive from their oral tradition.

In the contemporary world, writing is of paramount importance to our lives. The need for absolute clarity in communication, especially in areas such as science, government, business, and diplomacy, has obligated us to agree upon certain principles in the selection of vocabulary, the construction of sentences and their punctuation, the structures of paragraphs, and the development of compositions. These principles (or rules) are sometimes referred to as grammar, usage, mechanics, or conventions. Although you may often find them to be a nuisance, if not an irritation, these conventions do, in fact, ensure a clarity of communication that might not otherwise be achieved.

This appendix will help you become a more skillful sentence editor. The lessons in this section review the fundamental conventions of writing at the sentence level. You may already be familiar with most of these rules and find that your review of them reaffirms your confidence in your writing and editing skills. On the other hand, you may need to study certain sections quite closely either because you are unfamiliar with the conventions or because they cause problems for you in your writing. Your instructor may refer you to a specific section of this appendix as the need arises or may ask you to complete the entire appendix and then take a test.

LESSON ONE—Sentence Structure and Punctuation, Transitions

To be a good writer, you must be a skillful sentence editor—aware of the types of sentences you are using and how to punctuate them. Good writing is characterized by a variety of simple, compound, and complex sentences. Appearing at the beginning, in the middle, and at the end of sentences, phrases and dependent clauses create sentence variety and a fuller expression. Some sentences are long and complicated, but others are short, producing interesting contrast. Punctuation is used effectively to prevent confusion and to make reading easier. Smooth transitions are made between sentences and paragraphs. Always, whether by instinct or design, sentence structure enhances what is being said. The overall effect is sentences that flow with pleasing balance and rhythm. As you write, you will naturally be concerned with the task of saying what you want to say clearly. But you should try to write with style, rewriting, experimenting with options, correcting, trying different word combinations, until you are thoroughly satisfied with the results.

The Simple Sentence

By definition, a **simple sentence** is one that contains only one independent clause and no dependent clauses. Simple refers to one of anything: simple sentence means one independent clause in the sentence, simple subject means one subject, and simple predicate means one verb in the predicate.

By contrast, compound refers to two or more of any one thing: compound sentence means two or more independent clauses, compound subject means two or more subjects, and compound predicate means two or more verbs.

Examples

A massive oil *slick drifted* closer to the coast. (simple subject and predicate)

A massive oil *slick* and *debris* from the sinking tanker *drifted* closer to the coast. (compound subject and simple predicate)

A massive oil *slick* and *debris* from the sinking tanker *drifted* closer to the coast and *threatened* its delicate marine life environment. (compound subject and compound predicate)

A simple sentence can actually be quite complicated. But as long as it contains only one independent clause and no dependent clauses, it is still a simple sentence.

Example

To the dismay of the clean-up crews, the massive oil *slick* and *debris* from the sinking tanker *drifted* closer to the coast, threatening its delicate marine environment with irreparable damage from the sticky goo.

Phrases

A **phrase** is a meaningful group of words that does not contain a subject and a predicate. A phrase functions as a single part of speech, often as an adjective or adverb. Although a simple sentence contains no dependent clauses, it usually contains one or more phrases. These phrases are indispensable if you are to express yourself effectively. In order to punctuate a sentence correctly, you must be aware that you are using a phrase.

Examples

The scientist *has created* a perfect artificial emerald. (verb phrase)

She read *for an hour before lunch*. (prepositional phrases)

Falling asleep at the wheel, the truck driver drove off the highway, *demolishing a roadside fruit stand*. (participial phrases)

Eating a salad and fruit for lunch is healthier than *eating a hamburger and french fries*. (gerund phrases)

Her term paper finished, she let out a huge sigh. (absolute phrase)

Carol went *to find a newspaper*. (infinitive phrase)

His brother, *a track star at Borg High School*, suffered a pulled hamstring muscle. (appositive phrase)

One of the most financially successful movies of all time, *for example*, is *Titanic*. (transitional phrase)

Dirty and bedraggled, the puppy was obviously lost. (adjective phrase)

Two weeks earlier, he lost his watch. (adverb phrase)

Punctuating Simple Sentences

INTRODUCTORY PARTS

Commas may be needed in simple sentences to set off **introductory parts**.

1. Transitional Words and Phrases

Transitional words and phrases are used to build bridges between sentences. Use a comma to set off an introductory word or phrase.

Some Transitional Words and Phrases

In addition,	However,
Furthermore,	Nevertheless
First,	In other words,
For example,	Thus,
For instance,	Therefore,
Of course,	In conclusion,

Examples

They wanted to hike to the summit. *However*, the storm grew worse.

Nils had been acting differently for about a month. *For instance*, he would suddenly begin singing during class.

2. To Prevent Confusion

A comma after an introductory word or phrase may be necessary to keep the reader from mistakenly connecting the word or phrase to what follows, forcing the reader to reread the sentence.

Examples

Surprised, Fred barely had time to push his dirty clothes under his bed.

Three inches below, the heat shield tile had developed a crack.

3. To Create a Pause

You can direct a reader to pause after an introductory word or phrase by setting it off with a comma.

Examples

On the road to the enchanted castle, the miller's son met a wizard.
Somehow, the miller's son misunderstood the directions to the castle.
Two miles later, the fog began to form.
Warm and peaceful, the moss-covered tree looked inviting.

Sleeping peacefully under the branches of the tree, he did not notice the evil sorceress.
"*Miller's son*, you are trespassing on sacred ground."
Alas, he was turned into a frog!

INTERNAL PUNCTUATION

Words and phrases in the middle of a simple sentence may need to be separated from one another or set off from the rest of the sentence with commas.

1. Transitional Words and Phrases

Examples

The next day, *however*, the storm became worse.

He would, *for instance*, suddenly start singing in class.

2. To Prevent Confusion

Examples

Bill, *John's brother*, will visit us in December.

The ranger, *seeing the climber's plight*, radioed for a rescue helicopter.

3. To Separate Words and Phrases

Examples

It was a *hot, sultry* day in July.

They *rented sleeping bags, backpacks*, and *cooking equipment* for their camping trip.

The jeep *crossed the ravine, forded the stream*, and *began to climb* the steep slope below the cabin.

4. To Set Off a Word or Phrase

Examples

You see, *Dr. Jones*, you will never escape.

The miller's son, *alas*, was turned into a frog!

Leonard Greene, *my next-door neighbor*, has decided to sell his house.

The problem, *corrosion*, was discovered by a plumber.

In some cases the presence or absence of a pair of commas will tell the reader how to interpret the meaning of a sentence.

Examples

The car *stalled in the intersection* blocked traffic for miles.

The car, *stalled in the intersection*, blocked traffic for miles.

In the first version above, the one without commas, the participial verb phrase tells which car is being talked about perhaps there are many cars at the intersection. The phrase is essential to the identification of the car. In that sense it is a restrictive modifier and should not be set off with commas. In the second version, the pair of commas acts like parentheses, showing that the reader already knows which car is being talked about. The phrase, a nonrestrictive modifier, is information that is not vital to the meaning of the sentence.

END PARTS

A word or phrase at the end of a simple sentence may need to be set off with a comma. In general, however, end parts are less likely to need separation than are introductory parts.

1. Transitional Words and Phrases

Examples

The bird feeder remained standing after the windstorm, *however.*

Even while visiting England, most Americans want to start their day with a cup of coffee, *of course.*

2. To Prevent Confusion

Examples

The band performed in several states, *in Michigan, Florida, New York, and Ohio.*

The crack in the bridge upper deck grew more pronounced, *causing the Highway Department to close the crossing altogether.*

Eric darted up the street, *the county truant officer close behind.*

3. To Separate or Create a Pause

Examples

Lynne's report was late, *as usual.*

Thank you for an outstanding presentation, *Ms. VanderSchaaf.*

Joshua's large dictionary lay under his desk all during the test, *unconsulted and forgotten.*

Trenton received three dozen orders for the new printer during the first week it was available, *the direct result of his presale promotional mailings.*

She served his favorite dessert, *Jello with Cool Whip.*

The miller's son was turned into a frog, *alas*!

The Compound Sentence

When two or more simple sentences (independent clauses) are joined correctly, the resulting sentence is called a **compound sentence.** Study the following sentences.

Examples

The brakes failed, *and* the car crashed into the tree. (comma and conjunction)

The class was canceled; the teacher had chicken pox. (semicolon)

The road was covered with snow; *therefore,* the trucker drove very slowly. (semicolon, conjunctive adverb, and comma)

You can write compound sentences using any of the three methods illustrated above. However, the most common connector is the comma and conjunction shown in the first example. You must not omit any part of the punctuation, or you will create a sentence error.

Examples

Incorrect—   The brakes failed and the car crashed. (run-on)

Incorrect—   The brakes failed, the car crashed. (comma splice)

Correct—   The brakes failed, and the car crashed. (compound sentence)

The two independent clauses in a compound sentence are equal in importance and subject matter. The word used to describe any two things that are equal in rank or importance is called a coordinate. Logically the term **coordinating conjunction** describes any word used to join simple sentences to create a compound sentence. Other than using a semicolon, the only way to correctly join two simple sentences is to use a coordinating conjunction.

The coordinating conjunctions are often called FANBOYS, which is an acronym formed from the first letter of each conjunction. The acronym makes it easy to remember the coordinating conjunctions:

COORDINATING CONJUNCTIONS
The FANBOYS

For   And   Nor   But   Or   Yet   So

Whenever you use a coordinating conjunction to join two simple sentences, you must place a comma before the conjunction. Some authorities hold that when two short, closely related independent clauses are joined, a comma before the conjunction is not necessary. However, while working with this book you should use a comma. The comma and the conjunction work together; neither may be omitted.

Example

The storm-spawned waves rocked the boat, and the sailors became seasick.

Coordinating conjunctions confuse some writers because the same conjunctions that are used to join two sentences into a compound sentence are also used to join two subjects or predicates in a simple sentence. The difference is that no comma is used in the simple sentence while a comma must be used in the compound sentence.

Examples

Simple—   The storm hit the city just before dark and made the roads impassable by dawn.

Compound—The storm hit the city just before dark, and the roads became impassable by dawn.

Each of the previous example sentences has the same number of words, but one is simple and the other compound. In order to correctly punctuate each, you must first be able to distinguish one from the other.

Easy Test for Commas

When you see two sentence parts connected with the conjunction and, but, or, for, yet, nor, or so, conduct this simple test to determine whether or not a comma is needed in front of the conjunction.

1. Using your pen, cover the conjunction and the portion of the sentence after the conjunction.

Example

The storm hit the city just before dark *and the roads were impassable at dawn.*

2. Ask yourself, could the exposed portion before the conjunction stand alone as a sentence?

Example

Yes. "The storm hit the city just before dark" is a sentence.

3. Next, cover the portion of the sentence in front of the conjunction and the conjunction itself.

Example

The storm hit the city just before dark and the roads were impassable at dawn.

4. Ask yourself, could the exposed portion stand alone as a sentence?

Example

"The roads were impassable at dawn." Yes, is the answer.

5. Since your answer would be yes to both questions, you know you must use a comma before the conjunction to join these two independent clauses.

Example

The storm hit the city just before dark, *and* the roads were impassable at dawn.

6. If your answer is no to either question, you would not precede the conjunction with a comma.

Example

The storm hit the city just before dark and made the roads impassable by dawn.

Since the part of the sentence after the conjunction is not a complete sentence, you would not place a comma before the conjunction in the example.

USING A SEMICOLON IN COMPOUND SENTENCES

The **semicolon** can be used instead of the comma and conjunction in some compound sentences. In other words, the semicolon can sometimes be used to join two closely related simple sentences. Three possible reasons that you might want to use this technique are as follows:

1. Joining two closely related simple sentences is one way to achieve sentence variety, thus making your writing more interesting for your readers.
2. Joining two closely related simple sentences may help you develop smoother-flowing sentences.
3. Joining two closely related simple sentences emphasizes the close relationship of the ideas in the two independent clauses being connected.

The reader comes to a semi-stop upon encountering the semicolon instead of a full stop signaled by a period. The semicolon creates a tighter connection than the comma-conjunction combination. Study the examples below.

Examples

Ben and Jerry are active environmentalists; their business practices promote those causes.

Ruth spoke to the city council about bus service for the elderly last week; this week she is writing to seven state legislators.

Maria was so late to class that she had time to finish only half the test; her grade suffered because of her tardiness.

In each of the sentences above, the semicolon is preferable to a comma and the conjunction *and* or to two sentences, which would sound choppy. Notice that in each case the connection is brisk, and the sentences connect smoothly. Occasional use of semicolons will improve your writing style, but be careful not to overuse them.

Perhaps one of the most effective uses of the semicolon is in the *semicolon + conjunctive adverb + comma* connection between two simple sentences.

Examples

The funding for the new computer classroom has again been delayed; *however*, several businesses have agreed to lend the school some new computers for next year.

She wants to enroll in advanced science and math courses as soon as she starts college; *therefore*, she studies several hours each evening.

The fuel economy of American-made automobiles has not improved dramatically the past few years; *moreover*, their fuel technology now lags behind that of many imports.

Some Conjunctive Adverbs

; accordingly,	; clearly, then,	; for one thing,	; heretofore,
; afterward,	; consequently,	; fourth,	; however,
; afterwards,	; finally,	; furthermore,	; in addition,
; all in all,	; first,	; granted,	; in fact,
; also,	; for example,	; hence,	; in general,
; as a matter of fact,	; for instance,	; hereafter,	; in other words,
; in particular,	; nevertheless,	; second,	; thereupon,
; in short,	; notwithstanding,	; similarly,	; third,
; in summary,	; obviously,	; still,	; thus (,)
; indeed	; of course,	; then(,)	; to be sure,
; likewise,	; on the whole,	; thereafter,	; to make matters worse,
; moreover,	; otherwise,	; therefore,	; unfortunately,

The **conjunctive adverb** builds a smooth transition between the two sentences being connected. But be aware that it is the semicolon that connects the two sentences, not the conjunctive adverb. Notice in the following examples that the conjunctive adverb *however* could be omitted but that the semicolon could not be omitted without creating a punctuation error. Remember, too, that a comma is usually placed after the conjunctive adverb to complete the connection.

Examples

Incorrect— The swan was the Queen's favorite bird however, the poacher killed it. (run-on)

Incorrect— The swan was the Queen's favorite bird, however, the poacher killed it. (comma splice)

Correct— The swan was the Queen's favorite bird; however, the poacher killed it. (compound sentence)

Correct— The swan was the Queen's favorite bird; the poacher killed it. (compound sentence; conjunctive adverb removed)

> **Note:** Since many of the same kinds of words and phrases used in simple sentences are used in compound sentences, the same punctuation rules apply for both kinds of sentences. The following compound sentence, for example, contains an introductory participial phrase and a transitional word in the middle of the second independent clause. Such transitions must be set off with commas.
>
> *Example*
>
> > *Believing strongly in her principles*, his grandmother tried to convince Nicholas to be a lawyer for the elderly and poor; he, *however*, was determined to be a corporate lawyer in the electronics industry.

The Complex Sentence

In order to understand the **complex sentence**, you must first know the difference between independent and dependent clauses. An **independent clause** is any group of words that contains a subject and a predicate and can stand alone as a complete sentence.

Examples

Wolves / howl.

Julie / showed Bill the shawl.

By contrast, a **dependent clause** is any group of words that begins with a subordinating conjunction or relative pronoun and contains a subject and a predicate. The dependent clause cannot stand alone as a sentence.

Examples

when wolves howl (subordinating conjunction)

that she bought in Mexico (relative pronoun)

Every grammatically complete sentence must contain at least one independent clause. When a dependent clause is added to an independent clause, the idea contained in the dependent clause is of less importance. The dependent clause, therefore, is subordinated to the independent clause through the use of a **subordinating conjunction** (sometimes referred to as a subordinating connective). These conjunctions indicate the subordinate status of dependent clauses.

Some Subordinating Conjunctions

after	before	though	where
although	even though	unless	whereas
as	if	until	while
as long as	provided	when	because
since	whenever		

In addition to subordinating conjunctions, **relative pronouns** are used to create subordinate dependent clauses.

Relative Pronouns

that
what
which
who
whom

Relative pronouns and subordinating conjunctions are known collectively as **signal words**. These subordinating conjunctions and relative pronouns are used to join two clauses, making one dependent upon the other. That is, the clause to which one of these words is attached becomes a dependent clause and can no longer stand alone. Therefore, whenever one of these dependent clauses is created, it must be attached to an independent clause; the resulting sentence is a **complex sentence**. Complex sentences give your writing variety and life when interspersed among simple and compound sentences. While editing, you can convert some simple and compound sentences to complex sentences.

Examples

1. He did not like his new job. However, the salary was high. (two simple sentences)
   He did not like his new job, but the salary was high. (compound sentence)
   He did not like his new job *even though* the salary was high. (complex sentence with a subordinating conjunction)

2. She saw a police car. She stopped. (two simple sentences)
   After she saw the police car, she stopped. (complex sentence with a subordinating conjunction)

3. She wanted a Chinese basket. It would have to be large enough for her jade plant. (two simple sentences)
   She wanted a Chinese basket *that* would be large enough for her jade plant. (complex sentence with a relative pronoun)

Punctuating Complex Sentences

INTRODUCTORY DEPENDENT CLAUSES

Ordinarily, a dependent clause must be followed by a comma when the dependent clause is placed at the beginning of the sentence, preceding the independent clause. The effect of the comma is to create a pause.

Examples

Although an oil surplus developed, gasoline prices remained high.

When she saw Juan's picture, she screamed, "He's so cute!"

DEPENDENT CLAUSES IN THE MIDDLE

If a dependent clause in the middle of a sentence is essential to the meaning of the sentence (restrictive), no commas are used to separate it from the rest of the sentence.

Examples

The woman *who is wearing the bright red blouse* will show you the exhibit.

An automobile *that has a long wheelbase* often rides more comfortably on the highway.

But if a dependent clause that interrupts a sentence can be removed from the complex sentence without altering the intended meaning of the sentence, a pair of commas should be used to set the interrupting dependent clause apart from the rest of the sentence. In cases where you cannot decide whether or not a dependent clause is restrictive or nonrestrictive, ask yourself if the reader should pause at the beginning and end of the dependent clause in question. If pauses are necessary for proper reading, place a comma at the beginning and end.

Examples

Theresa, who is wearing the bright red blouse, will show you the exhibit.

Teri's truck, which she bought just last year, leaves her stranded at least twice a month.

DEPENDENT CLAUSES AT THE END

Whenever possible, refrain from using a comma to separate an independent clause and a dependent clause that follows it at the end of a sentence. You must have a good reason for using a comma to set off an end clause.

Examples

The magazine editor wore a smile *although she was obviously annoyed.*

They worked for a new car dealer *until they started their own auto parts business.*

However, a comma placed between an independent clause and the dependent clause that follows may be needed to create a pause or to prevent confusion. A pause may be needed so that the dependent clause will be read with more emphasis than if the comma were not used. Or the pause may be used to show that the dependent clause is not needed, an extra or a nonrestrictive clause.

Examples

The theater manager plans to begin evening productions one hour earlier, *whether the audience likes it or not.* (emphasis)

Devon and Sandra plan to buy a new refrigerator, *although their son Charles would rather have them buy a computer.* (signaling readers that the dependent clause is not essential)

A comma may be necessary to prevent confusion.

Examples

Jody has announced that she will return to college, *after she just told everyone she was going to quit school to find work.* (prevents confusion by separating main and subordinate ideas)

Carlton wants part of his mother's estate, *which he is entitled to according to the will.* (prevents confusion by separating thoughts)

Compound-Complex Sentences

A compound sentence may also contain one or more dependent clauses. This type of compound sentence is referred to as a **compound-complex sentence.**

Examples

After he ate dinner, Ryan went to the library, but he was too tired to study.

Judy wanted to keep working full time at Banana Republic; however, she decided to cut back to part time *because she didn't have enough time to study.*

[In each of the examples above, the dependent clause is italicized.]

TRANSITIONS

After you have made certain your writing contains a variety of sentence patterns, you may have to make another kind of revision. You may have to add transitional words and phrases that make your essay more coherent by more clearly showing the connection between different ideas.

Examples

Before revision—
A college education is very expensive. Typical college graduates earn much more during their lifetime than do typical high school graduates.

After revision—
Of course, a college education is very expensive. *But* typical college graduates earn much more during their lifetimes than do typical high school graduates.

Common Transitions

When you want to show that one idea is an **addition** to another, use—

too, also, furthermore, similarly, moreover, and, or, nor,
indeed, in fact, first, second

When you want to **illustrate**, use—

for example, for instance, for one thing, similarly, likewise

When you want to **summarize**, use—

that is, in short, in other words

When you want to **concede** a point, use—

no doubt, to be sure, granted that, it is true that,
of course, doubtless, certainly, admittedly

When you want to show a **contrast** between one idea and another, or when you want to refute any previously stated concession, use—

but, nevertheless, conversely, on the other hand, yet, however,
on the contrary, not at all, surely, no

When you want to **conclude**, use—

hence, accordingly, so, therefore, consequently, as a result, in conclusion,
thus, finally, on the whole, all in all, in other words, in short

Here are some additional points you should remember about the use of transitions:

1. Use transitions to make your sentences and paragraphs flow together smoothly. Study the way the italicized words and phrases have been used to smoothly connect ideas in the following student-written paragraph.

Example

Finally, on the topic of personal integrity, opponents of amnesty raise three points. *First*, they argue that to grant amnesty for acts done willfully would be a disservice to the individuals who performed them. *After all*, if the act of dissent is to have meaning, then it must not be forgotten. *Second*, opponents contend that most dissenters did not stand up for their beliefs in spite of the law and bear the penalty. Daniel Oliver speaks to this point in the *National Review*: "It is not the willingness of the man of conscience to break the law that impresses, but rather his willingness to pay the penalty for breaking the law." *In this way*, their protest does not show conviction and consequently does not have merit. *Third*, they argue that such a relaxation of the law will compound the problem in the future. Despite the fact that the Selective Service Act is no longer being used, there is still a principle of personal integrity with respect to the law which must not be violated.

2. Use the logical connections that will help your reader follow your argument. In other words, when you want to show contrast, use a transition from the contrast group, and so forth.

3. Avoid repeating the same transitional words or phrases in a short essay. They can become repetitious and cause the essay to seem awkward or mechanical.

4. Smooth transition can be achieved by repeating key words from a previous sentence.

Example

The District Attorney and the defendant's lawyer arranged a *deal*. *This deal* was contingent upon several *conditions*. The *first* condition was that . . . .

5. In longer essays a whole sentence (and in very long essays, even a complete paragraph) may be needed to establish the transition from one major point to another. These essays often develop two or more important concepts, and their relationship must be shown to the reader to justify their appearance in the same essay.

6. Parallel construction in sentences, especially in introductory phrases or clauses, can be used to effect transition. This device is very useful in showing the continuity of several topic sentences (see Appendix C).

Example

Winston's first act of rebellion is to purchase a diary.
Winston's second act of rebellion is to enter into a relationship with Julia.

[Parallel topic sentences]

LESSON TWO— Semicolons, Colons, Run-ons, Comma Splices, and Fragments

The Semicolon

Lesson One reviewed the use of the **semicolon** to join two simple sentences to form a compound sentence. That is its most common use. However, the semicolon can also be used to prevent confusion in long sentences that contain several commas. Perhaps the most common of these is the compound sentence in which a semicolon is used before a conjunction (*and, or, but, for, yet, nor, so*) to prevent confusion.

Example

War was inevitable, or so it appeared at the time; *but Americans*, as if denying reality would prevent it, continued to demand that President Roosevelt remain neutral.

The semicolon is used here before the conjunction because numerous commas are used elsewhere in the sentence. By using the semicolon to break the sentence into its two major parts, the sentence is made easier to read.

Some writers also use a semicolon in compound sentences with *yet* or *so*.

Example

> Gina was sure she understood how to drive in America two weeks after she moved here from England; *yet* she caused an accident almost immediately when she drove the wrong way on a freeway.

A semicolon may also be used in a sentence to separate the major items in the series from the lesser items.

Example

> Three people were killed in the boating mishap: Jerry, the skipper; Pamela, his fourteen-year-old daughter; and Adele, the skipper's sixty-four-year-old mother-in-law.

The Colon

Although the **colon** is not used as frequently as the semicolon, you must know when it is used to avoid misusing it. You will most commonly use the colon to introduce a list. Note that the lead-in should be a complete sentence; do not place a colon after a preposition or a verb.

Examples

> Long after the devastating hurricane, people remembered the three heroes: the 10-year-old girl who pulled the toddler from the pond, the 67-year old grandmother who pushed the car off the tracks, and the anonymous man who helped the children safely out of the wrecked school bus.

> "To be really successful, you will have to be trilingual: fluent in English, Spanish, and computer." —John Naisbitt, *Megatrends*

Colons and semicolons may not be used interchangeably. A colon is used to separate a sentence from a series or a phrase. A semicolon is used to join two complete sentences (unless it is used for clarification, which is rather rare.)

Colons are also used to introduce quotations in a formal manner.

Example

> Addressing the risks of voyaging in *Destination Mexico*, the authors remind would-be adventurers of an important point: "Whether in one's own backyard or on a remote island off the Mexican coast, the unexpected can occur. A sudden storm may appear. Accidents happen. But wherever we are, we all try to minimize the consequences of the unexpected by our preparations."

Finally, colons can be used to emphasize an appositive.

Examples

> Automobile accidents most often result from two dissimilar causes: alcohol and speed.

> Human beings are faced with many problems, but almost all of them can be attributed directly or indirectly to one single cause: overpopulation.

Run-ons and Comma Splice Errors

Many instructors assume that a student who does not correct run-on sentences in an essay is a poor writer. A **run-on sentence** consists of two or more independent clauses joined without any punctuation, thus giving the impression that two sentences have been fused, or run together.

Examples

Run-on error—

> He never seems to answer questions he always counters with questions of his own.

Revised—

> He never seems to answer questions; he always counters with questions of his own.

> OR

> He never seems to answer questions, and he always counters with questions of his own.

In the run-on sentence above, some indication of the relationship of the two clauses is necessary. Their relationship may be shown only through the use of appropriate punctuation or through the use of linking words and correct punctuation. The linking word you choose depends upon the emphasis and meaning that you want to give each of the clauses.

Independent clauses (IC) may be joined in the following ways:

1. semicolon
   <u>IC</u> ; <u>IC</u>

2. semicolon+ conjunctive adverb+comma
   <u>IC</u>; however, <u>IC</u>
   ; moreover,
   ; nevertheless,

3. comma+conjunction
   <u>IC</u>, and <u>IC</u>
   , but
   , or
   , for
   , nor
   , so
   , yet

Remember: Independent clauses cannot be joined with commas alone; the comma must be followed by a conjunction to avoid a **comma splice error.**

Examples

Comma splice error—

> Fossil fuel is not a perfect energy source, it is blamed for global warming.

Revised—

> Fossil fuel is not a perfect energy source; it is blamed for global warming.

> OR

> Fossil fuel is not a perfect energy source; *moreover*, it is blamed for global warming.

> OR

> Fossil fuel is not a perfect energy source, *and* it is blamed for global warming.

There is an exception to this rule. If a sentence contains a series of three or more short independent clauses, and the last two are separated by *and, or, or but*, commas may be used between the other independent clauses.

Example

She wanted equality, she demanded it, and she received it.

Fragments

Another convention of academic writing you must observe is the rule that all sentences will be complete sentences. A **sentence fragment** is an incomplete sentence, a piece of a sentence that cannot stand alone as a sentence. A sentence fragment is either a phrase or a dependent clause incorrectly punctuated as if it were a sentence.

Sentence fragments are used frequently in your everyday conversations, and they are easily understood for the most part.

Examples (Phone Conversation)

"Hi, Shawna. Can you help me with my calculus?"
"Sure. No problem, Maria."
"When?"
"After my soccer game Saturday morning."
"Okay. Great. See you Saturday. My house."

However, sentence fragments are not permitted in academic writing.

Sentence fragments frequently occur by mistake either because the writer does not realize that it is an incomplete sentence construction or because the fragment has inadvertently been separated from the independent clause that it modifies.

Fragment

Private ownership of guns escalated after the American Civil War. *Because thousands of soldiers were allowed to keep their guns and take them home after the war.*

In the above example, the fragment (underlined) is a dependent clause. The writer has set it apart and punctuated it as if it were a sentence. It should have been included in a complex sentence.

Correct

Private ownership of guns escalated after the American Civil War because thousands of soldiers were allowed to keep their guns and take them home after the war.

(Note that a comma is not used to separate an independent from a dependent clause if the dependent clause follows the independent clause.)

As with a great many rules and guidelines in the use of English, this prohibition against fragments may be broken for stylistic reasons. An occasional stylistic fragment can add emphasis if the technique is not overused. Fragments are sometimes used in novels and newspaper and magazine articles. Academic writing, however, is generally considered too formal to allow them. If you want to use them, be certain to obtain your instructor's permission.

Stylistic fragment—

"Man is the only animal that blushes. *Or needs to.*"

—Mark Twain

LESSON THREE—*Editing for Grammar Problems*

Another editing skill you must master is editing for **grammar problems**. This lesson is designed to help you with several of the conventions of Standard American English that may give you trouble. Most of these conventions have been around for generations and are now so rigidly adhered to in writing that they are called "grammar rules." Once mastered they are not usually difficult to apply, and they will seem quite logical after they have been in your "writer's vocabulary" for awhile.

Subject-Verb Agreement

The subject of a sentence **must agree** with the verb in number. A great many nouns and pronouns in English have one form to refer to a single item (the singular form) and another form to refer to more than one item (the plural form). Frequently, verbs also have two forms: one for singular subject nouns and another for plural subject nouns.

Singular	Plural
is	are
was	were
has	have
asks	ask

Examples

The average American **child** / *watches* too much television.
   [The simple subject, child, is singular; therefore, the singular verb, watches, is required. Singular verbs often end with -s or -es, but plural verbs never do.]

Many **women** / *watch* organized sports all year around.
   [The simple subject, *women*, is plural; therefore, the plural verb, *watch*, must be used.]

The **dandelion** / *is* a prolific plant.
   [The subject, *dandelion*, is singular; therefore, the singular verb, *is*, must be used instead of the plural verb *are*.]

Dandelions / *were used* for herbal medicines by our ancestors.
   [The simple subject *Dandelions*, is plural. Note that plural subjects often end with -s. To make the verb phrase, *were used*, plural, the helping verb, *were*, must be used instead of the singular *was*.]

She / *owns* a small red sports car.
   [The simple subject, *She*, is singular; therefore, the verb, *owns*, must be singular. Again note that a singular verb often ends with -s.]

They / *have* three hunting dogs.
   [The simple subject, *They*, is plural; therefore, the plural verb, *have*, is used instead of the singular verb *has*.]

Difficulty arises when you encounter expressions not obviously singular or plural. Words such as *each, either, neither, someone, one, any, anyone, nobody, nothing*, and especially *everyone* and *everybody* often seem to designate more than one person or item, but they all require singular verbs. These are called **singular indefinite pronouns**.

Examples

Everybody / *is expecting* higher utility bills.
>[The pronoun, *Everybody*, is the singular subject. It is singular because it refers to individuals one at a time. Therefore, the singular helping verb, *is*, must be used to make the verb phrase *is expecting* singular.]

Each of the Australian shepherds / *is losing* all ability to hear anything but the sharpest sounds.
>[The pronoun *Each* is singular because it refers to the shepherds individually. Therefore, the singular helping verb, *is*, must be used in the verb phrase to make it singular.]

Pronouns such as *all, few, most* and *some* may be singular or plural. When one of these pronouns is used as the simple subject, you must study the rest of the subject to determine whether a singular or plural verb is needed.

Examples

Singular: **All** of the advertising / *is* beginning to pay off.
>[The singular verb, *is*, must be used because the advertising should be considered a single unit.]

Plural: **All** of the advertisements / *are* beginning to pay off.
>[The plural verb, *are*, must be used because *All* refers to more than one advertisement, perhaps many.]

Compound subjects require the plural form even when each subject is singular.

Examples

Walking and bicycling / *are* both good exercise and invigorating.
>[Each of the compound subjects, *Walking* and *bicycling*, is singular, but the plural verb, *are*, must be used because there are two subjects.]

Ariel and **Alisa** / *are working* to register new voters before the next election.
>[Because there are two subjects, *Ariel* and *Alisa*, the plural helping verb, *are*, must be used.]

A mother **cat** and her **kittens** / *live* underneath the theater dress shop on campus.
>[Although one subject *cat* is singular and the other subject *kittens* is plural, the plural verb, *live*, must be used because there are two subjects.]

Even more troublesome for many students is the agreement of **quantities**. Even though they normally look as if they are plural, they must be treated as singular.

Examples

One thousand megabytes *is* a gigabyte.

When Cheryl was treasurer, **$500** *was* too expensive for printing the newsletter.

Sixty pounds of camping equipment and food carefully packed in a backpack *is* sufficient to make most anyone wish to have taken up a less strenuous activity.

Collective nouns, words that designate groups, are singular when you are thinking of the group as a whole, but they are plural when you are thinking of individual members of the group. Most contemporary writers, however, consider collective nouns to be singular.

Some Collective Nouns

audience	committee
family	group
jury	police

Singular—

The Heller *family* / is developing a web site that will include their family tree.

Plural—

The Brown *family* / are divided on the issue of private school vouchers.

Note—There are many other confusing and irregular singular and plural forms. If you are ever in doubt about the agreement of a sentence that you have written, consult a dictionary to be certain whether the verb you have used is singular or plural. Computer word-processing programs often feature a grammar-check function that may be useful when checking for agreement problems.

Pronoun Reference

A **pronoun** must refer clearly to its **antecedent**: the person, place, or thing substituted for by the pronoun. Do not, for example, let a pronoun seem to point to more than one antecedent, or the resulting sentence will create unintended double meanings.

Ambiguous—

The **painter** agreed to give the **writer** an interview because *she* knew *she* needed more media exposure.

Here the reader cannot tell who knew what, the painter or the writer. Sometimes the easiest way to solve this problem is to repeat the noun.

Revised—

The painter agreed to give the *writer* an interview because the writer knew the painter needed more media exposure.

Although this sentence is no longer ambiguous, it appears awkward. The apparent awkwardness may be overcome by reordering the sentence so that the pronoun comes before only one antecedent.

Revised—

Because the *painter* knew the writer understood the need for media exposure, **she** granted the writer an interview.

Just as the subject and verb must agree in number, so must a pronoun agree in number with its antecedent. Difficulty with pronoun agreement occurs typically when a pronoun is used to refer to an indefinite pronoun. Such agreement problems come about because informal, conversational English frequently includes these agreement errors. In conversations they are not considered serious errors, but in written work you do for class, agreement errors will be considered incorrect.

Informal— **Everyone** in the stands stood and clapped **their** hands.

Formal— **Everyone** in the stands stood and clapped **his** or **her** hands.

Formal— **All** of the spectators stood and clapped **their** hands.

Informal— **Everybody** in the class did **their** personal best.

Formal— **Everybody** in the class did **his** or **her** personal best.

Formal— **All** of the students in the class did **their** personal best.

Gender Fairness (Sexist Language)

Gender fairness in writing is desirable because sexist language offends many readers. Simply stated, the use of one gender, usually masculine, to refer to everyone, sounds sexist.

Example

Before selecting a doctor, check *his* qualifications carefully.

Those who are aware of sexist language would correctly assert that the speaker or writer does not know the gender of the doctor. Using the pronoun *his* completely ignores over half of the population. You should make it your goal to remove gender-specific references where they are unnecessary.

Examples

Sexist—   A *citizen* in a free society should be able to read, view, or listen to just about whatever **he** wishes, without fear of censorship.

Improved—   *Citizens* in a free society should be able to read, view, or listen to just about whatever **they** wish, without fear of censorship.

Sexist—   An *American* can be harshly punished if **he** violates the law in some foreign countries.

Improved—   *Americans* can be harshly punished if **they** violate the law in some foreign countries.

Notice that in each of the improved sentences above, the subject and pronoun were changed to plural. This is the preferred method of removing sexist language from your writing. However, you should be aware that you have other options.

Examples

Sexist—   *Nobody* should try to avoid **his** civic duty to serve on a jury.

Improved—   *Nobody* should try to avoid **his** or **her** civic duty to serve on a jury.

Better—   *People* should not try to avoid **their** civic duty to serve on juries.

While the "his or her" solution to the sexist language problem (the second example above) is technically correct, it is not favored because it too often produces wordy sentences.

Three Additional Pronoun Reminders

1. Always make pronouns refer to a basic element of a sentence; never let the pronoun refer to a modifier.

   Unclear—   He reached for the car door handle, but **it** rolled away.

   Clear—   The car rolled away as he reached for the door handle.

2. Eliminate indirect or indefinite pronoun reference.

   Unclear—   Riding across the mountains on horseback, **you** had to worry about rattlesnakes.

   Clear—   Riding across the mountains on horseback, **pioneers** had to worry about rattlesnakes.

   Clear—   **Pioneers** had to worry about rattlesnakes while riding across the mountains on horseback.

   Unclear—   In a surprise *attack* on June 25, rebel forces surrounded the capital. **This** caught the president and his military advisors off guard.

Clear—   In a surprise *attack* on June 25, rebel forces surrounded the capital. **This attack** caught the president and his military advisors off guard.

3. Avoid ambiguous use of **it** and **they**.

Unclear—   In last month's edition of *Oceans*, **it** presents a good explanation of whale migration.

Clear—   **An article** in last month's edition of *Oceans* gives a good explanation of whale migration.

Unclear—   **They** do not allow Olympic athletes to use steroids.

Clear—   Olympic **officials** do not allow Olympic athletes to use steroids.

Pronouns as Subjects and Objects

Different forms of pronouns are used, depending on whether they are subjects or objects. If a pronoun is a subject of a sentence or clause, use *I, you, he, she, it, we, they, who,* or *whoever.*

Examples

Incorrect—   **Him** and the **manager** / attended the computer conference.

Correct—   **He** and the **manager** / attended the computer conference.
[*He* is the correct form of the pronoun because it is one of the two subjects in the compound subject.]

Incorrect—   **Joan** and **him** / were the only ones who took notes at the meeting.

Correct—   **Joan** and **he** / were the only ones who took notes at the meeting.
[The pronoun *he* is correct because it is one of the two subjects in the compound sentence.]

Incorrect—   **Us two** / will conduct the project for the team.

Correct—   **We two** / will conduct the project research for the team.
[The pronoun *We* is correct because it is the simple subject of the sentence. The pronoun *We* is not an adjective modifying the pronoun *two* as it might seem. To more clearly see the simple subject, read the sentence without the word *two*.]

Incorrect—   **Whom** / is responsible for water purity testing in the city?

Correct—   **Who** / is responsible for water purity testing in the city?
[The simple subject of the sentence is *Who*. Note that all of forms of the verb *to be* require one of the subject forms of a pronoun. The *to be* verbs are *am, are, is, was, were, be, been,* and *being*.]

This same rule holds true for dependent clauses.

Example

Incorrect—   He is the only one (**who** I trust).

Correct—   He is the only one (**whom** I trust).
[The pronoun *I* is the subject of the dependent clause *whom I trust*. The pronoun *whom* is the direct object of the verb *trust*.]

When a pronoun is the **object of a preposition** in a prepositional phrase or the **direct** or **indirect object** of a verb, use *me, you, her, him, it, us, them, whom,* or *whomever.*

Examples

I am puzzled (by **her**).

[The prepositional phrase is *by her*. The pronoun, *her*, is the object of the preposition *by*.]

I want you to explain the reason for the delay (to **her** and **me**).

[The pronouns, *her* and *me*, are the objects of the preposition *to*.]

James likes **us**.

[The pronoun, *us*, is the direct object of the verb *likes*.]

My manager gave **me** a better schedule.

[The pronoun, *me*, is the indirect object of the verb *gave*. The direct object is the noun *schedule*.]

Again the same rule applies in dependent clauses.

Examples

Chris is the one (**who** helped **us** the most).

[The pronoun, *us*, is the direct object of the verb *helped*.]

Use the object form of a pronoun in verbal phrases.

Examples

(Counting on **her** for support,) Helen asked Judy to serve on her election committee.

[The object form, *her*, must be used because *Counting on her for support* is a verbal phrase. The verbal phrase functions as an adjective describing Helen.]

We hope (to visit **them** soon).

[The object form *them* must be used because *to visit them soon* is a verbal phrase.]

Some sentences are incomplete, so you must complete them in your mind to know whether to use the subject or object form of a pronoun.

Examples

Incorrect— Francis skis better than **her**.

Correct— Francis skis better than **she**.
[In your mind complete the sentence: Francis skis better than *she skis*. Then you can see that the subject form is needed because *she* is the subject of the dependent clause *than she skis*.]

Incorrect— My girlfriend is older than **me**.

Correct— My girlfriend is older than **I**.
[In your mind complete the sentence: My girlfriend is older than **I** *am*. Then you can see that the object form *me* would be wrong.]

Tense

When you write an essay, every verb and verb phrase helps create a sense of time. You may write as if events are happening simultaneously with your writing, as if they have already happened, or as if they will be happening in the future.

Present

A good education **gives** one a sense of self-worth.

Past

    A good education **gave** one a sense of self-worth.

Future

    A good education **will give** one a sense of self-worth.

Time perspective in a sentence tense is determined by the verb form or combination of verb forms you use.

Examples

    They **work** together to produce documentary films.

    They **worked** on a Civil War documentary.

    They **are working** on an animated documentary.

    They **had worked** for a small studio right after college.

    They **had been working** on the college newspaper during college.

    They **have worked** in film production for twelve years.

    They **will work** together on a new project.

    They **will begin working** on it as soon as they secure financial backing.

    They **will be working** in Mexico later this year.

    They **will have worked** on the final editing of the animated documentary by then.

    They **may work** on web-based documentaries.

    They **might work** on a documentary in Harlem.

    They **could have worked** for Steven Spielberg.

    They **should have worked** with digital formats earlier.

    Will you **work** with them?

    Have you **worked** as a multimedia artist?

    Work harder!

Although six tenses are considered basic, it is possible to identify thirty tenses, plus other word combinations within which these tenses work. However, you need not label all thirty tenses. What is important is that you use the verb-form combinations that will most accurately communicate the time of an action or state of being and most accurately show the time relationship of different actions and events within a sentence, a paragraph, and the various paragraphs in an essay.

The Six Basic Tenses

1. **Present tense**—designates an action or event taking place when the statement is made.

    Example

    They **see** the signals.

2. **Past tense**—designates an action or event that happened before the statement is made.

    Example

    They **saw** the signals.

3. **Future tense**—designates an action or event that will happen but that has not happened yet when the statement is made.

Example

> They **will** see the signals.

4. **Present perfect tense**—designates an action or event begun in the past and continuing to or into the present. To form the present perfect tense, add **has** or **have** to the past participle form of the verb. (Often the past participle will end -ed.)

Examples

> He **has seen** the signals.
> They **have seen** the signals.
> They **have worked** hard on the project.

5. **Past perfect tense**—designates an action or event begun and finished in the past before another action or event in the past. To form the past perfect tense, add had to the past participle form of the verb.

Examples

> They **had seen** the signals.
> They **had worked** hard on the project.

6. **Future perfect tense**—designates an action or event that will be completed in the future prior to some future time. To form the future perfect tense, add **will have** or **shall have** to the past participle.

Example

> They **will have seen** the signals.

Do not restrict yourself to the six basic tenses described above; use whatever verb form combination you need to communicate accurately and to follow the conventions of proper usage.

Once you begin writing in one tense, you must continue using it, avoiding **unnecessary shifts** in time perspective.

> Wrong— Although she **had** a stack of work on her desk she wanted to do, she **is** simply too sick to work. (Shift from past tense to present tense.)
>
> Right— Although she **had** a stack of work on her desk she wanted to do, she **was** simply too sick to work. (Past tense used consistently.)
>
> Right— Although she **has** a stack of work on her desk she wants to do, she **is** simply too sick to work. (Present tense used consistently.)

Shifts in tense sometimes are necessary to communicate a sense of time exactly, but you must carefully construct your sentences to avoid any confusion in time perspective when you write of two or more events that happen at different times or different places.

> Necessary tense shifts—
> Tonight Ronald Hammersmith **will discuss** (future) the actions Franklin Delano Roosevelt **took** (past) during his first one hundred days in office as he **attempted** (past) **to implement** (present—infinitive used as direct object) emergency measures against the depression **that had taken** (past perfect) America to the brink of disaster.

Person—First, Second, and Third

Everything is written in first, second, or third person, depending upon the writer's purpose and audience. Person is the perspective used to distinguish between the writer and those to whom or about whom the writer writes. **First person** is used when the writer or the character in the writing is speaking. **Second person** is used when someone is addressed. **Third person** is used when someone or something is written about. The writer must choose one of these three perspectives—first, second, or third person—and then use it consistently to avoid shifts in person, which can be awkward or confusing.

FIRST PERSON

First-person writing is characterized by the use of the pronouns *I, my, me, we, our,* and *us.* Either the author or a character in the writing is speaking firsthand. First person is commonly used in narratives, descriptions, anecdotes, fiction, and autobiographical essays. Traditionally, first person was avoided in explanatory and argumentative essays. Contemporary writers, however, are using first person references in their writing. Some instructors even go so far as to encourage their students to use the first-person *we* and *our* on the theory that first person promotes a feeling of involvement among the readers, thus making the writing more persuasive. Since this practice is not fully accepted, you should be careful to determine your instructor's preferences before using first person in your own writing.

Example

Unacceptable—

> *I* think *I* am right in saying that no woman can be denied the right to use her original name after she is married.

Better—

> Under *our* legal system, no woman can be denied her right to use her original name after she is married.

Best—

> No woman can be denied the right to use her original name after she is married.

Exceptions to this general rule occur when you are writing about activities or events in which you actually participated or at least observed firsthand, for example, when writing an anecdote or when writing an autobiographical essay. In these instances it is acceptable to refer to yourself.

Example (anecdote)

> A child's mind does not clearly comprehend death. When a traumatic event occurs that a child has never experienced before, however, it is not atypical for the child to decide death is near. I can still recall my first truly frightening experience. As the calf's head hit the side of my mouth, I felt the blow but no pain. However, when I had finally calmed the calf, and it had resumed eating, I began to feel a dull ache in my jaw. I felt my face in the darkness and suddenly realized that the sticky mess on my face and shirt was blood, my blood. As my fingers explored my face, my brain came to the realization that my face now had two mouths rather than one. As my brain attempted to comprehend this discovery, my fingers explored the hole to the left of my mouth. Suddenly, my composure dissolved; the pain, the blood, the hole, all overwhelmed my six-year-old mind. What started as a whimper ended as a yell of anguish that trailed along behind me while I ran into the barn to tell my mother I was dying.

While some instructors will not accept first-person *we* or *our* in persuasive writing, many will now accept this practice if used only occasionally and very carefully. Also, to be acceptable, the first person must refer to all people, not to first-person *I*.

Example

Unacceptable—

We should complete the Jackson County's light rail system in order to reduce the number of cars on the freeway. (Only the people of a special audience are the *we* in this sentence.)

Acceptable—

We must work to reduce the pollution of water and air if the planet is to remain habitable by the human species. (Presumably, the writer of this sentence is referring to all of the people in the world.)

SECOND PERSON

Second-person writing is characterized by the use of the pronouns *you* and *your*. The writer's intention is to direct his or her words directly to the reader as an individual. Commands (imperative sentences) are always written using second person because the subject of a command is always the **understood you**. Generally, second person is acceptable only in directions and textbooks; consequently, second-person usage should be carefully avoided in academic and job-related writing.

Example

Unacceptable—

When *you* are competing for a management job in a large company, *you* have to be better qualified than everyone else who applies.

Acceptable—

After *you* have formed the mold in the sand, melt the paraffin. *You* can use one of *your* old coffee cans to heat the paraffin until the wax is liquefied. As it is melting, mix pieces of crayon in with the wax until the color is right. *You* can also add a few drops of scented oil at this stage.

THIRD PERSON

In third-person writing, people, places, and events are referred to objectively by name or description. Third-person writing is characterized by use of the following pronouns: *he, his, him, it, its, she, hers, her, one, they, their,* and *them*. The writer is writing about someone or something. Most academic writing–essays, reports, and tests–are written in third person. The same holds true for reports, proposals, and other writing on the job.

Example

Three hundred years ago during the plague, London was not a very sanitary place to live. *Londoners*, both rich and poor, bathed infrequently. Most *families* bought a limited amount of water daily from *waterbearers*, and there were no private baths. *Samuel Pepys* wrote in *his* secret diary that *his wife* actually dared to wash *herself* all over at a public "hothouse" and that a few days later *he* bathed also, an unusual event. The city had no underground sewer system. Instead of sewers, kennels (open gutters) were used for waste liquids from chamber pots and wash-up water.

Keeping a Consistent Point of View

You must use pronouns consistently to avoid awkwardly **shifting your point of view.**

Incorrect— *We* get together every August for a reunion, and *you* start by going to a huge bar-becue in the park.

Correct— *We* get together every August for a reunion, and *we* start by going to a huge bar-becue in the park.
[The incorrect example shifts awkwardly from the first person plural *we* to the second person singular *you*.]

Incorrect— *One* needs to research carefully before *you* invest in mutual funds.

Correct— *One* needs to research carefully before *he* or *she* invests in mutual funds.
[By using *he* or *she* the awkward shift from the third person *one* to the second person *you* is avoided.]

APPENDIX B: *Documentation*

INTRODUCTION

Appendix B has only one purpose: to help you write your Works Cited section. An example or two of an entry for almost every type of source is listed in the following section. You only need to be sure you find and follow exactly the example of the source you have referred to in the body of your paper. Be exact: every comma, period, and colon must be used accurately.

PART ONE: BOOK ENTRIES

A BOOK WITH ONE AUTHOR

Herbert, Frank. Heretics of Dune. New York: Putnam's, 1984.

> [Author is listed last name first.]

Hill, Ruth Beebe. Hanta Yo. New York: Warner, 1979.

> [Name of publishing company is shortened—Warner Books becomes simply Warner.]

King, Stephen. Pet Sematary. New York: New American, 1983.

> [Cite city of publication and date of publication.]

TWO OR MORE BOOKS BY THE SAME AUTHOR

Wouk, Herman. War and Remembrance. New York: Pocket, 1971.

---. Winds of War. Boston: Little, 1978.

> [Give author's name in first entry only; in subsequent entries show three hyphens followed by a period to repeat the author's name. Note that publisher's name—Little, Brown and Company—has been shortened to Little.]

A BOOK WITH MORE THAN ONE AUTHOR

Collier, Peter, and David Horowitz. The Kennedys: An American Drama. New York: Summit, 1984.

> [First author is listed last name first; second author is listed first name first.]

Gibaldi, Joseph, and Waiter S. Achtert. MLA Handbook for Writers of Research Papers. 2nd ed. New York: MLA, 1984.

> [Second edition becomes 2nd ed. Modern Language Association of America shortened to MLA.]

Rose, Turner, et al., eds. U.S. News & World Report Stylebook for Writers and Editors. Washington: U.S. News, 1981.

> [If a book has more than three authors or editors, list the first person's name and use "et al."—meaning "and others"—in place of the authors' names. Use "eds." to indicate editors or "trans." to indicate translators.]

AN ANONYMOUS BOOK

Information Please Almanac: Atlas and Yearbook 1983. 37th ed. New York: Information Please, 1982.

> [If a work has no author, begin the entry with the title; ignore the articles "a," "an," and "the" when arranging items alphabetically.]

Urdang Dictionary of Current Medical Terms. New York: Urdang, 1981.

A TRANSLATION OF A BOOK

Ende, Michael. <u>The Neverending Story</u>. Trans. Ralph Manheim. Illus. Roswitha Quadflieg. New York: Doubleday, 1983.

> [After the author and title are listed, the translator is listed following the abbreviation "Trans." Here the name of the illustrator is given after the abbreviation "Illus."]

Kawabata, Yasunari. <u>The Sound of the Mountain</u>. Trans. Edward G. Seidensticker. New York: Berkeley, 1971.

Maude, Aylmer, trans. <u>Anna Karenina</u>. By Leo Tolstoy. Ed. George Gibian. New York: Norton, 1970.

> [List the translator's name first if you are documenting the comments of the translator. The author of the literary work being discussed is preceded by "By." The editor is listed after the author.]

A FOREWORD, AN INTRODUCTION, OR A PREFACE

Gannett, Lewis. Introduction. <u>The Sea Wolf</u>. By Jack London. New York: Bantam, 1972. v-xvii.

> [When you are citing what is written in an introduction, first give the name of the author of that section, followed by the word "Introduction" with the first letter capitalized but without underlining or quotation marks. The author of the work under discussion follows the word "By" after the title. The page numbers of the entire introduction, usually in lower case Roman numerals, are listed at the end of the entry. Note the use of periods throughout.]

Matlaw, Ralph E., trans. Preface. <u>Fathers and Sons</u>. By Ivan Turgenev. New York: Norton, 1966. vii-ix.

> [If the translator included a preface to explain the work, as is often the case, begin the entry with the translator's name if you wish to make reference to those comments.]

Naisbitt, John. Introduction. <u>Megatrends: Ten New Directions Transforming Our Lives</u>. By Naisbitt. New York: Warner, 1982. 1-9.

> [When citing something in an introduction that was written by the author of the work itself, the author's last name only is given after the word "By". Again, the total span of pages covered by the introduction being cited is listed at the end of the entry.]

A WORK IN AN ANTHOLOGY

Espinosa, Luzmaria. "La Cultura Chicana." <u>Sacramento Edition</u>. Ed. Ben L. Hiatt and Bill Howarth. Sacramento: Sacramento Poetry Exchange, 1982. 39.

> [A poem in the anthology is cited by author and title; the page number is listed.]

Wells, H. G. "The Country of the Blind." <u>Science Fiction: The Future</u>. Ed. Dick Allen. New York: Harcourt, 1971. 66-68.

> [Begin by giving the author's name and then list the title of the work you are citing, placing quotation marks around the title. The name of the editor is placed after the title of the anthology; underline the anthology title. The total number of pages covered by the article is listed at the end of the entry.]

Worth, Helen. "Get Cooking!" <u>The Complete Guide to Writing Nonfiction</u>. Ed. Glen Evans. Cincinnati: Writer's Digest, 1983. 477-85.

> [Helen Worth is the author of the article, and "Get Cooking!" is the title of the article; Glen Evans is the editor of the anthology. The article appears on pages 477-485.]

A BOOK IN A SET OF VOLUMES

Crane, Stephen. "The Bride Comes to Yellow Sky." The Norton Anthology of American Literature. Ed. Ronald Gottesman et al. 2 vols. New York: Norton, 1979. 2: 926-35.

> [When referring to a work in a multi-volume anthology, begin the entry with the author's name and proceed as with any anthology, but insert the total number of volumes in the set after the editor's name. At the end of the entry, place the number of the volume the work is in, followed by a colon and the total page span of the work.]

Synge, J. M. The Playboy of the Western World. J. M. Synge: Collected Works. Ed. Ann Saddlemeyer. 4 vols. London: Oxford UP, 1968. 4: 51-175.

> [If the work being discussed is a play in a collection, it must be underlined and followed by a period if the play was originally published as a book. The title of the volume, the editor, and the number of volumes follow. The publishers name, Oxford University Press, Inc., has been shortened to Oxford UP.]

Wallbank, T. Waiter, and Alastair M. Taylor, eds. Civilization Past and Present. 4th ed. 2 vols. Chicago: Scott, 1961.

> [Place the number of the edition between the title and the volumes; the publisher's name, Scott, Foresman, and Company, has been shortened to Scott.]

Robinson, Charles Alexander, Jr., ed. An Anthology of Greek Drama. Classical Literature in Rinehart Editions 1. New York: Holt, 1964.

> [When you are citing a work in a series, you must include the name of the series. The name of the series will be given on the title page or the page facing the title page. Do not underline the series title or place quotation marks around it.]

ORGANIZATIONAL AUTHOR

The Carnegie Foundation for the Advancement of Teaching. Three Thousand Futures: The Next Twenty Years in Higher Education: Final Report of the Carnegie Council on Policy Studies in Higher Education. San Francisco: Jossey-Bass, 1980.

> [A book may have an organizational or corporate author. In this example, Jossey-Bass is the publisher, but in some cases the organization may be both the author and the publisher.]

A REPUBLISHED BOOK

Auel, Jean M. The Valley of Horses. 1982. New York: Bantam, 1983.

> [When citing a paperback printing of a book that was originally a hardbound, place the date of the first publication before the information about the book cited.]

Michener, James A. Centennial. 1974. Greenwich, CT: Fawcett, 1975.

> [If your reader may not recognize the location of the city of the publishing house, include the ZIP code abbreviation of the state.]

Toomer, Jean. Cane. 1923. New York: Liveright, 1975.

> [The original date of publication is often many years prior to the date of the edition you use.]

PUBLISHER'S IMPRINT

Thackeray, William Makepeace. Vanity Fair: A Novel Without a Hero. New York: Signet-New American, 1962.

> [A publisher's imprint is the special name used to identify a certain series or division of

the publishing company. Place the publisher's imprint before the name of the publisher—separate the two with a hyphen. In this example the imprint, "A Signet Classic," is shortened to "Signet"; the publishing company name, "The New American Library," is shortened to "New American." Although this old novel (first published in 1837) is republished, no original publication date is needed.]

A PLAY OR POEM

Baldwin, James. Blues for Mister Charlie. New York: Deli, 1964.

[A play presented in a book is treated just as any other book.]

Field, Edward. "She." Variety Photoplays. New York: Grove, 1967. 15-16.

[Title of poem is placed in quotation marks. Pages covered by poem cited are given.]

Jones, LeRoi. "The Death of Malcolm X." New Plays From the Black Theatre. Ed. Ed Bullins. New York: Bantam, 1969. 1-20.

[This play title is placed in quotation marks because it was not published first as an individual book. Page numbers of entire play are listed at end.]

A REFERENCE BOOK

Bettelheim, Bruno. "Autism." Encyclopedia Americana. 1983 ed.

[Encyclopedia entries need no page numbers since such books are alphabetically arranged. If the entry lists an author, list the author's name first; otherwise, alphabetize according to article title.]

Fink, Donald G., and Donald Christiansen, eds. Electronic Engineer's Handbook. 2nd ed. New York: McGraw, 1982.

[Reference book with full publishing information, including the editors.]

Moody's Analytical Overview of 25 Leading U.S. Cities. New York: Moody's Investor Service, 1977.

[In the case of reference works not commonly used by students and instructors, cite the full publication information.]

Neuman, Gerhard. "Ocean Currents." Encyclopaedia Britannica: Macropaedia. 1981 ed.

[Specify "Macropaedia" or "Micropaedia." For articles in Macropaedia the author's initials are given consult the "Propaedia: Outline of Knowledge" for the author's full name.]

"Draconian." American Heritage Dictionary. 1982 ed.

[List dictionary entries by subject heading. No page or publisher is needed.]

A PAMPHLET

Air Pollution Primer. New York: National Tuberculosis and Respiratory Disease Association, 1969.

[A pamphlet entry is written as a book entry.]

Mulligan, William. Dyslexia: Specific Learning Disability and Deliquency. N.p.: California Association for Neurologically Handicapped Children. N.d.

[The sponsoring agency is considered to be the publisher. Use "N.p." if no place of publication is given; use "N.d." if no date of publication is given.]

AN UNPUBLISHED DISSERTATION, THESIS, OR PROJECT REPORT

Bettcher, Margaret A. "Teaching Reading in the Innercity: A Focus on Teacher Training." Thesis. California State U., Sacramento, 1971.

> [The title of an unpublished thesis or dissertation is not underlined; the title of a published one would be underlined.]

Pinney, Theodore Charles. "The Biology of the Farallon Rabbit." Diss. Stanford U, 1965.

> [University is abbreviated as "U" to shorten length of entry.]

GOVERNMENT REPORTS

Asimov, Isaac, and Theodosius Dobzhansky. The Genetic Effects of Radiation. Understanding the Atom Series 1. Oak Ridge, TN: USAEC Division of Technical Information Extension, 1967.

> [Example of government publication not published by Government Printing Office in Washington. Note that the authors' names are given and that United States Atomic Energy Commission has been abbreviated "USAEC." Note also that the pamphlet is from a series.]

Berns, Waiter. "Affirmative Action vs. The Declaration of Independence." New Perspectives: U.S. Commission on Civil Rights. Washington: GPO, Summer 1984: 21+.

> [Use common sense when you are not sure how to list a government publication. In this case, an article is cited in a quarterly periodical published by the U.S. Commission on Civil Rights but printed by the Government Printing Office.]

Greenwalt, Kent. Legal Protections of Privacy: Final Report to the Office of Telecommunications Policy, Executive Office of the President. Washington: GPO, 1975.

> [With author]

United States. Commission on Civil Rights. The Federal Civil Rights Enforcement Budget: Fiscal Year 1983. Washington: GPO, 1982.

> [If no author is given, consider the sponsoring agency to be the author. Note the period after United States. Most U.S. Government publications are published by the Government Printing Office (GPO) in Washington, D.C.]

PART TWO: MAGAZINE AND NEWSPAPER ENTRIES

AN ARTICLE FROM A MAGAZINE

Franklin, D. "Embryo Transfer: It's a Boy." Science News 11 Feb. 1984: 85.

> [No colon or period is placed between magazine name and date of publication.]

Moritz, Michael. "A Hard-Core Technoid." Time 16 Apr. 1984: 62-63.

> [Weekly or biweekly magazines require complete date with day of month first. Do not include volume and issue numbers. Abbreviate the name of the month if it is in excess of four letters.]

Nolen, William A., M.D. "New Ways to Treat Arthritis." McCalls June 1982: 31+.

> [If the magazine appears once a month or every two months, give month and year; omit volume and issue. The + shows that the article continues on various other pages.]

"Vatican Warning: Cardinal Joseph Ratzinger's Report." Time 26 Mar. 1984: 70.

> [If the author's name is not given on an article, alphabetically arrange the article by title.]

AN ARTICLE FROM A JOURNAL

Axelrod, Pearl, and Natalie Trager. "Directing a Day Care Center." <u>Innovator: the University of Michigan School of Education.</u> 4.10 (1973): 10-13.

> [When the article cited appears in a journal that begins with page one each issue, list the title followed by a period and the issue number (volume 4, issue ten above). The year appears in parentheses.]

Bodmer, George R. "The Apple Ate My Paper." <u>College English</u> 46 (1984): 610-11.

> [If the article cited appears in a journal that uses continuous pagination throughout the year, (that is, each issue begins with the next number after the last page of the previous issue) give the volume number and follow it with the year of publication in parentheses. End the citation with a colon and the pages covered by the article.]

AN ARTICLE OR EDITORIAL FROM A NEWSPAPER

Campbell, Don G. "Autistic Child's Quick Recovery." <u>Los Angeles Times</u> n.d.: n. pag.

> [When the newspaper article being cited has been found in the vertical file, it will occasionally have no date of publication or page number listed. The abbreviation "n.d." for no date and "n.pag." for no pagination explains to your reader that the information is missing.]

Kirp, David. "A Civics Lesson in the Suburbs." Editorial. <u>Sacramento Bee</u> 3 Dec. 1984: B10.

> [If you cite an editorial in a newspaper, include the word "Editorial" after the title of the editorial. If no author's name is included, arrange it alphabetically according to the title.]

Mercer, Kathy. Letter. <u>Sacramento Bee</u> 3 Dec. 1984: B11.

> [A letter to the editor is identified by the word "Letter" immediately after the writer's name. Do not underline the word or place quotation marks around it.]

Sheehan, Thomas. "The Vatican Errs on Liberation Theology." <u>New York Times</u> 15 Sept. 1984, sec. 5: 23.

> [Note that the name of the newspaper is <u>New York Times</u> not The New York Times. If the newspaper is paginated continuously as is the Saturday edition of the paper above, list the section before the colon.]

"Vatican Reported to Have Sought Rebukes for Two Other Latin Clerics." <u>New York Times</u> 11 Sept. 1984: A14.

> [In the instance where the author is not listed, alphabetically arrange the article according to the article title.]

A REVIEW OF A BOOK, PLAY, OR OTHER WORK OF ART

Dewey, Phelps. "This World." Rev. of <u>The Old Ones of New Mexico</u>, by Robert Coles. <u>San Francisco Chronicle</u> 17 February 1974: 9.

> [When citing a review in a newspaper, after you give the reviewer's name and review title, identify the book being reviewed and its author or authors.]

Hedgpeth, Joel W. "Shifting Sands." Rev. of <u>Living with the South Carolina Shore</u>, by William J. Neal, et al. <u>Oceans</u> Nov. 1984: 59-60.

> [When citing a review in a magazine, arrange the information the same as for a newspaper.]

PART THREE: ELECTRONIC SOURCES

MAGAZINE ARTICLE

Waller, Douglas. "The Battle of the Yucca Mountains." Time 25 Mar. 2002: 20. Infotrac.
Time, Inc. 19 Mar. 2003 <http://web1.infotrac.galegroup.com>.
[An online magazine includes the author, the title of the article in quotations, the publishing date, the page number(s) preceded by a colon, the database name (underlined), the article's publisher, the access date, and the URL.]

JOURNAL

Ornoy, Asher. "The Effects of Alcohol and Illicit Drugs on the Human Embryo and Fetus." The Israel
Journal of Psychiatry and Related Sciences 39.2 (2002). 25 Mar. 2003 <http://
0-proquest.umi.com.laasiii.losrios.edu>.
[An online journal includes what information you can find: the author's name, followed by the title of the article in quotations, the title of the journal (underlined), the volume and issue numbers, the publishing date in parenthesis, the access date, and the URL.]

NEWSPAPER ARTICLE

Wade, Nicholas. "Grappling With the Ethics of Stem Cell Research." New York Times 24 Jul. 2001.
Proquest. 20 Mar. 2003 <http://0-proquest.umi.com.lasiii.losrios.edu/pqd>.
[An online newspaper article begins with the author's name, the title of the article in quotations, the title of the newspaper, the publishing date, the database used (underlined), the access date, and the URL.]

CD-ROM

La Rue, Steve. "The El Nino Effect." San Diego Union-Tribune 15 Mar. 1998: A-1. NewsBank News-
File. CD-ROM. NewsBank. May 1998.
[For a CD-ROM citation, begin with the author, title of the article in quotations, the title of the work (underlined), date of publication, the title of the database (underlined), the medium (CD-ROM), name of the vendor, and the electronic date.]

GOVERNMENT DOCUMENT

Office of Civilian Radioactive Waste Management. Yucca Mountain Project. 22 Apr. 2003 <http://
www.ocrwm.doe.gov>.
[For a government online document, include the government agency as the author, the title of the document (underlined), the publishing date, the access date, and the URL; note this document has no publishing date.]

PART FOUR: MISCELLANEOUS

AN INTERVIEW

Steck, Harold. "Waterfront Interview: Master of a Lost Art." Waterfront: California's Boating News
Magazine Dec. 1984: 70-71.
[When citing an interview in a magazine or newspaper, list the name of the person interviewed first. After the name of the person interviewed, give the title of the interview, if it is given, and the publication in which it appears.]

Steen, Lynn. Interview. <u>New York Times</u> 5 Dec. 1984: B17.

> [If an interview has no title listed, identify it by using the word "Interview" in place of the title. Do not underline the word or place quotation marks around it.]

Taylor, Horace. Personal Interview. 6 May 1984.

> [A personally conducted interview only shows the name of the person interviewed, the type of interview (i.e., private or telephone interview) and the date of the interview.]

A LECTURE OR SPEECH

Blanton, Marian. Lecture. San Francisco City College. 17 May 1984.

> [A class lecture can be cited by giving the lecturer's name, the title of the lecture (if one was given), the location of the lecture and the date. When no title is given, identify the citation with the word "Lecture" or "Speech" as appropriate.]

Smith, William E. "Integrating Writing Curriculum with Computers." Weber State College Conference. 11 May 1984.

> [When the title of a speech or lecture is given, list it immediately after the speaker's name.]

RADIO AND TELEVISION PROGRAMS

"Lena Horne: The Lady and Her Music." <u>Great Performances</u>. PBS. KQED, San Francisco. 9 Dec. 1984.

> [Radio and television entries begin with the program and series titles and include the network, the local station, the city where it was aired, and the date of the broadcast. Other information can be inserted as necessary to help readers identify the program.]

Hemingway, Ernest. <u>The Sun Also Rises</u>. NBC miniseries. KCRA, Sacramento. 9 and 10 Dec. 1984.

> [Here Hemingway is listed first because the work is primarily based on his novel. In the case of a miniseries, give the dates of all parts of the production.]

MOVIES AND VIDEOTAPES

<u>2010</u>. Dir. Peter Hyams. With Roy Schieder. MGM, 1984.

> [In citing a movie, list title, director, primary actor or actors, distribution, and year.]

<u>West Side Story</u>. Videocassette. Dir. Robert Wise. CBS Video, 1961.

> [When citing a videocassette, filmstrip or slide program, list the medium just after the title.]

RECORDINGS

Goodall, Jane. <u>A Lecture by Dr. Jane Goodall: Chimpanzee Behavior and Its Relationship to the Study of Man</u>. Everest 33179, n.d.

> [A cassette recording of a lecture. Include the name of the speaker, the title of the cassette, the name of the recording company, and, if available, the recording date.]

Lennon, John, and Paul McCartney. "Eleanor Rigby." Revolver. Capital SW 2576, n.d. [A song on a record album]

PERFORMANCES

<u>Rigoletto</u>. By Giuseppe Verdi. Dir. Jean-Pierre Ponnelle. With Ingvar Wixell. War Memorial Opera House, San Francisco. 2 Dec. 1984.

> [In citing performances, give information about production, author, director, performer, place, and date.]

PART FIVE: ABBREVIATIONS

ABBREVIATIONS

Use the following abbreviations when necessary in your documentation.

n.p.	No publisher given; no place of publication
n.d.	No date of publication given
n. pag.	No page numbers given—or page numbers missing
(*sic*) or [*sic*]	Quotation is accurate; error is in original publication.
trans.	Translator(s)
ed.	Editor(s)
rpt.	Reprinted by, reprint
illus.	Illustrated by, illustrator
e.g.	For example; set off by commas
i.e.	That is; set off by commas
c.or ca.	About, used with approximate dates
+	And other pages
qtd.	Quoted
qtd. in	Quoted in (for indirect quotation)
Apr.	April (Do not abbreviate May, June, or July.)
NE	Nebraska (Use ZIP code abbreviations for states.)

APPENDIX C: A Guide to Stylistic Revision

INTRODUCTION

Good writing is clear, terse, and forceful. No reader should misunderstand what you are saying. Furthermore, your sentences should not drone on and on in a haphazard succession of excessively worded and loosely connected thoughts. And, finally, your style should engage the reader because your sentences are interesting and lively. Think about what you want to say; then write and rewrite relentlessly until you have stated your ideas plainly but gracefully.

The connection between sound thinking and good writing cannot be overstressed. Responsible writers must heed George Orwell's warning in Politics and the English Language:

> It is clear that the decline of language must ultimately have political and economic causes. . . . But an effect can become a cause, reinforcing the original cause and producing the same effect in an intensified form, and so on indefinitely. A man may take a drink because he feels himself a failure, and then fail all the more completely because he drinks. It is rather the same thing that is happening to the English language. It becomes ugly and inaccurate because our thoughts are foolish, but the slovenliness of our language makes it easier to have foolish thoughts.

The style guide that follows offers some suggestions to help you avoid the stylistic abuses that pervade much of what you read today. By studying "A Guide to Stylistic Revision," you can improve your style and your grades.

Avoid Trite Introductory Phrases

Purge your writing of trite introductory phrases, such as "Since the beginning of time," "Since the days of the cavemen," "Throughout time," "Throughout history," and "In generations past." Typically these introductory phrases are overused and too general. They are rarely used as they should be: to introduce a passage summarizing authentic historical information. Instead, they are used to falsely create the impression that the writer knows what happened millions of years ago. For example, a writer might assert that, "Since the days of the cavemen there has been a generation gap between the young and the old." This statement is far too general. Has there been a generation gap in all societies? Is the writer implying that the supposed generation gap caused conflict between ancient tribal elders and the young? The writer has not really thought through the matter and does not know exactly what happened and, therefore, should have avoided such careless generalizing. One technique of revising trite introductory phrases is to substitute verified concrete examples. For example, the statement "Since the beginning of time man has suffered degenerative diseases" might be changed to "The Stone Age dwellers of Great Britain, the Romans, the early American colonists, and modern-day Americans have all suffered from the same degenerative diseases." Using the specific examples makes the introduction more authoritative and more apt to engage the reader's interest because the examples create images in the reader's mind.

Eliminate Platitudes

Also omit or rewrite sentences containing platitudes. Platitudes are trite, space-wasting statements of what every reader already knows. For example, a writer might state, "Millions of Americans drive automobiles," or "Television sets may be found in almost every American home," or "Advertisements are communicated through a variety of media: radio, television, magazines, and newspapers." What reader needs to be told any of this? These platitudes become even more offensive when combined with trite introductory expressions.

Example

TRITE INTRODUCTORY PHRASE	PLATITUDE
Since the beginning of time,	people have found it necessary to eat.

331

Be especially cautious when writing the opening statement of your paper. Try to begin with a meaningful, thought-provoking generalization, one that will intrigue the reader. The platitude "Millions of Americans drive automobiles," for example, might be changed to "The Environmental Protection Agency wants millions of Americans to stop driving their automobiles." Almost every reader should be affected by that statement. If you are not sure whether or not a statement is platitudinous, ask for advice.

Support Your Generalizations with Specifics

1. Explain your ideas.

    Rising college costs are causing problems. This year a fresh group of parents and students must grapple with grim economic realities as admission notices arrive. Savings accounts are smaller, more inflation is almost certain, and competition for loans and scholarships is increasing.

2. Use examples.

    Johnson notes, for instance, that one of every three students filing for admission now asks for financial aid, compared with one of every four last year. For example, fewer students major in liberal arts programs to "learn how to work with people." But more students enroll in accounting programs.

3. Use facts and figures.

    The report estimates tuition and fees will cost $1,388, room and board on campus $3,054, books and supplies $350, and miscellaneous personal expenses (not counting transportation) $1,455, a total cost of $6,247.

4. Use quotations.

    Warren stated, "A family must save almost two thousand dollars a year for nine years for each child planning to attend four years of college."

5. Use anecdotes.

    When I attended the University of Michigan, costs were much lower. Tuition, for example, was only $125 per semester. Yet we were always short of money and welcomed the summer vacations when we could replenish our depleted bank accounts.

Reword Clichés

Avoid the use of clichés. In French, cliché means stereotype; in English, cliché means a prefabricated phrase, one that is commonly known and commonly used. Admittedly, some clichés are colorful; the problem with the use of these prefabricated phrases is that they show lack of imagination. Clichés are phrases that are so common that when you are given the first part, you can usually fill in the last part yourself.

Examples

common as dirt	the spirit is willing, but the flesh is weak
warm as toast	the blind leading the blind
old as the hills	a parting of the ways
sell like hotcakes	diamond in the rough
sleep like a log	the full flush of victory
bolt from the blue	the patter of rain drops
politics makes strange bedfellows	a fly in the ointment
left high and dry	part and parcel
variety is the spice of life	the old song and dance
point the finger of suspicion	live to a ripe old age
sly as a fox	to grow by leaps and bounds
slippery as an eel	to withstand the test of time

stubborn as an ox	to let bygones be bygones
goose is cooked	to be unable to see the woods for the trees
covers a multitude of sins	eat crow
	to upset the apple cart

Other phrases, such as *"in today's society"* and *"in today's world"* are less colorful but just as trite. Although these phrases should ordinarily be avoided, occasionally they may be used with some effectiveness, but when they are used, they should be put in quotation marks to indicate to the reader that the writer knows full well that they are clichés, for instance, *"When in Rome, do as the Romans do."*

Euphemisms

Euphemisms are expressions employed to make unattractive ideas more pleasing or disturbing thoughts less troublesome. There are some topics about which people are reluctant to talk candidly. Therefore, they believe that if they can clothe them in words or phrases that are less disturbing the unpleasantness will be avoided. For example, people are reluctant to discuss death, toilets, disease, old age, sex, and menial jobs. People do not die; they *"pass away," "pass on, "enter into rest," "go to Heaven," "become deceased," "kick the bucket," "cash in their chips," "give up the ghost,"* or *"go to the happy hunting ground."* Hopelessly injured animals are not killed; they are *"put to sleep."* Secretaries are given the title *"Administrative Assistant"* but still given secretary's pay. Many less obvious euphemisms are used regularly by educated Americans: *"residential restrictions"* instead of *"no minorities allowed," "disadvantaged"* or *"under-privileged"* rather than *"poor," "credibility gap"* instead of *"lie," "underachievers"* rather than *"lazy."* Euphemisms are inescapable, but have the courage to screen them from your writing as much as possible. Most euphemisms are motivated by kindness, but many are condescending, and some are ruthlessly intended to delude and mislead—the tools of dictators and propagandists. Euphemisms reduce clarity and should be banished from your writing because they mask truth and reality.

Jargon

Omit any jargon in your college papers. Jargon, or "shoptalk" language, is the unique vocabulary or language used by a particular trade or profession, for example, police, military, education, business, law, or government. Instead of writing about burning houses and buildings, firefighters write about "structure fires." Instead of using forceful action verbs, military writers add "-tion" to make long, dull nouns: *"pacify"* becomes *"pacification,"* and *"demobilize"* become *"demobilization," "defoliate"* becomes *"defoliation."* Government writers *"finalize"* and *"definitize."* Business and management people seem fond of adding *"-wise"* to nouns to make adjectives, such as *"newswise," "moneywise,"* and *"taxwise."* Educators refer to counselors and advisors as *"student personnel counselors,"* to tutors as *"peer mediators"* or *"peer facilitators"* and to teaching as *"facilitation of learning."* Participants in the Watergate hearings in 1974 used considerable jargon: the words *"operative, " "inoperative," "transmission," "confidentiality," "parameter," "a highly sensitive matter," "deniability,"* and *"expedientiability"* were frequently employed. Business and legal writers often use words and phrases such as *"heretofore"* and *"herewithin enclosed."* Avoid jargon, especially if you are writing a technical paper for the nontechnical reader. Jargon reduces the clarity and conciseness of your writing and may confuse a reader not familiar with your terminology.

Gobbledygook

Gobbledygook is pretentious writing, the wordy and unnatural style that results when student writers try, unsuccessfully, to impress instructors with a more "intellectual" vocabulary and prose style. Remove or revise any pretentious writing in your papers. Do not make the mistake of thinking that your best written English is not good enough for your instructors and that you must use longer words, wordy phrasing, and long, involved sentence constructions to impress them. Use your own language—your natural written style. Specifically, you should avoid two types of gobbledygook.

The first type of gobbledygook to be' avoided is excessively wordy phrasing: the use of several words and long phrases when all that is needed is a short phrase or a single word. The simplest way to eliminate this type of wordiness is to reduce wordy phrases to their smallest one- or two-word equivalents.

announced himself to be in favor of	—	said he favored
met with the approval of Jones	—	Jones's approval
at the theoretical level	—	theoretically
a long period of time	—	a long time
at that point in time	—	at that time OR then
resembling in nature	—	like
finally, to conclude	—	finally
exhibits a tendency	—	tends
in many instances	—	often
paid a compliment	—	complimented
reach a decision	—	decide
make an attempt	—	try OR attempt
local level	—	locally
utilize	—	use

The second type of gobbledygook, or pretentious writing, occurs when the writer unsuccessfully attempts to be more impressive by using a more complex vocabulary. What happens, however, is that the larger words are often used improperly or in such a way that they cloud rather than clarify meaning. When pompous vocabulary is combined with excessive wording, the results may be very embarrassing for the writer, ludicrous in fact.

Read the following excerpt taken from a student's paper that argues for a particular interpretation of a poem by Leonard Cohen:

> . . . In an explication of this poem the archetypal is used to illustrate the foremost degree of definition and understanding.
>
> To solidify the lucidity of the poem, it is a necessity to briefly recapitulate the account. In the beginning, the man asks the subject, whom he has met on the train, to meet with him later in an apparent endeavor to begin a liaison. In response, the subject accepts the invitational proposal. The affair results in being parasitic; meanwhile, the man seems to be wandering in search of mortal happiness. At the end of the poem, the man believes that the subject is preventing his independency of the search; therefore, he decides to leave the subject and catch a train. He apologizes for his departure in dubious concern.
>
> By using the archetypal approach, the reader can detect a sense that man is a preginator in the first stanza . . .

The student's instructor was flabbergasted when she read this paper. In class discussion the student had always been straightforward and to the point. In a conference, the student revealed that because he was afraid his own vocabulary and sentences would not impress the instructor, he tried to imitate the way professional literary critics wrote. Obviously, the attempt was a disaster, and although this excerpt is an extreme example of how garbled writing can become when writers do not use their own vocabulary and writing style, it does serve as a warning. State what you are saying concisely and simply. Have no qualms about removing pseudo-intellectual language from your paper.

Slang and Obscenity

Slang (including obscenity) is not appropriate in your writing. Do not become overzealous in your attempts to combat euphemisms. For example, do not write an obscenity instead of *"sexual intercourse."* The obscenity may not be euphemistic, and while it has rhetorical impact, the word disturbs or angers too many readers for you to risk using it (just as the word has carefully been avoided here).

Other obscenities used for emphasis usually fail to achieve their intended effect, also. "Americans must take action immediately" will sound better to most readers than "*Americans must do something damned quick.*" "*Social Security laws are in a hell of a mess*" might be an appropriate sentence in a conversation, but in a written argument the sentence would be better worded "*Social Security laws desperately need revision.*"

Slang, for all its energy and colorfulness, is just not appropriate for your writing. "*This dude makes it to the meeting*" should be changed to "*The delegate attended the meeting.*" "*Chick*" should be changed to "*woman*" and "*busted*" to "*arrested.*"

Use the Correct Word or Phrase

Students commonly misuse certain words and phrases. For example, *affect* and *effect* are frequently used improperly. *Affect* should never be used as a noun; it should be used as a verb:

> He wondered how the new plan would *affect* the others.
> The north wind *affected* his sinuses.

Effect, on the other hand, can be used as a noun:

> He wondered what *effect* the new plan would have on the others.

But *effect* can be a verb, too:

> She wanted to *effect* changes in the organization.

Another misused expression is "the reason is because."

> *The reason* most students have difficulty finishing freshman composition *is because* they do not do enough homework.

The sentence reads much better after "The reason . . . is because" has been dropped:

> Most students have difficulty finishing freshman composition *because* they do not do enough homework.

Your instructor will point out inappropriate wording in your writing and explain how to correct the errors.

Repetition

Repeating words and phrases can be an effective and sometimes dramatic way of achieving emphasis and clear transition.

> *Example*
>
> Now what does "let students move at their own pace" mean? Too often it means letting them come to class only when they want to. Too often it means let them do no homework. Let them take two semesters to finish a course that they should finish in one. But "let students move at their own pace" should mean let them know they must produce. Let them know they must attend class regularly and do homework every night. Let them work hard and be proud of what they write. Let them accept and master the challenge of meeting self-imposed deadlines. Let all of those who are able finish their work early, but let a deserving few continue their work another semester. Let students realize from the very beginning that a self-paced course is rigorous, but let them understand too that it is rewarding, and make them want to work.

Repeated words are sometimes ineffective and bothersome to the reader. While proofreading, you may discover that you have overused a transitional word or phrase, perhaps *of course, however,* or *moreover.* Or you may have created a monotonous tone by using one too many times in an attempt to keep your writing in the third person. All writers have words and phrases that they overuse. Watch for this kind of repetition in your writing. Reword or rephrase whenever necessary. using a dictionary or thesaurus to find synonyms.

Impersonal Use of "One"

In converting first or second person writing to third person, resist the temptation to use the impersonal **one**. When "one" is overused, the writing becomes boring and wordy.

Impersonal—

> *One* never knows where forest fires will occur. Many times *one* finds the hottest spots are in difficult places, deep in a box canyon or similar area—difficult to fly into and even more difficult to fly out of—places where maneuverability and good rate of climb absolutely must be there when *one* pulls up after *one's* fire retardant drop. *One* can do just that with the S-2 aerial tanker.

Revised—

> Forest fires never seem to break out where they can be reached easily. Many times the hottest spots are deep in box canyons or similar areas—tough to fly into and even tougher to fly out of—places where maneuverability and good rate of climb absolutely must be there when the pilot pulls up after a fire retardant drop. The S-2 aerial tanker can do just that.

Use Active Verbs

When the subject of a sentence performs an action, as in the sentence "Bertie mashed the garlic," the verb is **active**. The writer is using the "active voice." When the subject of a sentence receives an action, as in the sentence "The garlic was mashed by Bertie," the verb is **passive**. Whenever possible, use active verbs to give sentences force and clarity. Avoid passive verbs when they make writing wordy, unclear, impersonal, evasive or dull.

Example

> PASSIVE *It has been decided* that you are not ready for graduate school at this time.
>
> ACTIVE The Dean of Admissions has *decided* that you are not ready for graduate school at this time.

In some situations passive verbs are more desirable than active verbs, as when the subject is perfectly obvious or when the subject is not known.

Example

> PASSIVE The huge old jade plant *was stolen* from the front porch during the night. Only a forlorn pile of broken leaves *was left* scattered in the street. It was as if a member of the family *had been abducted, forced into a car,* and *spirited* away to some unknown fate.
>
> ACTIVE Someone *stole* the old jade plant from the front porch during the night. Only a forlorn pile of broken leaves *lay* scattered in the street. It *seemed* that someone *had abducted* a member of the family and *spirited* him away to some unknown fate.

Using the active voice in the second version caused problems. Since the abductor is not known, the word *Someone* has been inserted, taking away emphasis from where it should be, on the jade plant, as in the first version. Furthermore, the next sentence is not as accurate in the second version as in the first, since, strictly speaking, leaves do not "lay" anywhere. And then in the last sentence, the intrusive someone has been employed again, and because there is no alternative, the awkward sounding "him" has been used. A "family member" could not be referred to as *it*, but a jade plant is customarily an *it*, not a *him* or a *her*.

Editing for "It Is" and "There Is"

To liven up your sentences, cut the *"it is's"* and *"there is's"* and their cousins, such as *"it was's,"* *"it will be's,"* *"there was's,"* *"there were's,"* and *"there seemed to be's."* Writers overuse these phrases, mistakenly believing that these adverb-linking verb constructions make their sentences flow more gracefully. But actually all these weak expressions do is slow down sentences, drearily stretching them with unnecessary words. Unless your objective is to put your reader to sleep, edit most of them from your writing.

Wordy—

[It is] unfortunate that people do not have the gift of looking into the future.

Edited—

Unfortunately, people do not have the gift of looking into the future.

Wordy—

To assure society a satisfactory future, [it is] imperative that a program of zero population growth be implemented immediately.

Edited—

In order to assure society a satisfactory future, a program of zero population growth must be implemented immediately.

Wordy—

At present the world population is approaching 4¹/₂ billion, and [it is] doubling every thirty to thirty-five years.

Edited—

At present the world population is approaching 4¹/₂ billion and doubling every thirty to thirty-five years.

Wordy—

[There are] numerous problems [that are] caused by overpopulation.

Edited—

Numerous problems are caused by overpopulation.

Cut Unnecessary Words

Do not rely on needless verbage to meet the required word limit for an assignment. Edit each paragraph for general wordiness. Ordinarily you can revise a wordy paragraph to say the same thing better, in half the words.

Wordy—

High school, college, and university students have the knowledge now more than they ever did in the past that a degree from an institution of higher learning can be the key leading down the trail to jobs that are better and lives that are richer. But the prospects of a degree, especially for members of the lower middle class and the working class of society, have a tendency to descend with costs which are rising. Already a son or daughter who wants a college education for four years can expect to pay four years of payments which can total up to a total of fifteen thousand dollars or possibly even more. (112 words)

Revised—

Students know a college degree can lead to better jobs and richer lives. But the prospects, especially for the lower, middle, and working classes, descend with rising costs. Already four years of college can cost fifteen thousand dollars or more. (40 words)

Study the following breakdown:

—High school, college, and university students (6 words)	—students (1 word)
—know more than they ever did in the past now that (11 words)	—know (1 word)
—a degree from an institution of higher learning (8 words)	—a college degree (3 words)
—can be the key leading down the trail (8 words)	—can lead (2 words)
—to jobs that are better and lives that are richer (10 words)	—to better jobs and richer lives (6 words)

Awkward Sentences

Sentences can be awkward for many reasons. Much of the advice in Chapter Two and in "The Guide to Stylistic Revision" is given to help you avoid awkward writing. For example, vague pronoun reference, tense shifts, passive verbs, faulty parallelism, and misplaced modifiers all cause "awkward" sentences. When these problems and other kinds specifically covered in *Survival* show up in your writing, your instructor will mark them so you can refer to the appropriate sections for suitable remedies. Suppose, for example, an instructor reads the following sentence:

In the early days of our grandparents: the supposition could be made that crime and corruption were not unknown since by way of tradition they have handed down their feelings.

The author would be directed to study the section on *Gobbledygook*. Sometimes, however, a sentence will be marked *Awkward* because this general label offers an easy way for the instructor to point out a bad sentence—one that does not read well, or one that does not "sound good." Awkward sentences should be rewritten. Reading the sentence aloud may make you "hear" the problem. If after reading a sentence marked *Awkward* you cannot see how to revise it, request assistance. Here are some awkward sentences and suggested revisions:

Awkward—

The meaning of "The Bear" by William Faulkner deals with the close alliance with nature when people learn the ritual of the hunt.

Revised—

"The Bear" by William Faulkner deals with people's close alliance with nature when they learn the ritual of the hunt.

Awkward—

The reason for legalizing off-track betting is on the grounds of lost tax money.

Revised—

Off-track betting should be legalized to prevent the loss of tax money.

Awkward—

This statement was about the only one which all of the Indians who fought in the Battle of Little Bighorn agreed.

Revised—

This statement was one of the few about which all of the Indians who fought in the Battle of Little Bighorn agreed.

Awkward—

Attempting the insulation of television viewers by taking for granted they are complete idiots is poor taste.

Revised—

Attempting to insulate television viewers by assuming they are complete idiots is in poor taste.

Awkward—

All along for their struggle to reach equality with the male officer, the women have run into much opposition.

Revised—

All during their struggle for equality with male officers, women have run into much opposition.

Parallel Construction

Parallel construction—or parallelism—is stylistic symmetry achieved by repeating grammatical constructions. The basic tactic in achieving parallelism is to use the same kinds of words, phrases, or clauses in pairs or series—for example, a noun paired with a noun, or three adjectives teamed in a row.

Example

1. Three Adjectives—Predicate Adjectives
   His tie is ‖ red,
              ‖ white, and
              ‖ blue.
2. Three Verbs—Compound Predicate
   The cornered mountain lion ‖ snarled,
                              ‖ snapped, and
                              ‖ lunged.

A breakdown in parallelism occurs when an item in a pair or series is not the kind of construction the reader expects. Sentences lacking parallelism lack balance and rhythm—they do not flow well, and they should be revised.

Example

For breakfast John has two scrambled eggs, a mound of fried potatoes full of bacon bits, three pieces of buttered toast, and drank coffee until he finished the whole pot. (not parallel)

In the above example, the reader is thrown off balance upon encountering "and drank coffee until he finished the whole pot." That part of the predicate should be revised to read, "and a potful of coffee." Here are some general suggestions about parallel construction:

Correlative Pairs

Be on the lookout for these correlative conjunctions—they work in pairs.

either — or
neither — nor
both — and
not — but
not only — but also
first — second . . .

Place each conjunction in the pair next to the sentence part being correlated.

Example

Not Parallel	*Parallel*
Either automation is one of the major enemies of the American worker *or* the means to provide future employment and prosperity.	Automation is *either* one of the major enemies of the American worker *or* the means to provide future employment and prosperity.

Team Modifiers

When separated modifiers are teamed, fewer words are needed and parallelism is improved. Use similar grammatical constructions, such as two adjectives, and place them together either before or after the word or word group being modified.

Example

Not Parallel	*Parallel*
The *gusty* north wind, *which was cold,* blew steadily for three days.	The *cold, gusty,* north wind blew for three days.

Phrases in a Series

Try to use similar grammatical constructions in a series of phrases—a succession of coordinate phrases.

Example

Not Parallel	*Parallel*
For many, college is a time filled *with constant mental strain, with feeling physically fatigued, and by periodic depression.*	For many, college is a time filled *with constant mental strain, physical fatigue,* and *periodic depression.*

Note that the preposition *with* in the example above has not been repeated in the parallel version.

with ‖ constant mental strain,
‖ physical fatigue, and
‖ periodic depression.

Unless special emphasis is desired, the introductory word—an adjective, a preposition, or a pronoun—need not be repeated in each phrase in a series of short phrases. But when one or more of the phrases in the series contains five or more words, repeat the first word at the beginning of each phrase.

Examples

> *to* investigate, prosecute, and publicize (single words and short phrases)
> *to* investigate, *to* prosecute, and *to* publicize (special emphasis)
> *to* the store near his aunt's house and *to* the Mercury Cleaners on Broadway (more than five words)

Dependent Clauses in a Series

When writing a series of dependent clauses, keep them parallel. The first clause in the series ordinarily can be used as a model for the rest.

Example

Not Parallel	*Parallel*
Jimmy believes that the lost continent of Atlantis is below the Bermuda Triangle, and an underwater civilization flourishes there.	Jimmy believes that the lost continent of Atlantis is below the Bermuda Triangle and that an underwater civilization flourishes there.

As can be seen in the example above, the signal word "that" is repeated in the second dependent clause to make the two clauses parallel. Also note that it is the missing signal word that makes the example "not parallel."

In a series of long dependent clauses beginning with the same signal word, repeat the signal word in each dependent clause. (A long dependent clause is one that contains five or more words.)

Example

A state treasury surplus of 4 billion dollars can be expected by the end of next year || *if* the economy continues to improve, *if* proposed income tax reform laws are implemented, and *if* the state budget for next year can be cut eight percent.

If the dependent clauses are short (fewer than *five* words), there is usually no need to repeat the signal word.

Examples

Although Frank lost his ring *and* Jamie became seasick, || everyone else had a good time sailing on San Francisco Bay.

Those students *who* studied daily *and* completed every exercise || finished the course before those who tried to take shortcuts.

Position Modifiers Accurately

A modifier is a word, phrase, or clause that describes, limits, qualifies, or distinguishes another word. Modifiers must be positioned accurately to make the meaning of a sentence clear. Avoid the squinting modifier, one that can modify either the sentence part before it or after it.

Squinting modifier—

She asked the salesman *tactfully* to express his opinion.

Revised—

She *tactfully* asked the salesman to express his opinion.

Or—

She asked the salesman to express his opinion *tactfully*.

Also avoid placing modifiers in the wrong parts of the sentences. Misplaced modifiers can be confusing and occasionally embarrassing.

Misplaced modifier—

The president and vice-president of the company were forced to show the memo to the board of directors *that implicated them in the plot.*

Revised—

The president and vice-president of the company were forced to show the memo *that implicated them in the plot* to the board of directors.

Misplaced modifier—

After they finish taking the pretest, the instructor wants to have a conference with the students.

Revised—

The instructor wants to have a conference with the students *after they finish taking the pretest.*

Be especially careful not to write *dangling introductory phrases and clauses* that do not modify the subjects of the main clauses immediately following them. The subject of a main clause must be the "doer" of the action in the introductory word, phrase, or clause.

Dangling introductory phrase—

Hopefully, all students will complete the course early.

Revised—

All students *hope* to complete the course work early.

Or—

The instructor *hopes* all students will complete the course work early.

Dangling introductory phrase—

Naive and innocent, the intrigues of politics amazed him.

Revised—

Naive and innocent, he was amazed by the intrigues of politics.

Dangling introductory phrase—

A good buy, many people purchased the tool kit.

Revised—

Because the tool kit was a good buy, many people purchased it.

Dangling introductory clauses—

While riding on the freeway, the truck ran over the bicyclist.
After learning the art of throwing pots, a modest living was made.
Because it was too dull, the grass would not cut evenly.

Revised—

While riding on the freeway, the bicyclist was run over by a truck.
After learning the art of throwing pots, he was able to earn a modest living.
Because the mower was too dull, it would not cut the grass evenly.

Capitalization Rules

Capitalize the following:

1. Persons, races, nationalities, languages

   Examples

George	But not—
William B. Smith, Jr.	blacks
Asian	white
African-American	
Indian	
American	
Italian	
Chinese	

2. Specific places

   Examples

Boston	Detroit River
North Carolina	Lake Tahoe
Mexico	Pacific Ocean
Appalachian Mountains	West (section of the country)

3. Specific organizations

   Examples

   The Sierra Club
   The State Air Resources Board
   The National Aeronautics and Space Administration
   NASA
   The House of Representatives
   Senate

   But not—

   government
   state government
   the state
   the federal government
   the legislation

4. Historical events, documents, and periods

   Examples

   the French Revolution
   World War Two
   Declaration of Independence
   Magna Carta
   the Dark Ages

5. Days, months, holidays

   Examples

Monday	But not seasons—
April	spring
Christmas	summer
Memorial Day	fall
	winter

6. Titles of courses

   Examples

   The West as an Idea in American Literature
   English
   Spanish
   Math 101
   Anthropology 2
   But do not capitalize—
   mathematics
   anthropology
   sociology
   chemistry

7. Titles of books magazines, journals, newspapers, movies, plays, poems, songs, record albums, articles, chapters, speeches, papers, and other publications.

   Capitalize the first word and all other words in the title except—
   articles (a, an, the)
   prepositions (in, on, over . . .)
   conjunctions (and, but, or . . .)

   Examples

Catcher in the Rye (book)	"My Last Duchess" (poem)
Encyclopaedia Britannica (book)	"America the Beautiful" (song)
Time (magazine)	*Nashville Skyline* (record album)
English Journal (journal)	"Automakers Urge Mandatory Belts" (article)
New York Times (newspaper)	"The White Race and Its Heroes" (chapter)
The Godfather (movie)	"Inaugural Address" (speech)
Hamlet (play)	"Nature Symbolism in 'The Bear' " (paper)

8. Official titles

   Examples

   Dr. Robert Lee, Jr.
   Professor Johnson
   Treasurer James E. Burns
   President John F. Kennedy
   Mr. Pong
   Mary B. Jorgenson, Doctor of Pharmacology
   John Marshall, Chief Justice, United States Supreme Court

   But not—

   Mary B. Jorgenson, pharmacist
   James Johnson, a chemistry teacher

9. Religious names, terms, titles

   Examples

God	Hinduisim
Christ	the Bible
Allah	the Koran
Buddha	Jews
Saint John	Muslims
Holy Communion	Hindus
Christianity	

10, In addresses

Examples

20178 Park Street
Ford Motor Company
English Department
Claims Department, Pacific Mutual Life Insurance Co.
Mountain View, California

11. Names of buildings, ships, airplanes, automobiles, brand names

Examples

Empire State Building (building)	But not—
Titanic (ship)	shepherd in German shepherd
Boeing 747 (airplane)	oak
Mercedes (automobile)	roses
Tide (brand name)	

12. Outlines

Examples

I. Background of Project Mercury
   A. Impact of Sputnik
   B. Creation of NASA
   C. Objectives of the Project

Abbreviations and Symbols

In general, avoid abbreviations in the text of a paper. Spell out the names of months (e.g., "February"), units of time (e.g., "hours," "century"), units of measurement (e.g., "miles per gallon," "centigrade," "kilometers"), geographical names (e.g., "New York," "United States"), and items often abbreviated in conversation and journalism (e.g., "television").

Some terms, however, are almost always abbreviated in a paper (e.g., "Mrs.," "a.m.," "PhD," "BC"). Current style favors omitting periods and spaces in abbreviations consisting entirely of capital letters and in some almost entirely capitalized (e.g., "AD," "USSR," "PhD"). The intitials in names are followed by periods and spaces (e.g., "J. F. Kennedy," "Franklin D. Roosevelt"). Most abbreviations made up of single lowercase letters contain periods but not spaces (e.g., "a.m."), but some have neither periods or spaces (e.g., "rpm").

Although the general rule is to avoid abbreviations, use common sense. In some papers it may be easier for readers to read abbreviations, such as "US" or "FBI," rather than the spelled-out versions many times. What is important is that readers should not have to puzzle over the meaning of an abbreviation. Some writers will spell out the term once and accompany the full name with its common abbreviation placed in parentheses, for example, "National Aeronautics and Space Administration (NASA)" and then use the abbreviation in the rest of the paper or even alternate between the spelled-out and abbreviated forms. In some cases the abbreviation placed in parentheses is not necessary, for example, in a paper referring to the United States many times.

The above guidelines apply only to the text of a paper. Abbreviations should be used according to directions in parenthetical documentation, Notes, and Works Cited. For further information and examples, consult Appendix A and Lesson Five of Chapter Four (page 214).

Symbols may be used (e.g., "$1,200," "47.33%," "-11°F"); you may prefer not to when a paper contains only a few figures (e.g., "1,200 dollars," "47.33 percent," "– degrees Farenheit" or "eleven degrees below zero"). [Also see "Numbers," page 382.] Symbols likely to be unfamiliar to your readers should not be used.

[*Sic*] or (*Sic*)

Errors within quotations may be designated by the word *sic* in square brackets or parentheses, i.e., [sic]. Any error found in quoted material will be considered yours unless you designate it. Never correct an error in a quotation, however. Instead use the [*sic*], placing it immediately after the error.

Numbers

Write as words numbers one through nine, but use numerals for 10 and above.

Examples

The witch granted her *three* wishes.
Greta saw *11* grotesque statues lining the driveway.

As an alternative to the above convention, you may spell out numbers that can be said in one or two words when you are writing a non-technical paper containing only a few numbers.

Examples

For more than *twenty* miles the road twisted and turned through the mountains.
The new school will cost at least *seven million* dollars.
More than *two-thirds* of the parts were defective.

No matter which of the above conventions you follow, dates, years, addresses, and times followed by a.m. or p.m., pages, dimensions, and decimal fractions should be stated as numerals.

Examples

His big break came on *July 12, 1973*.
The artifacts were probably used before *11,000 BC*.
Deliver this package to *21533 Hastings Avenue, Apartment 3C*.
At *10:33 a.m.* a sharp earthquake shook the building.
For your research notes use *4-by-6-inch* index cards.
Only *33.5%* of the recruits passed the examination.

Always use symbols or abbreviations when numerals are used.

Examples

The telephone company sent him a bill for *$263*.
Currently, *55%* of the college population is female.
Raise the connecting rod *12 cm*.

With very large numbers—millions, billions, trillions—numerals and words may be mixed.

Examples

Electronics sales may surpass *$400 billion* by 1990.
That image of Saturn was obtained when Pioneer 11 was *2.5 million* kilometers from the planet.

Never begin a sentence with a numeral. Either write the number in words or reorganize the sentence so that the number appears later.

Examples

Fifteen thousand dollars was more than he could afford for tuition.
He could not afford to pay *$15, 000* for tuition.

For the sake of appearance, numerals should be used consistently in a paper.

Examples

Don't write *3%* in one place and then *five percent* in another.

Don't write *$36.25* in one place and then *fifteen dollars* in another.

Don't write *18th* century in one place and then *twentieth century* in another.

Do not change the numbers in a passage you are quoting. Quote the passage exactly as it appears, no matter how you have been stating numbers in the rest of your paper.

APPENDIX D
Suggested Subjects

The following list presents 400 subjects used by many students in papers they have written. You should be aware that not every subject will be considered acceptable to your teacher. Furthermore, some instructors will offer other subjects for consideration. Select two or three from the following list and discuss the merits of each before you begin writing. Keep in mind, too, that almost every subject listed is a general subject and will need to be narrowed.

Abortion
Academy Awards
Accidents
Actors/Actresses
Acupuncture
Adoption
Advertising
Affirmative Action
Agent Orange
Agnosticism
Agriculture
AIDS
Airline Industry
Air Pollution
Airline Safety
Alcoholism
Alternative Energy
American with Disabilities
    Act
Amnesty
Androgyny
Animal Experimentation
Animal Rights
Arab-Israeli Conflict
Architecture
Art
Artificial Intelligence
Artists
Astrology
Astronomy
Atheism
Athletes
Attention Deficit Disorder
Autism
Auto Emissions Control
Automation
Automobile Safety
Automobiles
Balanced Budget
Baseball
Battered Women

Beauty Contests
Behavior Modification
Best-sellers
Bicycles
Bilingual Education
Biodiversity
Birth Control
Black Humor
Books
Bovine Growth Hormone
Boxing
Boycotts
Budget Deficit
Busing
Camping
Cancer
Capitalism
Capital Punishment
Careers
Caregiving
Carpal Tunnel Syndrome
Cell Phones
Censorship
Central America
Character Education
Charities
Child Abuse
Child Custody
Child Rearing
Childbirth Methods
Children's Rights
Church and State Separation
Civil Disobedience
Civil Rights
Civil War
Class Action Suits
Clichés
Cloning
Clubs
Collective Bargaining
College Education

Comedy
Computer Crime
Computer Games
Computer Hackers
Computers
Congress
Conscientious Objectors
Conservation
Conservatives
Corporate Welfare
Cosmetic Surgery
Cost of Living
Crafts
Crib Death (SIDS)
Crime
Cuba
Cults
Cultural Diversity
Cyberspace
D.C. Statehood
Date Rape
Dating
Designer Genes
Down-Sizing
Drug Testing
Drugs: Legal and Illegal
Eating Disorders
Ecology
Elections
Electoral College
Endangered Species
Environmental Groups
Ethics
Euro
Families
Family Reunions
Famines
Feminism
Fetal Alcohol Syndrome
First Amendment
Floods

Folk Medicine
Folklore
Food
Food Banks
Fourth Amendment
Gambling
Garbage
Gays in the Military
Genealogy
Genetically Modified Crops
Gerontology
Globalization
Global Warming
Graduation Requirements
Gulf War Syndrome
Handicaps
Hate Crimes
Hawaiian Sovereignty
Heath Care
Helmet Laws
Hispanic Americans
Holistic Healing
Hostages
Housing
Human Rights
Hunger
Hunting and Fishing Rights
Illiteracy
Immigration
In Vitro Fertilization
Income Taxes
Indigenous Peoples
Information
Institutions
Insurance
Interest Rates
Internet
Internet Censorship
Internships
Inventions
Jingoism
Junk Foods
Jury Trials
Justice System
Juvenile Delinquency
Ku Klux Klan
Land Use Planning
Latin America
Law Practice
Laws
Learning Disabilities
Liberal Arts Education
Liberals
Lifestyles

Literacy
Lobbyists
Lottery
Luxury Taxes
Lyrics
Mad Cow Disease
Marriage
Martyrs
Mass Transit
Materialism
Matriarchy
Medical Costs
Medical Practice
Mental Illness
Mental Retardation
Mexican Americans
Middle East
Military Draft
Military Life
Military Spending
Militias
Minimum/Subminimum Wage
Minorities
Mixed Marriages
Money
Moon
Motorcycles
Movie Rating System
Movies
Music
Music Pirating
Music Videos
Musicians
Mythology
NAFTA
NASA
NEA Grants
National Debt
National Park System
Natural Disasters
Neighbors
Nobel Prize
Noise Pollution
Nuclear Non-Proliferation
Nuclear Power
Nuclear Waste
Nuclear Weapons
Nudism
OSHA
Occult
Oceans
Off-Road Vehicles
Oil Drilling
Oil Spills

Old Growth Logging
Olympics
Orphanages
Overpopulation
Ozone Layer
Parenting
Parole
Patriarchy
Performance Art
Personality Disorders
Pesticides
Philanthropy
Photography
Plea Bargaining
Police
Political Campaigns
Political Prisoners
Politicians
Pollution
Pornography
Prayer in School
Presidents
Prisons
Private Schools
Professional Sports
Proficiency Tests
Provincialism
Psychiatry
Public Television and Radio
Puerto Rico Statehood
Quality of Life
Racism
RU-486
Racial Profiling
Rainforest
Rap
Rape
Rapid Transit
Real Estate
Recessions
Recycling
Refugees
Registration for Classes
Rehabilitation Programs
Relatives
Religious Fundamentalism
Renewable Energy
Rent Control
Reservation Casinos
Right to Know
Robotics
Rock Music
Rodeos
Rural Poverty

Satellites
SATs
School Lunch Program
Schools
Science
Science Fiction
Second Amendment
Secondhand Smoke
Sex Education
Sexism
Sexual Harrassment
Shelters
Sibling Rivalry
Smoking
Smoking Bans
Social Class
Social Security
Software
Solar Energy
Space Colonization
Space Programs
Space Weapons
Speed Limits
Spirituality
Sports
Stadiums
Standard of Living
Standardized Tests
States Rights
Stem Cell Research
Stereotypes
Steroids
Sting Operations
Stock Market
Stress
Strikes
Strip Mining
Student Government
Subliminal Messages
Suburbia
Subversive Organizations
Success

Superfund Clean-up Sites
Superstition
Supreme Court
Surgical Implants
Tariffs
Taxes
Technology
Teenage Marriage
Teenage Pregnancy
Telecommunications
Television
Term Limits
Terrorism
Theater
Theologians
Third World Debt
Third World Politics
Three Strikes Law
Tobacco Settlements
Tolerance
Tourette's Syndrome
Toxic Wastes
Trade Deficits
Trade Embargoes
Traffic Congestion
Transportation
Trauma Care
Truancy
Trucking
Tuition
U.S. Postal Service
Unemployment
Unions
United Nations
Urban Decay
Urban Planning

Urban Renewal
Values
Veterans
Videos
Vietnam War
Violence
Virtual Reality
Satellites
Volunteer Work
Voter Redistricting
Wages
War
War Crimes
Water Quality
Water Resources
Weapons Treaties
Welfare
Wetlands
Wilderness Preservation
Wind Power
Wolves in Yellowstone
Women in Military Academies
Women in the Military
Workers' Compensation
Working Parents
World Bank
World Court
World War I
World War II
Writers
Writing
Yoga
Youth
Zen
Zoning Laws
Zoos

Index